Acclaim for Robert Blair Kaiser's

A CHURCH IN SEARCH OF ITSELF

"An important book for Catholics and non-Catholics alike, because of the power and the influence of the Church. It's written in a lively style by a liberal Catholic journalist who wants his beloved Church restructured in a major way." —*Huntington News*

"Kaiser is a master of the Catholic world. Those interested in the future of the Church would do well to pay careful attention to his work." —*Publishers Weekly*

"Kaiser is tops in Vatican coverage, playing confessor to cardinals and giving us not only an inside account of the conclave that elected Benedict XVI, but also a way to salvage today's much-battered Catholic Church." —Ted Morgan

"A compelling depiction of the making of a pope and a rallying cry for a revolution of sorts among the faithful." —*The Social Edge*

"Well written. . . . A work of both journalism and activism." —*The Catholic News*

"If you are looking for a book that sees recent Church history with a strong Vatican II approach, *A Church in Search of Itself* is the book for you." —*Inland Register*

A Church in Search of Itself

A Church in Search of Itself

Benedict XVI and the Battle for the Future

Robert Blair Kaiser

Vintage Books
A Division of Random House, Inc.
New York

FIRST VINTAGE BOOKS EDITION, MARCH 2007

The Library of Congress has cataloged the Knopf edition as follows:
Kaiser, Robert Blair.
A church in search of itself : Benedict XVI and the battle for the future /
Robert Blair Kaiser.—1st ed.
p. cm.
1. Catholic Church—History—20th century.
2. Christianity—Forecasting. I. Title.
BX1389.K35 2005
282'.09'0511—dc22
2005044961

Vintage ISBN: 978-0-307-27814-2

Author photograph © Julian Wasser
Book design by Virginia Tan

www.vintagebooks.com

Printed in the United States of America
10 9 8 7 6 5 4 3 2 1

For Polly, John, and Bill,
my three brilliant and beautiful children,
their spouses, Tim, Amy, and Cheryl,
and their intelligent kids, all readers,
Callum, Phoebe Olivia, Dylan,
Amelia Blair, and Lucy

Here below to live is to change, and to be perfect is to have changed often. John Henry Newman

The royalty of Christ means democracy. Hans Küng

We feel bound to disagree with these prophets of doom who are forever forecasting calamity—as though the world's end were imminent. Today, rather, Providence is guiding us toward a new order of human relationships, which, thanks to human effort and yet far surpassing human hopes, will bring us to the realization of still higher and undreamed of expectations.

Pope John XXIII

The Gospel is totally political. What use is "Love as I have loved you" if we think nothing, pray nothing, and do nothing about making that love real? Politics moves love from charity to justice. Yes, we are given different gifts, different vocations. But politics is a dimension of all of us. Robert Brophy

Contents

Author's Note

THE GOSPEL OF JOHN tells us that after Jesus died and went missing from his tomb, the disciples met behind locked doors "in fear of the Jewish leaders." Almost two thousand years later, in April 2005, another band of disciples, 115 cardinals, were meeting behind locked doors at a papal conclave, this time in fear of "the media"—a term that symbolized all the dizzying diversity of a world these hierarchs needed to put behind them. This book is, in part, a story about how they proceeded to elect a man who knew how to play to their fears.

But there is another story here as well: one about Catholics who aren't buying into the fear; rather, they are making efforts to seize citizenship in their own Church. This may have a whiff of revolution about it, but if the last century was about anything, it was about the passing of power, from old elite institutions to the people, an idea that was formulated in the American Constitution and voiced in a new way by Abraham Lincoln in the Gettysburg Address, when he called for a government "of the people, by the people, and for the people." That gave rise in the 1960s to a rallying cry of "Power to the people" during civil rights battles in the American South. Years before, that same sentiment was planted early in the history of the American labor movement. It germinated notably under the leadership of Mohandas Gandhi in India. It was given test plantings in colonial revolutions around the globe. It took root during World War II in the mind of the German Lutheran minister Dietrich Bonhoeffer, who saw what the Nazis were doing to his country and told his people they had to resist because they were part of "a world coming of age." When people come of age, they pass from one culture to another, from a kind of slavery as unthinking pawns of others, to a new kind of life as men and women who can think and act on their own.

The Second Vatican Ecumenical Council (1962–1965) was a part of the history of the world's growing up, an attempt to write a charter for a Church of the people, by the people, and for the people. That charter was meant to be only a beginning, an invitation to the people of God from an inspired parliament of the world's bishops to take ownership of what was, after all, their Church—not the pope's Church. A people's Church.

It was no surprise that the lords who stood to lose their long-standing power in a clerical Church resisted the revolution and succeeded in suppressing it by electing two popes, John Paul II and Benedict XVI, who raised higher the walls of patriarchy, so they could keep control. It was no surprise, either, that the people, their hands and their feet so newly unshackled, didn't quite know how to walk on their own at first. The people of God are still in the process of learning how to do that, to think and assert themselves, and speak their own needs. We will see some of them in action in the pages that follow, and their stories should embolden others to join in an inexorable process—the ever-growing awareness of who we are and what we can be.

Christian theologians have another name for the people of God. They call them members of the Mystical Body of Christ, a collectivity that takes in almost half the human race, many of whom are now reaching out to the other half of the race in a new way, as spiritual, loving neighbors, and downplaying their old absolute claims of God's special favor.

I would consider betting on this Christ of history. I can imagine this mystical Christ bursting into a gathering of fearful disciples—in a future conclave, perhaps—and telling the hierarchs, "Put your fingers into my hands. Put your hands into my side. And do not be unbelieving, but believe."

Believe in Christ, in Christ's Body, in the people, in a people's Church, in the reign of justice and peace in this world. In yourselves.

—Robert Blair Kaiser

August 2005

Introduction

JOHN EMERICH EDWARD DALBERG, the first Lord Acton, who is most famous for noting that absolute power corrupts absolutely, spent his most productive early years as a news correspondent in Rome at the First Vatican Ecumenical Council in 1869–70. Acton filed passionate reports on that Council's battle over papal infallibility from his apartment on the Via della Croce, which became a salon where the Council's finest bishop-theologians could meet, break bread, exchange information, and hatch strategies.

Acton, an English lord with blood ties to the nobility of two European nations, opposed any declaration of papal infallibility, convinced that Pope Pius IX was promoting it in order to shore up his temporal power against the advancing forces of the Italian Risorgimento. Acton not only reported on the debate inside this Council; he even wrote speeches for some of the bishops who were arguing against a declaration of papal infallibility. When one of the bishops dared tell the pope that infallibility had no precedent in ancient Church tradition, Pius IX exploded. *Traditio sono io. Sono io la chiesa* is how he put it: "I am tradition. I am the Church."

A third of the bishops fled Rome rather than give this pope the absolute power he wanted. Those who were left at the Council (547 of them) agreed with Pius IX's self-promotion and set the Church up for the papolatry that has bedeviled it ever since. Their vote, however, didn't stop the forces of Garibaldi, who marched into Rome even before the Council ended and ran the pope out of his palace on the Quirinal Hill and into what is now called Vatican City.

Acton's dispatches were carried in the *Augsburger Allgemeine Zeitung* and reprinted all over the world under the pseudonym Quirinus. He wrote them in a hurry, often finishing at 4 a.m. and smuggling them out of Rome via diplomatic pouch to avoid confiscation by the pope's secret police. His accounts warned readers about the dangers of making the pope into a kind of god. But he did not have the final word. The Quirinus collection, his account of the battle, was put on Rome's *Index of Forbidden Books,* and its editor, Ignaz von Döllinger, the best German theologian of his day, was excommunicated.

A CENTURY LATER, I tried to emulate Acton when I became a reporter for *Time* magazine at Vatican II, the Second Vatican Ecumenical Council. Few wanted to admit it, but this Council's agenda corrected that of Pius IX at Vatican I. There, Pius IX asserted his primacy over the Church and over all the princes of Europe as well, as medieval popes had done routinely. At Vatican II, a majority of bishops fought to move the Church away from that kind of papal absolutism; in fact, they wrote a charter to give the Church back to the people.

Like Acton, I took sides in this battle, cheering in my reportage the huge majority of bishops who had (to the great surprise of many) voted for the updating that Pope John XXIII called his "aggiornamento." A long tradition in the Church, dating back to the hermit-monks in fourth-century Egypt, feared the world and set up false dichotomies—between the sacred and the secular, between grace and nature, between (as Saint Augustine would have it) the City of God and the City of Man. When those false dichotomies made the Church largely irrelevant to the twentieth century, some pioneering theologians reversed that negative view of the world. They liked to quote Jesus' mission statement: that he had come so that we might have life and have it more abundantly—life in this world as well as in the next. John XXIII embraced that idea, and blessed it, because it accorded with his own down-to-earth approach to the world. He loved the world, and encouraged his Council to love it, because, after all, it was a world redeemed by Christ. It would continue to be redeemed when other Christs carried on with the work of justice and peace. That is how they passed the love on.

I learned all this at the feet of the Council's forward-looking bishops and theologians in my apartment on Monteverde Vecchio, which became a kind of salon where these bishops and theologians could meet, break bread, exchange information, hatch strategies, and write speeches—most of them aimed at creating a humble, serving, listening Church that didn't have any qualms about talking with (and learning from) Moslems, Buddhists, Hindus, and Jews.

In the fall of 1999, a little more than thirty years after Vatican II, I again took up residence in Rome to begin research for this book. It started out to be a book about the making of a pope, the next one, someone who I hoped would try to explain Vatican II without explaining it away or, worse, dumbing it down. I found then that the institutional Church had one overriding concern—to put on shows (several hundred of them in the Jubilee Year 2000 alone) designed to delight millions of visitors with glimpses of a pope who had become a media icon. I watched these shows with horrified fascination, chronicled the contradictions of John Paul II's waning years, and set about a more challenging and important task, learning about the other Church, outside the Vatican (whose officials like to think they are the real Church). The other Church I am talking about is the people of God Church. I wanted to focus on this Church because I hoped it would demand or produce out of its own heart a new kind of papal leadership to meet the needs of the whole Church, which was suffering because it had a pope who couldn't listen.

I traveled the world and sought out men and women of deep faith with different ways of "being Church" in the context of their daily lives. Being Catholic did not stop them from being people of their own time and place, with startling differences in language, liturgy, and local devotion. But their differences did not detract from the purity of their faith; their differences contributed, rather, to its beauty—in the spirit of the poem "Pied Beauty" by the English Jesuit Gerard Manley Hopkins.

Glory be to God for dappled things—
For skies of couple-colour as a brinded cow;
For rose-moles all in stipple upon trout that swim;
Fresh-firecoal chestnut-falls; finches' wings;
Landscape plotted and pieced—fold, fallow, and plough;
And áll trádes, their gear and tackle and trim.

All things counter, original, spare, strange;
Whatever is fickle, freckled (who knows how?)
With swift, slow; sweet, sour; adazzle, dim;
He fathers-forth whose beauty is past change:
Praise him.

I found Catholicism around the world to be a dappled thing. The various ways that Catholics "become Church" for one another told me a great deal about their faith—so different in its various enculturations and yet so zeroed in on the person of Christ. It also told me something about the irrelevancy that the institutional Church had become, such a far cry from its beginnings as a simple assembly. The Greek word for "assembly" is εκκλησία, which also came to mean "church." That *ecclesia* grew, for good and for ill. It grew through the blood of martyrs who died at the hands of Roman emperors; and then later, under the canny calculation of popes who became emperors themselves, it became wealthy (sometimes on the strength of forged documents giving it title to vast real estate), and set up a network of laws and institutions that came to be known as Christendom.

"Europe is the faith, and the faith is Europe," declared Hilaire Belloc in the early twentieth century, when many Catholics had a sense of imperium, something that other Christians in the east and the north had rejected centuries before. Those left on the barque of Peter (an ancient metaphor for the Church), their hearts contracted after the schism (for which they had to bear more than a share of the blame), pulled back within themselves and erected walls of defense, not only around their *ecclesia,* but also around their minds, so that even when they followed Jesus' command to go out to all nations, they went not to minister and serve, but to conquer and reign, with a rule-book mentality that did not commend Christ as a light to the world.

Then, at a peculiar turning in time, came a simple man whose name was John, the 260th successor of Peter. He was the most open of all the popes in history, a man who challenged the Church to become more democratic, more free, more human, more humble in the face of history. In some places, it has become that. In other places, the challenge still stands.

. . .

THOUGH POPES AND BISHOPS appear often in my account, so much so that it often seems like they *are* the Church, I have written this book for the whole Church, the people of God Church chartered at Vatican II, the Church that gives the pope and the bishops their reason for being: to serve. I have gone back and forth across many borders to gather stories that tell us more about this other Church, a thinking, loving, pulsing-with-energy people's Church.

I decided to focus on six cardinals around whom I could tell those stories. I could have chosen six more ordinary people—six priests or six nuns or six lay catechists or six Catholic families—to make the part stand for the whole (a literary trope called synecdoche). I chose six cardinals for their iconic value, as Shakespeare preferred princes and kings for his protagonists (rather than artisans and accountants), and because these cardinals would participate in the drama that ends this account, the election of a new pope. Each of the cardinals, of course, is accountable to the people he serves—as the pope himself is.

If that sounds like a cheeky statement, to hold a pope accountable, consider the British historian Eamonn Duffy's charge that we have surrounded the recent papacy with "a superhuman mystique and an aura of sanctity" that has obscured the real relationship that ought to exist between the pope and the people of God. "We have idealized the popes, dehumanizing them and turning them into holy icons or superstars, and have then projected onto them unreal dreams and expectations." Popes, he said (and, we must assume, cardinals, too), are men like other men, with likes and dislikes, prejudices and presuppositions, virtues and vices, all of which shape, for good or ill, their actions and their policies.

And if the pope isn't a hero, a genius, a saint, a star, what then? Duffy maintains that in the end this isn't what matters most. We stick with our popes "not because they are clever or nice, but because they hold all the churches to a common vision, and help prevent them collapsing back into the parochialism of their own regional or cultural agendas." Duffy gives us a practical corollary: "Because we must all live with the papacy, we are all enabled to live with each other."

I chose five cardinals from five continents, and a sixth cardinal who represented the Church's headquarters in Rome. I chose the five I did because they were the kind of men who didn't come to their positions thinking they had all the answers; I was looking for men who had learned to lead by listening to their people. To my delight, I found some of these men were not in denial about the parlous condition of the Church and the perilous condition of the world. Some of them did not believe their people had to change but, rather, that the clerical Church had to change in order to meet the needs of the people they were vowed to attend. Some believed their people had been drifting away from the Church, not because they rejected the Jesus message but because those charged with proclaiming it had made that message so banal, so unbelievable—and so unbelievably boring.

Jesus, of course, was the whole point. But many scholars were arguing at the beginning of the twenty-first century that the institutional Church had hijacked Jesus, rubbed his message smooth with mindless repetition, and obscured it with rote ritual.

Who was Jesus? What was Jesus? When a Boston Jesuit named Roger Haight attempted to answer those questions in a work called *Jesus, Symbol of God,* the Vatican's Congregation for the Doctrine of the Faith (which we will call by its former name, one that is still used most often in the Vatican itself, the Holy Office) subjected him to a four-year inquisition and ended up notifying the world in February 2005 that Haight could no longer teach as a Catholic theologian. Haight was asking the kinds of questions that every generation of theologians has to ask—and then answer in language its contemporaries can understand.

The Catholic Church hasn't been doing a very good job of that. I will never forget the time when my twelve-year-old nephew, who had been going to mass every Sunday since the day he was born, asked his father, "Dad, are Catholics Christians?" He and many of his contemporaries were not finding Jesus at mass, as visitors to almost any parish church from Rome to Recife to Denver could tell on any given Sunday by looking around and seeing only gray heads—and not too many of them. "I used to go to church," one of the most respected physicians in Arizona told me when he learned I was headed to Rome in 1999. "I almost joined the Benedictine order back in Indiana. But this pope we've got. He's like something out of the seventeenth century." He shrugged. "I don't go to church anymore." He paused for a few seconds. Then he said, "Is there any chance we will get someone who can take us into the twenty-first century?"

I noticed how this physician spoke of "we" and "us." He was still a Catholic. But he didn't know that Vatican II had written a charter for a people's Church. He didn't know that because John XXIII's successor, Paul VI, only made some halfhearted stabs at building a people's Church. The man who followed him, John Paul II, never even tried.

Talk about a people's Church may sound political. But the Catholic Church has been, from its very beginning, the most political of all the world's religions. Peter and Paul were locked in a first-century argument over their tiny new community's own identity: would it, could it, include non-Jews? A Roman emperor called the Council of Nicaea in 325 to settle a raging dispute between two factions in the Church. The Council of Constance met in 1415 to sort out the conflict between three men claiming the papacy. The twenty-two cardinals and thirty laymen who were voting members of that Council put those pretenders aside to elect a noble layman from Rome. They also took a historic (though now largely unnoticed) step toward a more collegial governance by decreeing that councils should meet at regular intervals to put a check on absolute papal power. The popes that followed Constance largely ignored that decree. What man in power, if he is a man, wants to see his power checked?

Before readers reject the term "politics" as something unseemly in the followers of the man who said his kingdom was not of this world, they should realize that most of the planet's species govern themselves with one form or another of what we call politics. Social psychologists tell us that every group's agendum, from ants to elephants, revolves around a single question: who's in charge here? That is a political question.

Just exactly how Churchmen come to their high estate is also a lesson in politics. Some cardinals, for example, like to pretend politics has had nothing to do with getting the prime symbol of their office, a red hat. If they were candid, they would have to admit how well they managed their climb to the top by going to the right seminaries (preferably in Rome), finding their first jobs close to the center of power (also in

Rome), and networking with powerful prelates (in Rome, of course). Politics is one of the games that people, even Church people, play.

But Church politics is not just a game about who's in charge inside the Church. Papal politics—the choice of this bishop or that pope—has consequences in the real world. In the nineteenth century, Pius IX spent most of his more than thirty-five years on the papal throne (an all-time record) battling for temporal power by playing off the principal nations of Europe against one another. In 1962, Pope John XXIII helped the United States and the Soviet Union avoid a nuclear exchange over Cuba. In 2004, Church politics threw the American election to George W. Bush.

During Vatican II, Protestants were surprised by John XXIII's political leadership, not only for calling a Council, but for suddenly taking an irenic stand toward all other Christian religions as well. To the good Pope John, Presbyterians, Methodists, and Lutherans were no longer the Church's enemies, but "separated brethren." This was a change of language that bespoke a change of attitude that the Catholics and Protestants who had battled over the course of the previous four hundred years would have never understood. The change in attitude led to unprecedented cooperation between Christians in every arena—civic, social, and academic.

Church politics (even and especially papal politics) also had an effect on Jews, who didn't pay much mind to the Church until the Fathers of Vatican II (and three popes) tried to repeal the verdict that had been levied against them for centuries by many Christians (including some popes): that Jews were "Christ killers." Reversing that verdict led to a general tearing down of the walls of fear and hatred between Christians and Jews. (Some fear remains; it will and should continue as long as even a few Christians believe there's something wrong with Jews who do not convert to Christianity.)

Today, papal politics continues to affect public policy, at city, state, national, and even international levels. John Paul II had mixed results when he tried to influence the population policies of the United Nations at a Cairo conference in 1994, and when he tried to "put God" into the preamble of the constitution being drafted by the European Union in 2000–04. He had some success at the UN and failed with the EU. But the point is that when a pope in Rome pushes a boulder into the sea, the waves roll up on every shore.

And as the history of John Paul II's reign demonstrated, politics inside the Church—a battle between the Catholic right and the Catholic left over the very notion of a people's Church—has continued to rage. Talk about a people's Church makes conservative Catholics uncomfortable. The Church, they insist, is not a democracy. True, the Church is not a democracy (not now, though it was for centuries) and the pope is not a president. Both wings in the Church have agreed, however, that the pope's job description calls for him not to dominate but to serve the people at large. Once both the Catholic right and the Catholic left agreed on that proposition, then, I thought, anything could happen in this Church and in the conclave of 2005. If serving the people (and, therefore, listening to them) was the raison d'être of the papacy, then it followed that the people, too, had to have a role in the making of a pope.

As we shall see, the virtual presence of more than a billion Catholics at the conclave influenced the electors, but I didn't know how that would play out before it began. This was one of the questions I had to ask myself as the conclave loomed: would a significant percentage of the people hold these cardinal-electors accountable for the man they chose to succeed Pope John Paul II? How would they do that? And the most important question of all: would the cardinal-electors elect a pope of the people?

More than a billion Catholics and a billion other Christians had a stake in this election, too. So did the millions of Moslems, Buddhists, Hindus, and Jews who had come to know, however slightly, that a pope could help bring the world's warring peoples together in ways that no other man could even conceive. No single religious or political figure can unite people as a pope can. It took centuries for the great men in the history of religion—Moses, the Buddha, Jesus, and Muhammad—to rise to the kind of worldwide visibility and credibility that John Paul II attained over the course of less than twenty-seven years as pope. True, he could not stop the American-British invasion of Iraq in 2003. But he raised the papal profile in such a radical way that the new pope, or the next one—a man with more flexibility and more charm, perhaps—might well stop the next war by the very force of his religious witness. A man of religion can do that, as presidents and prime ministers cannot.

The very word "religion" comes from the Latin verb *religare,* to retie. This is what religion does: it ties people back together, with God and with one another. And so, since the pope is a man of religion, people have come to expect that a pope will help tie things back together, within his own Catholic community and, following the sometime example of the twentieth-century popes, within the world community as well—at a time when both the Catholic family and the family of nations seem to be coming apart for lack of meaning.

At the beginning of the conclave of 2005, many were wondering which papal candidate could help reweave the rope of meaning. Maybe it was too much to ask that any single individual on earth, much less any of the cardinal-electors in the first conclave of the twenty-first century, had the people skills to enlist humankind in the work required to do that—in the Church and in the world at large. Whoever the cardinals picked would simply have to try to do his best and hope for the best, knowing that he was not God, just a man. We would have to take some consolation in this, that he knew he would have a great deal of help from the heavenly prayers and the earthly efforts of at least a billion people.

And he would have the help of God. At the end of his day, Pope John XXIII would pray for the needs of the Church throughout the world, naming several that were troubling him most. Then he would conclude, full of trusting confidence, *Signore, è la vostra chiesa. Vado dormire!:* "Lord it's your Church. I'm going to bed."

That's enough help.

A Church in Search of Itself

CHAPTER ONE

Politics

Toward a People's Church

FOR MORE THAN SIX HUNDRED YEARS, it has been the same scenario. A pope dies. The cardinals assemble. After a good many prayers calling on the Holy Spirit, they lock themselves in the Sistine Chapel, surrounded by some of the most stunning art in the history of humankind, to vote, twice each morning and twice each afternoon, in a series of solemn, silent, and secret paper ballots, until a two-thirds majority agrees on the successor. When he responds, he does so with the same single Latin word used by so many of his predecessors—*Accipiam*—"I will accept." He proceeds to announce his new name, while over in a corner of the chapel the papal chamberlain burns the ballots with some dry straw in a centuries-old stove, sending three white puffs of smoke above the Roman rooftops to tell a waiting world, *We have a pope!*

The same prayers, the same ballots, the same three puffs of smoke—always the scrupulous insistence on sameness by a group of men as committed to their history as any community on the face of the earth, to emphasize the fact that they didn't invent all of these formalities yesterday, that they are only following ancient traditions, and passing them on to the next generation.

But in the spring of 2005, the cardinals coming to Rome to elect Pope John Paul II's successor were being challenged to play new kinds of roles in a different kind of story. It was different because, although every element in their protocol mirrored the conclaves of 1378, 1566, 1846, and 1978, one important dynamic fact had changed: the waiting world had changed, changed more in the past quarter century than it had changed in all of human history. The old waiting world was a passive world—except in Rome, where its people, at least for the first thousand years of the Church's history, were asked to ratify, viva voce, the man chosen to follow in the steps of Peter. But for almost a thousand years since then, the cardinals who gathered and voted were *verbs,* and every other Catholic in the world a passive recipient of the action of the verbs. We have given you a pope, the cardinals said in effect. Rejoice and be glad—in our choice.

In 2005, however, in a world that had suddenly shrunk to the size of a village, new mass-mediated channels of communication among the people of the world marked a shift in the grammar of the Roman Catholic Church, one that scholars predicted would have a profound, positive effect on the Church's existence for the rest of the twenty-first century. Through these channels, Catholics were finding the kind of active voice not exercised in the Church since the first few centuries of its existence in Rome.

Electronic miracles have compressed time and space, so that now we live and work in new kinds of microcosms and macrocosms that alter our perceptions of everything, accelerate the pace of change, and create the need not only for a new grammar, but for a new geometry of power, moving from the pyramidal to the circular. The shift was largely driven by new information technologies that made it possible, for example, for a cameraman working for RAI, the Italian state-owned television giant, to stand on a Vatican City rooftop, focus his Sony Betacam SX television camera with the fourteen-inch X2 Yashinon telephoto lens on the golden pectoral cross of a cardinal crossing Saint Peter's Square, and flash that image out to every television on earth—and to many cell phones—instantaneously and in color.

And so, when the cardinals gathered in the spring of 2005 to prepare for the Church's change of command, the whole world was present in Rome, courtesy of the mass media. Interviews and commentary about the event started beaming out from Rome to every corner of the planet. CNN had a rooftop aerie high above Saint Peter's Square, with glib reporters who had done their legwork and solemn analysts who had done their homework. CBS, with more than a hundred on its papal news team, had another view of Saint Peter's from the rooftop of the Atlante Star Hotel. Other networks had huge crews: NBC, ABC, Fox, and the BBC; Sky News in Asia; and Televisa, the network that covers all of Latin America, home to almost half the world's Catholics. Intelligence about the papal election, which had once been the private concern of no more than a few thousand Church insiders, had suddenly become common to all the world, so that Rome itself could be present to a nun in Tokyo and a lawyer in Riobamba and a mayor in San Francisco, giving them reason to care about the implications of this papal election in a way their parents and grandparents were never informed enough to care about as they did.

More important (and this is what made 2005 so completely different), Catholics everywhere—and not only Catholics, but every man and woman on earth with a spark of religion in them and a feel for history—could also have a real presence in Rome because they could now express themselves about the kind of pope they wanted with an unprecedented ease and an incalculable power. They did it on the Internet, that miraculous child of the geosynchronous satellite and the personal computer that has so revolutionized the planet's communications. Suddenly, the Internet allowed people to make their opinions known in a realm where many of the cardinals also dwelled—in cyberspace. Insofar as the cardinals surfed the Internet (and many of them did, almost obsessively), one wondered whether they could fail to pay attention to the hopes and prayers of the people who were cheering for them to make the right choice.

Many cardinals told me they were paying attention. They told me they felt blessed—as no other cardinal-electors had ever been blessed before—because they had new ways of understanding what their people wanted of them. The College of Cardinals had no formal machinery for promoting their own understanding. They wouldn't be taking any public opinion polls, for example, before this conclave. So some of them relied on their local press to reflect public opinion. And thanks to the Internet, they had new windows on the rest of the world. They could read every major publication in the world as easily as they could read their local daily newspaper. The Internet had another treasure for them: a myriad of Web sites where they could listen in on people of every class, free from censors or gatekeepers, saying what they wanted to see in a new pope—and saying it there on a daily basis.

These people with an Internet voice hoped many of the cardinals were listening, but they knew, of course, that the cardinal-electors were members of the pope's senate, not the people's senate. They had won their positions by appointment, not by a popular vote, and they didn't come to the conclave like delegates to a political convention, committed to a particular man. Still, after the Second Vatican Ecumenical Council of the early 1960s redefined the Church as all the people of God, many ordinary folks expected the cardinals to take the lead in building a new kind of Church, a Church that listened—even, some hoped, a people's Church. In effect, and in a new way, the people of God thought they had some kind of consultative role in this election, and they voiced their opinions in cyberspace.

Christine Roussel, a legal researcher in New York City, put a prayer on the Internet, asking God "to part the Red Sea of fear, power, and bureaucracy and give us the pope we need!" Andrew Greeley, an American priest-sociologist, published an online survey that had asked 4,278 Catholics in five countries if they wanted a new pope who would give more autonomy to the local bishops, show more concern about the life of ordinary laypeople, permit more change in the Church, appoint lay advisers, return to the practice of local election of bishops, ordain women, and allow priests to marry. He found surprising support, as high as 78 percent in Germany and as low as 55 percent in Poland, for all of these mostly democratic reforms. And We Are Church, an umbrella for 140 reform organizations, issued a three-page statement on the Internet calling for a bishop of Rome who would share leadership with other bishops and the whole people of God. Its statement focused on qualities of leadership, not on specific candidates for pope.

These people could speak boldly because they were now so much more well informed. On the eve of the conclave, anyone with a computer could make the acquaintance of the Nigerian cardinal Francis Arinze, now featured on more than two thousand Web sites. Internet surfers could visit no less than 250 sites to learn about the background of Brazilian cardinal Cláudio Hummes, his record as archbishop of São Paolo, and what he had said about the family, eternal life, and Pope John Paul II's teachings on social justice. Anyone who knew how to use Google could find more than a hundred thousand entries on Cardinal Joseph Ratzinger, John Paul II's doctrinal chief; many of these sites gave the full text of one or another of Ratzinger's important speeches over the past decade. And millions of people on thousands of electronic bulletin boards could share their feelings with like-minded spirits about what they were reading. John Wauck, a priest and professor of communications at Rome's Santa Croce University, said, "I run into housewives who are telling me about Cardinal So-and-so, and I'm wondering, where do you get that information? I can't help but think the Internet is feeding that."

Some asked, rightly enough, how many of the cardinal-electors would pay attention to these newly vocal Christians. In a 1996 directive on papal elections, John Paul II decreed that cardinals could not speak with the outside world during the conclave, or be spoken to by anyone but another cardinal. No telephones. No radios. No television. No e-mail. Electors should be attentive to the voice of the Holy Spirit, no other.

As far as we know, that rule was observed during the conclave of 2005, but only during the days when the cardinals were actually casting their ballots. Before then, in fact for several years before Pope John Paul II passed to his reward, many of the cardinal-electors haunted the Internet. Only one of many, Cardinal Julius Darmaatmadja of Jakarta (sometimes with the help of his aides) had been reading the *New York Times*, the *Los Angeles Times*, and *The Times* of London on the Internet. He could type in "next pope" on a half-dozen search engines and be ushered into hundreds of Web sites that gave him a sense of what people were thinking and feeling all over the world. He could (and did) correspond by e-mail with a number of his favorite theologians, and with friends from his own polyglot community in Jakarta who were not too shy to tell him what kind of pope they wanted. He could (and did) lurk on the fringes of any number of electronic bulletin boards and Listservs, allowing himself to ponder a mighty range of Catholic opinion (and even Muslim opinion, too, for Darmaatmadja lives in a predominantly Muslim country) that could not fail to tell him what kind of pope people wanted to see in John Paul's successor. If the Holy Spirit was speaking to Cardinal Darmaatmadja, this is how She was doing it, through the voices of other men and women or, as Pope John XXIII would have said, through history—that is, through events themselves.

Furthermore, when Cardinal Darmaatmadja and the other cardinal-electors arrived in Rome for a last good-bye to the deceased, long-reigning pope, they came determined to make maximum use of their weeks of freedom to compare notes with their fellow cardinals, during a period called the "preconclave," before they were finally rendered incommunicado inside the Sistine Chapel to cast their first ballots.

Cardinals are political animals. They couldn't have achieved their eminence otherwise. Whether these cardinals had started their careers as diocesan clergy or as members of a religious order, they, like the executives in any corporation, had networked their way to the top. They learned the art of politics, closely allied to the arts of conversation and of compromise, trading information for power. Now, at this conclave, information was power—power, at least, to make the most intelligent possible choice for the 264th successor of Peter, and thus shape the future of the Church.

Yes, they were cardinals, appointed by the pope to do two things: advise the pope (but only when asked to do so) and elect a new pope when he passed on. But no one could expect them to make their choice in an information vacuum. They were also bishops, with a mandate to serve their people. In biblical terms, they were shepherds, called upon to feed their sheep. In 2005, that call had become far more complicated than ever before. For one thing, the sheep-shepherd metaphor did not much work for city dwellers, many of whom will never see a living shepherd or a live sheep. For another, their people did not much like to think of themselves as sheep. They had adult ideas, and more and more, they were demanding that those ideas be heard.

But this is what made the cardinals' task more complicated: their people did not speak with one voice, but two.

Ever since the French Revolution, two factions in the Church had been battling, not so much over the meaning of their faith but over ways to advance and give an account of that faith. One side said the Church was outside history. It was a perfect society, with no need of help from anyone but God; it didn't have to worry about giving an account of itself to anyone else. The other side said that because Jesus had been part of history, the Church was also part of history—which meant that it had to grow up as the world was growing up. And growth means change. "In a higher world it is otherwise," said the famed English cardinal John Henry Newman, "but here below, to live is to change, and to be perfect is to have changed often."

One side bought into the zeitgeist—the spirit of the age that hailed progress, pluralism, freedom, and democracy. The other side looked upon the very notion of progress as a sacred cow.

The two sides fought at Vatican II in the early 1960s, and they were about to fight again in this conclave, a little more than forty years later—two parties, the party of change versus the party of no change. The change party wanted to update the Church. The no-change party despised the word "updated" and its sister word "reform," a word they had looked on with some suspicion ever since Martin Luther nailed his theses to a church door in sixteenth-century Germany. "Reform" sounded like "Protestant."

The change party knew their Church had to reform or die (or as Pope John XXIII had warned in 1962, become a museum). The no-change party said that the main thing the Church had to offer a world that was caught up in chaos was its solid, unbroken tradition.

The change party said the Church had to reach out to sinners and people at the margins and help them face their chaotic condition by looking ahead to the future, not by dreaming about days past. The no-change party wondered how inclusive the Church could be and still be the Church; people needed to obey the pope and the bishops.

The change party said that what the people needed most was freedom. The no-change party said that this freedom had created a runaway Church—priests rewriting the mass in popular jargon, or consecrating potato chips and Coca-Cola instead of bread and wine; Catholics joining Planned Parenthood; priests asking for "reduction to the lay state" so they could marry; nuns asking to be dispensed from their vows so they could marry young curates. They cited the words of Pope Paul VI, uttered in 1974 as if they were a judgment on the state of the Church in 2004: "The smoke of Satan has entered the temple of God."

The no-change people, many of whom had been trained in the court culture of the Vatican, clung to the notion of the pope as monarch. The change people wanted to see a pope who would not only listen to people but heed their words, too, so he could serve them with what they said they needed, rather than what he thought they ought to have. To the no-change people, this sounded too much like democracy. And democracy frightened them.

In 2002, Cardinal Giovanni Battista Re, one of John Paul II's company men, spoke at a conference in Milan concerning democracy in the Church. In a democracy, said Re, the people are sovereign, whereas the Church is ruled by a pope whose authority is "instituted from above." Re explained that in the Church the people are protected from themselves by "the hierarchical constitution of the Church," which "must not be seen as a limitation to the freedom and spontaneity of Christians, but as one more manifestation of God's mercy toward men." How so? Because that hierarchical constitution can remove the Church from the "variations, mutations, and competitions that occur in history."

The word "hierarchy" is from the Greek. It means "rule by the holy," and in an extended sense, "rule from above." Over centuries, Catholics accepted that rule from above as God-given. The pope and his bishops issued orders. The people followed them—or else. Even when the Church's hierarchy finds more democratic ways of doing things (as, inevitably, though ever so slowly, it will), its pyramidal structure will probably remain for some time to come. Catholics are not Congregationalists. For many of them, there is something solid about a pyramid. They take comfort in having a pope in Rome—and a bishop in downtown Detroit, Dublin, and Dar es Salaam—who can connect them to the men who walked and talked with Jesus.

But Catholics in the twenty-first century live in a different kind of world than the people who walked and talked with Jesus. They aren't too sure they want to follow orders, even from a man who can trace his authority back to Saint Peter himself. And while an administrator like Cardinal Re could well be forgiven for trying to avoid the "variations, mutations, and competitions" of history, many men and women are now exhilarated by precisely those elements. They live more intensely and more awarely *in history* than ever. They see events unfolding on a global stage, where time is accelerating, and they are sometimes asked to climb up on that stage themselves and take a speaking part. "When things speed up like this," Marshall McLuhan wrote in 1980, "hierarchy disappears. As a bureaucratic figure, the pope becomes obsolete, but as a role player, he is more important than ever."

McLuhan was a little ahead of his time. Within the Church at least, John Paul II still possessed a curious omnipotence at the top of the old pyramidal structure. He enjoyed an almost slavish devotion from many of his flock, and at the beginning of the year 2005, he was able to demand strict obedience from a huge professional class—4,695 bishops, 405,000 priests, 802,000 nuns, 143,000 lay missionaries, and 2.7 million catechists—who ran thousands of churches, schools, hospitals, orphanages, and programs promoting everything from an end to the death penalty to wars on hunger and plague. It was a community devoted to service, men and women giving their lives for others. Most of them didn't really have any daily sense of "working for the pope." They knew that, in the words of an American Jesuit theologian, "the primary church is the church on the ground, the local church. Rome and the Vatican can do and say all sorts of things that are relevant or not. But what most affects people is what happens in their local church, the local praying community."

Still and all, Rome mattered. Most Catholics respected the pope, much more than most Americans respected their president, and the pope's rules meant something to them, even (maybe especially) in the most intimate, personal parts of their lives. If members of the Catholic community broke one of those rules—if, for example, a priest "attempted marriage" or if a Catholic married someone who was divorced—they were automatically excommunicated. This meant that, unless they repented, they were barred from the sacraments and, some believed, barred from heaven itself.

Outside the Church, John Paul II used his power to project an authority that secular rulers admired. On their travels to more troubled places, presidents and prime ministers felt fortunate indeed to stop in Rome, to see the pope and secure ten to fifteen minutes in his presence. When the pope died, kings and queens and presidents and prime ministers jetted into Rome to occupy prime seating close to the pope's bier, to be seen by a television audience of 3 billion people as pass holders in what one of them called "the prime drawing room of international politics."

The heads of many major international corporations, Catholic or not, also found ways of seeing the pope. As a result, almost any day of the week when John Paul II was still quite able to speak, he could raise a half million dollars with a single phone call to a wealthy Catholic. His art collection alone was worth an estimated $63 billion and his basilica—Saint Peter's—was priceless. Spoken from Saint Peter's Square, or indeed from any microphone in the world, his words could unite people or push them apart, foment hatred or heal it. In the fall of 1962, a pope brought together the leaders of the two great atomic powers to help avert a nuclear exchange. This is the kind of power a pope has when he takes the helm of the barque of Peter, power in the family of the Church, power in the wider world.

But how should a pope exercise that power now, in a world where hierarchy is fading away? That was one of the things the cardinals would have to talk about at the conclave. Some were quite prepared to agree with McLuhan, that in the cybernetic world we live in now, the new pope would have to climb down from the apex of power's pyramid and be satisfied with an iconic presence in the world—not imposing his rule over the people, but listening to them in their needs. More traditionally minded cardinals said that, by all means, the new pope should listen to the people's needs, but then follow Pope John Paul II's example by giving them firm, solid, unequivocal, moral leadership.

The question was, what did the people need? Many said the people could find all their needs fulfilled by sticking close to the faith of their fathers. Others pointed out that people of faith were finding the Church less and less able to meet their needs for meaning and for community. In many countries of Western Europe, once so solidly Christian, less than 10 percent of the population went to Sunday services of any kind. In April 2001, a poll conducted by London's *Sunday Telegraph* found that 49 percent of the nominally Christian English population did not know why they were celebrating Easter. In the United States, people joked about the second-largest denomination of Christian believers: former Catholics. Obviously, the Church wasn't getting its message across. True, John Paul II had become the most visible man on the planet and, according to some polls, the most admired. It was strange, however, that so many young people seemed to love the singer but so few listened to his song.

During his entire papacy, John Paul II had called seventeen international assemblies of bishops in Rome to help him make the Church more relevant. But in many of these meetings—officially called "synods"—the bishops had tried to make the pope more relevant by, paradoxically, seeing how they could diminish his power. It was a delicate subject, and the pope had been touchy about it, so they used a code word that emerged during Vatican II. The word was "collegiality," a term that invited the pope to recognize that the Catholic bishops had responsibilities that were every bit as real as the pope's.

To put it more bluntly than many bishops would dare at these synods (with John Paul sitting in on every session, glaring at them), the pope had too much power, and the local churches had too little. Worse, the longer the pope stayed in office, the more absolute he had become in its exercise. "It is not good for a pope to reign for more than twenty years," John Henry Newman observed in 1873, referring to Pope Pius IX, who, then twenty-seven years into his papacy, had become a complete tyrant. "He begins to think he is a god."

Through most of his papacy, John Paul II had given members of the Church's change party ample excuse to make the same charge. Eamonn Duffy, the historian from Cambridge, judged that this pope had disempowered local churches, stifled intellectual inquiry, disparaged women, encouraged clericalism and curial bullying, and in his repudiation of liberation theology and his campaign against condoms in AIDS-ravaged Africa, betrayed the poor.

Duffy, a subject all of his life to an English queen with not much more than symbolic power, was only one of thousands of thinking Catholics who wanted the pope to be less a monarch and more a democrat. A monarch, thinking Catholics said, will preside over one kind of Church, a democrat over another. A monarch will try to provide the people of God with things that he believes are for their own good. A democrat will ask the people of God to define their own good. A monarch will demand uniformity, a one-size-fits-all clerical Church. A democrat will listen to his bishops, put his blessing on their diverse local solutions to their most pressing problems, and soft-pedal "the divinely instituted hierarchical constitution of the Church."

Members of the change party scorned the very notion of hierarchy itself, and had huge objections to its "divine institution." When they saw the pomp of a papal mass in Saint Peter's Basilica, or noted the fear in the eyes of a lowly Vatican functionary, they asked, would Jesus have ever wanted this? They observed that hierarchy was not a popular notion through much of the twentieth century, not in a world that looked with some skepticism on the self-professed holiness of a rule that translated into the self-righteousness of its rulers.

But the no-change party, which had a strong presence in this conclave, would defend it. "There's nothing wrong with hierarchy," Cardinal George Pell of Sydney, Australia, told me before the conclave. In Pell's view, his hierarchical Church had existed for two thousand years and it seemed to be doing just fine. Didn't most of the world's Catholics regard the pope as holiness itself, almost a god? Didn't those of other faiths continue to see him as a man of God? John Paul II had spoken of God so often, with such familiarity, and with such reach, because of the mass media. And didn't the Church's solid success through the centuries prove everything? How else could it have become so big? Pell said there was "something fine about a monarchic papacy."

Pell knew some who were hoping for the chance to lead. In fact, on the eve of the conclave of 2005, the same ten cardinals were featured on almost every Vatican watcher's list of *papabili* (the Italian word is literally translated as "pope-able") because they—or their champions—had already given subtle signals of their ambition. Only one of these *papabili* was from Italy, and six were from the third world, a fact that seemed to portend that this conclave might hold some surprises for the veteran Vatican watchers, who, going with the historical odds, were predicting another Italian pope. Italians had owned the papacy for 455 years before a Pole took it away from them in 1978.

There was a time during previous conclaves when Italian cardinals were so numerous they could have their own nominee locked in before any group of foreign cardinals could start lobbying for a candidate of their own. But in 2005, there were only twenty Italian electors and no one believed that an Italian background alone would make a man pope. All the candidates were pious enough; that was a given. What set them apart was their attitude to change in the structures of Church government. Of the ten men who made one widely distributed list in early

2004, it turned out that half were open to some kind of radical, even constitutional, change that could make the Church more accountable to its people, and half were not. In alphabetical order, the *papabili* were

- Francis Arinze, 71, from Nigeria, prefect of the Congregation for Divine Worship in Rome. *No change.*
- Jorge Mario Bergoglio, 68, archbishop of Buenos Aires, Argentina. *Change.*
- Godfried Danneels, 70, archbishop of Mechelen-Brussel, Belgium. *Change.*
- Ivan Dias, 67, archbishop of Bombay, India. *No change.*
- Cláudio Hummes, 69, archbishop of São Paulo, Brazil. *Change.*
- Walter Kasper, 70, the German president of the Pontifical Council for Promoting Christian Unity in Rome. *Change.*
- Norberto Rivera Carrera, 61, archbishop of Mexico City. *No change.*
- Oscar Andrés Rodríguez Maradiaga, 61, archbishop of Tegucigalpa, Honduras. *Change.*
- Christoph Schönborn, 59, archbishop of Vienna. *No change.*
- Dionigi Tettamanzi, 69, archbishop of Milan. *No change.*

A Web site called freeserve.betting.com listed many of the same names, along with a betting line that established Tettamanzi as the favorite (at 31–10); Arinze was close behind at 9–2, and Hummes at 5–1. Freeserve had two members of the party of change on its list at 21–1: Carlo Martini, the retired archbishop of Milan, and Cormac Murphy-O'Connor, of Westminster, in London.

At that time, in 2004, Cardinal Joseph Ratzinger did not make any lists. He said he wasn't a candidate because of his age, then seventy-seven, and because he was weary after serving for twenty-three years as John Paul II's guardian of orthodoxy—prefect of the Congregation of the Doctrine of the Faith, once called the Holy Office of the Inquisition. But in giving his approval to some candidates and lobbying against others from his undisputed place near the top of the Church's pyramidal structure, many thought Ratzinger would have much to say about his choice to shape the future of the Church. He would be a kingmaker.

For years, Cardinal Carlo Martini, then also seventy-seven, had been on almost everyone's list of *papabili,* and he was still the giant in the College of Cardinals—a biblical scholar, author of more than two dozen works, and a prepossessing preacher who could draw admiration from audiences across the globe. (In the summer of 1999, he spoke to the faculty at Harvard and received a standing ovation.) Most prognosticators removed Martini from their list of *papabili* when he resigned Milan in 2001 at the age of seventy-five. They assumed he was too old to be in the running for pope any longer. But in the spring of 2004, Martini was still a cardinal, the same age that Angelo Giuseppe Roncalli was in 1958 when he was elected John XXIII.

Roncalli was elected *because* he was old: after the almost twenty-year-long papacy of Pius XII, the college wanted a man who wouldn't be around for another twenty years. If in this conclave the cardinals were looking for such a man (and some said they were), then it was possible for them to choose Martini. He was still a giant, and perhaps as much a kingmaker as Ratzinger.

But who would be the king? None of the most-mentioned *papabili* could even admit they were in contention. Partly because of the papacy's shocking history (when some candidates had their rivals poisoned so they could assume the role of Christ's vicar on earth), every one of these cardinals had to hide even an innocent ambition to lead.

In the United States and in England—in fact, in any democratic nation—candidates for the highest office struggle openly for the top job, and spend hundreds of millions of dollars to attain it. In the Church, papal candidates like to suggest that the Holy Spirit would rule the outcome—an effort to conceal the fact (perhaps even to themselves) that, in a conclave, real men are locked in contention for power, which need not be a dark word. Even the angelic popes of the twentieth century lobbied for the papacy. They told themselves they didn't want the papacy for its own sake, but because they wanted to make a difference in the world.

In 1939, on the eve of World War II, Eugenio Pacelli, from his high post in the cabinet of Pius XI, had his election arranged in advance; he won a unanimous vote on an early ballot and became Pius XII. Angelo Giuseppe Roncalli went around charming the kingmakers before the conclave that elected him John XXIII in 1958. Giovanni Battista Montini remained conspicuously and calculatingly absent from Rome almost until the cry of *Extra omnes!*—"Everyone out!"—began the proceedings inside the Sistine Chapel in 1963. Once there, before he became Pope Paul VI, he had to promise a majority of the electors that his papacy would carry on the revolution that began with John XXIII's efforts to make a people's Church. In October 1978, the cardinals arrived in Rome to elect a successor to John Paul I, who had died of a heart attack a month after his election. The electors were eager to find a man who would last somewhat longer than that. They found just the one, a smiling, macho cardinal from Poland, Karol Wojtyla. He was only fifty-eight, and he had the concrete proof of his fitness in his cassock pocket, his recent electrocardiogram.

They elected Karol Wojtyla on the seventh ballot, and he took the name John Paul II, an indication that he (like his predecessor John Paul I) intended to follow the lead of John XXIII and of Paul VI, who, during the 1960s, made some moves to democratize the Church's governance. Instead, Papa Wojtyla (as he was called by the Italian press) did all he could to reimpose a more rigid hierarchical model on the Church, something that some of those who voted for him hadn't foreseen. In a crucial moment during the last ballot of the October 1978 conclave, Cardinal Franz Koenig of Vienna made a silent nod toward Wojytla that gave him the last votes needed for a two-thirds majority. Koenig later lamented that move, professing that he didn't really know how much Wojytla would pull back from the charter that was written at Vatican II.

John Paul II feared a runaway democracy in which, he said, "everyone gets to vote on everything." This was a rhetorical exaggeration, one that the pope employed whenever he needed to quash loose talk in his synods about collegiality. "The Church is not a democracy," he said many times, occasionally adding, "and no one from below can decide on the truth." But calls at many of John Paul's synods for more democratic structures never included suggestions that people vote on Catholic "truth." What Christians believed had been pretty well fixed since the Nicene Creed of A.D. 325. What their leadership did—that is to say, how the Church governed itself—was something that had changed through the centuries in very human ways. And because the Church was human, it was always in need of reform.

Which means change.

Which means political struggle.

The passing of power (and the politicking that goes with it) is a fact of life, even in the Church. The very word "church" comes from a Greek word referring to the gathering of free citizens called to debate matters of civic import. When the early Christians emerged from the catacombs, their assembly patterned itself on an imperial Roman political model. In medieval times, the Church followed a feudal model—serfs at the bottom, then vassals, then lords—with local lord-bishops exercising their authority without much reference to Rome. Pope Gregory VII, in an effort to centralize authority during the eleventh century, made the papacy into an absolute monarchy. Subsequent popes were frozen in kingly postures and took on new titles that summed up the gathering of power represented by the papacy.

When the new pope uttered his word of acceptance, he acquired nine titles: Bishop of Rome, Vicar of Jesus Christ, Successor to the Prince of the Apostles, Supreme Pontiff of the Universal Church, Patriarch of the West, Primate of Italy, Archbishop and Metropolitan of the Province of Rome, Sovereign of the Vatican City-State, and—a commission that comes as something of a surprise in this lineup, for it implies that this supreme pontiff is called to a most unusual kind of leadership—Servant of the Servants of God.

Taking servanthood seriously in 2005 had many liberal Catholics calling for a new kind of governance in the Church. They complained because their bishops, hampered by a rigid, top-down autocracy, couldn't make a move without consulting Rome. On the other hand, could the cardinals gathered for the conclave of 2005 choose a candidate who threatened to change the way things had been done for most of the twentieth century?

The quick answer was no. Some 25 percent of the cardinal-electors held offices in the Roman Curia, and all but two of them had been created by John Paul II. Few expected that either the curialists or the cardinal who served as leaders of dioceses would be all that willing to vote for someone who would turn John Paul's pyramid upside down. Curial cardinals who voted for such a man (never mind upsetting history and tradition) might be abdicating their own power. And most of the other cardinal-archbishops, especially those who had spent some of their early years in Rome, seemed cut from the same clerical cloth. Justin Rigali of Philadelphia worked for more than twenty years in the Vatican before he was assigned to his native United States. Ivan Dias of Bombay began in the Vatican diplomatic corps, took junior postings elsewhere, and then, back in Rome, worked as a desk officer in the Secretariat of State. Both Rigali and Dias were firmly in the party of no change.

Many Vatican watchers believed the cardinals would elect a clone of John Paul II—another monarch, another centralizer, another pope frozen in old formulas. Others disagreed. Richard McBrien maintained in his *Lives of the Popes* that every conclave in the last two centuries had elected a pope who was quite different from his predecessor. He fell back on admittedly oversimplified political categories to identify them: liberals and conservatives.

On this model, McBrien could trace a surprisingly consistent pattern of first one party in the winner's circle, then the other. Pius IX, a conservative elected in 1846, was followed in 1878 by Leo XIII, a liberal, who was followed in 1903 by Pius X, a conservative, who was followed in 1914 by Benedict XV, a liberal, who was followed in 1922 by Pius XI, a conservative, who was followed in 1939 by Pius XII, a complicated liberal-conservative, who was followed in 1958 by John XXIII, a liberal, who was followed in 1963 by Paul VI, a liberal who turned dour in his last decade, who was followed in 1978 by John Paul I, a liberal, who was followed a little more than a month later by John Paul II, a conservative. Not a perfect pattern, but a pattern nonetheless.

McBrien's theory was born of simple historical observation, but it was predicated on a biblical image: the cardinals represented a pilgrim church, one that was picking its zigzag way through history, trying, like the members of any human institution, to figure out what works. One could claim that the cardinals were simply good sailors who would move the barque of Peter through the seas of the world by learning to tack.

Possibly on that theory alone, McBrien approached the conclave expecting change. Other pope watchers thought the conclave would elect a candidate committed to change because of their own simple conclusions about the current turbulence in the Church. There was something in the Church that was not working, something that needed changing. But since pope watchers didn't get to vote in the conclave, the real question was, how many cardinal-electors had the same perception? From their perches on top of the Church's power pyramid, it was not always easy for these eminences to see the turbulence on the plain below.

Perhaps the greatest cardinal temptation was a sin of sloth—not wanting to see. History is full of tales about great men who make wrong decisions because they do not want to see what is obvious to all around them. General Custer did it at Little Big Horn in 1876. President George W. Bush made the same kind of obstinate, nobody-can-tell-me decision before he launched Operation Shock and Awe in Iraq in 2003. In a democracy, there is an antidote for this willed blindness. It is called public opinion—not often wrong, according to James Surowiecki in his book *The Wisdom of Crowds,* which argues persuasively that large groups of people are smarter than an elite few (no matter how brilliant): better at solving problems, fostering innovation, coming to wise decisions, even predicting the future.

It seemed quite unlikely on the eve of the conclave that the College of Cardinals, one of the most elite clubs in the history of the world, could be swayed by the wisdom of their crowd, some billion souls around the world who called themselves Catholics. But some believed that even the most autocratic cardinal-electors such as George Pell could be moved by public opinion.

Public opinion, in fact, had already proven how it could upset even the usually detached monsignori who worked inside the Vatican. It was public opinion, specifically an editorial in the *New York Times,* that forced John Paul II to order all the American cardinals to Rome in April 2002 to tell him about the priest sex-abuse scandal. Revelations of how perhaps 5 percent of the priests in America were seducing little boys and young men had emerged day by day during the winter of 2002; the stories appeared on the front page of the *New York Times* for all but one of forty-six straight days.

The problem called for radical reforms. Rushing the American cardinals to Rome was pure public relations, a media event that culminated in a news conference during which some of the cardinals made vague promises about what they would do with their wayward priests. They did not speak of any radical reforms, because the pope already had a simple answer to the complicated question of wayward priests: they simply had to become men of prayer.

Some of the pope's closest advisers even denied there was a sex-abuse crisis. One high-ranking curial cardinal who had been touted in the papal sweepstakes as a possible successor to the pope suggested this was strictly an American problem. Another *papabile* blamed the press for concocting stories to denigrate the Church. In fact, by the beginning of 2005, American bishops had already paid hundreds of victims combined settlements of almost a billion dollars.

The situation clearly called for a closer look at the priesthood itself from the cardinal-electors who were summoned to Rome for the conclave. For two or three weeks, these cardinals would never have more power to influence the future course of the Church. Could they cut through all the denial and find enough honesty within themselves to probe deeper into the possible cause of the problem? Recent scholarly analysis (and their own experience) told them that a majority of priests were suffering from what one of the Church's most admired moral theologians once called an "ecclesiogenic pathology." This meant that the Church's sex-fearing, woman-hating system itself was making some priests ill, not to mention those Catholics who had been listening their whole lives to spokesmen for that system.

John Paul II had seen no need to launch a thoroughgoing reevaluation of the Church's pathogenic system, or reexamine the training given in the seminaries, or question the value of celibacy, or restructure the priesthood itself. He not only failed to do that; he intimidated others who tried to discuss these issues.

What could a new pope do?

Celibacy was not a doctrinal question. It had nothing to do with what Catholics believed. It had everything to do with the way the Church had operated under an absolute monarch surrounded by celibate males for more than a thousand years. But how could a new pope change this system in the face of a previous pope's insistence that there be no change? Popes are quite reluctant to veto the policies of their predecessors. "The structure of the Church," John Paul II said in January 2004, "cannot be conceived according to simple political models. Its hierarchical constitution is based on the will of Christ and, as such, forms part of the deposit of faith, which must be preserved and totally transmitted through the centuries."

If John Paul was right, then it seemed the Church was stuck. But Church scholars maintained that it was only the pope who was stuck—in a myth. The very week John Paul spoke these words, a group of American Catholic historians published a symposium that would put the pope's theory of the Church in context. Brian Tierney, a former president of the American Catholic Historical Society, and a member of that symposium, wrote:

> The early Church was a community in which all participated in community life; when the first major doctrinal issue arose, it was settled by "the apostles and elders with the whole Church" meeting in council in Jerusalem (Acts 15:22). The first popes did not even claim the powers that modern ones take for granted. They did not exercise jurisdiction over the whole Church; it did not occur to anyone that they were infallible; they did not appoint bishops; they did not summon general councils. Bishops were elected by their clergy and people, and general councils were summoned by emperors. It is a long way from there to here. The Church has been governed in different ways in the past and it may be again in the future.

Had the time now come to start thinking of different ways? Not necessarily. This conclave was not a council. The cardinals weren't here to reform the Church, but to elect a pope. Still, their choice would say a great deal about the strength of their commitment to reform.

Historically, the cardinals have made their choices at a conclave for a multitude of fascinating reasons, never entirely free of outside pressures—usually from one or another faction in the Church, sometimes from potentates, princes, and prime ministers, who have not been shy in expressing their preferences for one candidate rather than another. "Where you have human beings involved," wrote Richard McBrien, "you have the human factors of politics, self-interest, greed, and desire for power. How the two—the divine and the human—interact in a papal election, one cannot determine."

The human players were here in Rome. Not only the cardinal-electors—a whole host of men and women who represented special interests inside the Church filled Rome on the eve of the conclave to lobby the cardinal-electors, either directly, if they could get access to their favorite cardinals, or indirectly, by giving interviews to members of the media. (The cardinals, they presumed correctly, would see or hear the interviews.)

Those from the party of no change were in Rome, standing on the edge of almost every crowd. Members of Opus Dei, the notoriously secretive "personal prelature" of the pope, and their ideological allies, international organizations called the Neo-Catechumenate, Communion and Liberation, and Focolare, along with priests belonging to the Legionaries of Christ, together with their friends and supporters, all came to the conclave to tell the world how numerous they were, and lobby for the kind of man who would continue the current programs and policies.

Representatives of the Church's party of change flocked in, too, looking to influence electors on behalf of a candidate who might move the Church in new directions. There were representatives and spokespersons, for example, of the Women's Ordination Conference; of CORPUS, an international association of inactive priests (most of them married) who yearn to be active again; and the leaders of We Are Church, an international group that was first launched at the 1995 *Kirchenvolksbegehren* in Austria, when a half million people signed a petition demanding reform in the Church. (More than 2 million did so later in Germany.)

These special interests couldn't help but give the conclave a political cast, for they brought an air of high contention to Rome, one not seen since the end of Vatican II. This pleased the war lovers in the media, tumbling into the city to cover another kind of battle, looking for heroes and villains. They rejoiced in the prediction of George Weigel, John Paul II's almost-official biographer, who said that since the cardinals didn't know one another very well, and didn't have a single common language, it would take them some time to find a successor. Weigel said the conclave would be "complex, difficult, probably lengthy—and perhaps quite surprising."

Thomas J. Reese, editor of the Jesuit weekly *America,* did not think the conclave would produce any surprises (though it would turn out to have a personal one for him). After John Paul II had named his last batch of new cardinals in the fall of 2003, Reese sent an e-mail advisory to his select list of journalists covering the Church.

> John Paul II has done what anyone would do if they were pope—he has appointed men who agree with him on the major issues that face the Church. The next conclave, as a result, will not elect someone who will reject the legacy of John Paul. With the next pope, we will see more continuity than change.

CHAPTER TWO

Death

A Call to Serve by Suffering

POPE JOHN PAUL II died more than twenty years after Vatican watchers had written him off. The experts first started doing so in May 1981, when he was felled by an assassin's bullet—and survived. They did so again in July 1992, when he had a large benign tumor removed from his large intestine. At the time, the Vaticanologist Peter Hebblethwaite announced that the pope was dying of cancer and wrote a book called *The Next Pope.*

Hebblethwaite died before the book appeared, and John Paul II carried on for more than a decade, despite more ills than most men are heir to. He had an appendectomy. He had four more minor surgeries. He developed Parkinson's disease, not officially confirmed until the end, because, inside the Vatican, the only time a pope is sick is when he's dead. And with each report or rumor about the pope's fading health, major newspapers ran stories about potential successors. Their stories never held up for long, because candidates had a way of dying, or becoming too ill to be taken seriously.

During the Jubilee Year 2000, signs of the pope's Parkinson's became more visible. His left hand trembled, and he walked with a cane in an obvious attempt to maintain his balance. Inevitably, reporters wondered whether the pope could or would resign. Sometimes, they would coax a cardinal to give them a commonsense response: "Certainly, if he's no longer able." Indeed, if the pope were the CEO of a major corporation, the board might have asked for his resignation long before. All too often, however, newspapers would blow the casual response into a major news item, as *The Times* of London did in January 2000 with a story that was headlined: "Critics Join Chorus for Pope to Quit."

From time to time over the next four years, despite pleas from the Holy See's house organ, *L'Osservatore Romano,* that the press "mind its manners," almost every major news organization in the world printed wild guesses about possible successors. The stories were triggered not so much by the pope's obviously fading health but by the impatience of editors.

The pope not only sailed through the Jubilee Year, he continued over the next four years with a schedule that would have taxed men twenty years his junior. He continued to travel the world, he continued to chide its leaders, he continued to "run the Church," as he put it, with increasing self-assurance. In February 2001, he created forty-four new cardinals, bringing the College of Cardinals to an all-time high of 155. No pope had ever made so many on a single day.

By the late spring and summer of 2002, however, it was apparent that John Paul was fading. He started to drool in public, and he could hardly walk. But that didn't stop him from carrying on as before—appearing at his weekly audiences, greeting visiting foreign bishops, and entertaining the heads of various countries passing through Rome. He made three more international trips. He flew to Azerbaijan and Bulgaria in May 2002, jetted halfway around the world in July to preside over another World Youth Day in Toronto, visited Mexico City on his way back to Rome for the beatification of Juan Diego. Then, no sooner in Rome, he turned, somewhat unsteadily, toward his Polish homeland.

He spent four nostalgic August days in Poland and told his countrymen with a pardonable note of pride that he wasn't going to resign as some newspapers predicted he would. "Would Jesus come down from his cross?" he asked. He returned to Rome, spent the rest of August at his summer villa outside Rome, and in the fall of 2002, he was still "pope-ing it up" (as one admiring teenager had described his public posture in Toronto).

In November 2002, John Paul II made a historic trip to Italy's seat of government, to patch up a quarrel between church and state that had been raging since 1870. He told the Italian parliament that as far as he was concerned, the traditional enmity between the Church and the Italian government should end (an enmity that was triggered when revolutionary forces invaded Rome and expropriated the Papal States, which comprised not only Rome but all of central Italy). They all had to work together, he said, for the common good of the most Catholic nation in Europe. As he made his halting way out of the Chamber of Deputies, many applauded, filled with admiration for this heavyweight who was still on his feet in the last round, punching away. But many said they couldn't understand why the pope didn't resign. He gave one good, personal reason: if he did, he wouldn't be able to travel anymore, and that seemed important, as he explained on June 12, 2003, to a group from Alitalia, the Italian airline.

> Right from the day I was elected as bishop of Rome, October 16, 1978, with special intensity and urgency I heard the echo of Jesus' command: "Go into all the world and preach the gospel to all of creation"—to tell everyone that the Church loves them, that the pope loves them, and likewise to receive from them the encouragement and example of their goodness, of their faith.

His critics said this wasn't his job. He was elected to be the bishop of Rome, but in logging 690,000 miles on 104 trips to 129 countries, he became a kind of CEO for Christianity, Inc., and took the holiness business to a new level by canonizing 482 saints and beatifying 1,338 men and women (all but a few of them priests and nuns), more saints and blesseds than all the popes of the last five hundred years combined. In October 2003, he celebrated his twenty-fifth anniversary as pope, beatified Mother Teresa of Calcutta, one of the world's contemporary heroines, and, to everyone's surprise, created thirty-one more cardinals, expanding the college to 184. One hundred thirty-five of them were electors, under the age of eighty, exactly fifteen more than the mandated maximum of allowable electors, 120. Those who wondered how the pope could break the rules were reminded that if the pope could make the rules, he could also unmake them.

Most of the cardinals and the cardinals-designate who gathered that October in Rome (the largest group of cardinals in history) found a sadly disabled man presiding over their Church. When the new cardinals marched up for their red hats, they realized the pope could barely lift his head. Some asked why the Vatican officials were putting the pope through this torture. Then they learned this was his own idea. He was making a statement that though he was old and weak, he was still the pope.

Of those who understood this, some gasped at his courage. Others felt some sorrow, because they knew the pope had already abdicated his responsibility to others. He could last through almost any ceremony with the right medication, but he let Cardinals Joseph Ratzinger and Angelo Sodano (his secretary of state, or prime minister) take care of everything else. He was reading whatever he was given to read. He was signing whatever he was given to sign. Few of the new cardinals had a private meeting with him. He was seeing almost no one. And his few encounters were turning out to be farce.

Two weeks before, on October 4, the pope had received Rowan Williams, the new archbishop of Canterbury, along with a large entourage that included the Roman Catholic primate in England, Cardinal Cormac Murphy-O'Connor. After an exchange of short speeches and the usual picture taking, the historic meeting was over. But the pope hardly knew how historic. As everyone was filing out, one of the archbishop's aides overheard the pope say, "Who were those guys?" His secretary shouted in his ear, "They're from England."

On October 10, John Paul received the president of East Timor and his entourage. After they greeted each other and had photographs taken, the pope and the president retired to the pope's study for a private one-on-one chat. The two of them talked for four minutes or so. Then the pope dozed off—for seventeen minutes. The president didn't know what to do. So he looked at his watch. Eventually, the pope roused himself, said, "Nice talking to you," and rang for his aide.

Now more and more cardinals were saying publicly and privately that the pope ought to think about retiring. John Paul II said he had no plans to do so. He said it again at the beatification of Mother Teresa on October 19.

He carried on like this for another year, letting others craft the solemn sermons and the speeches and even one more pious, theologically dubious encyclical on the Eucharist. But on February 1, 2005, stricken with the flu, he began gasping for breath, and after protesting vehemently for more than four hours that he didn't need to go to the hospital, he started choking and finally gave in. Doctors at the Policlinico Agostino Gemelli received him and rushed him to an emergency room. The pope's spokesman said the visit was "purely precautionary," but a staff member at the hospital said the pope almost died. Indeed, John Paul's condition warranted a nine-day visit. Halfway through that stay, wanting to assure everyone that he was all right, he appeared in a hospital window to give his usual Sunday blessing to the people of Rome, and said he would "continue to serve the Church."

Papal critics were appalled. Hans Küng told German television, "A pope can resign for the need and the necessity of the Church. I think this need and necessity has now risen."

On the ninth day of his stay at the Gemelli, John Paul tried to refute such talk by returning to the Vatican as visibly as he could. Instead of calling for his black Mercedes with the darkened windows, he had his secretary, Stanislaw Dziwisz, order up his popemobile. When it arrived at the Gemelli on the bed of a large white truck, the pope was eased into it by Dziwisz and a brace of hospital attendants and proceeded on a two-mile, sixteen-minute parade through the streets of Rome with an eight-man police motorcycle escort. His trip was hailed by applauding bystanders on the streets and by a large dinner-hour television audience; RAI TV's remote trucks followed the popemobile into Saint Peter's Square, normally dark at this hour, but now ablaze with floodlights.

Marco Politi, longtime Vatican reporter for the Rome daily *La Repubblica*, called the whole solemn scene "*uno* show." He used the English word instead of the Italian *mostra* to indicate the international importance of this televised tour that was carried by satellite "from the metropolises of the United States to villages of the Arab East, so that everyone could know the pope's flu had passed and his command was stronger than before."

Physically, John Paul II was hardly as strong as before. With advanced Parkinson's, he could lose his balance and go crashing to the floor in an instant. His every move—rising, retiring, even going to the bathroom—needed assistance. But he wanted to leave no doubt about his command. He was back at work the next day, or at least seemed to be by making some headlines. A banner in *Le Monde* said the pope had appointed a new archbishop for Paris, and an Associated Press story out of Rome said the pope had reaffirmed his wish to attend a World Youth Day in Germany in August. Resign? Certainly not. *L'Osservatore Romano* carried a page-one headline: "The Rudder Is Still in His Hands."

Two days later, on Sunday, February 13, John Paul II appeared in the window of his third-floor apartment in the papal palace, stood there stiffly, and croaked out his word of welcome, *Benvenuti!*—"Welcome." It was an unseasonably warm day and twenty-five thousand people were gathered in the square to gaze at him. They applauded. Then another voice took over. It was Archbishop Leonardo Sandri, who spoke for two minutes. The gist of the message, after thanking the people for their prayers, was in one sentence: "I always need your help before the Lord, for carrying out my mission that Jesus has entrusted to me."

The pope got his point across, even in the secular media. He had a call, now, to serve by suffering. Christopher Dickey wrote in *Newsweek* that debate about John Paul's "ability to administer the church, as if he were the CEO of a secular corporation, essentially misses the point."

> This pope is not doing a job, he is carrying out a divine mission, and his pain is at its core. This exaltation of suffering may be difficult for many non-Catholics to understand. But suffering, scholars point out, is at the very core of the faith; it is the vital link between the human experience and that of Christ as savior.

Dickey quoted a White Father from Africa, Justo Lacunza-Balda: "The pope is not just an icon. He represents the very essence of Christianity, which is the cross—and resurrection. He is the incarnation in his whole life of the message of Christ." In the meantime, Joaquín Navarro-Valls, the longtime papal spokesman, was telling the press the pope was improving. When John Paul made another brave appearance in his apartment window and croaked out, *Buona Domenica, a tutti*—"Happy Sunday, everybody"—the Associated Press reported he was "on the rebound." The *Newark Star-Ledger* headlined that story "Pope's Return a Godsend for Catholics."

Less than ten days later, the pope was back in the Gemelli for a tracheotomy to help him breathe. It was the pope's seventh surgery, and it left him unable to speak and confused. Though he had reportedly elected the tracheotomy himself, he wrote on a pad when he woke up the next morning, "What have they done to me?"

For seven more days, John Paul II fought for his life. When he had massive heart failure on March 30 and went into septic shock, everyone knew the end was near. He probably died in the early afternoon on Saturday, April 2, but it is likely that the pope's Polish handlers held back the news for more than six hours until an expected crowd of more than a hundred thousand could gather in Saint Peter's Square to say the rosary for him. Only when that prayer was over did a Vatican official tell the crowd that the pope had died a short while before, at 9:27 p.m.

The crowd, which had been agonizing in union with the pope's suffering for several weeks now, broke into spontaneous applause, and sang an ancient Marian hymn, the *Salve Regina,* and then, as the bells of Saint Peter's began to clang, chanted a litany of the saints. Fewer than 20 percent of the throng dispersed. Most of those who remained just stood there regarding the pope's window—priests and seminarians, nuns, couples of all ages, teenagers, children—while the giant bells of Saint Peter's tolled mournfully. When a hundred thousand people gather in one place, there is nothing they can do that is more powerful or more stirring than to be quiet. And they were. Silent.

And so Karol Wojtyla ended his papacy as it had begun, with a show in Saint Peter's Square. He had dazzled humankind for almost twenty-seven years, a record for longevity in the papal office surpassed only by Saint Peter and Pius IX. This multilingual priest-professor-poet, this laborer-turned-actor, this skier, canoeist, and swimmer, this smiling Slav, this sovereign of the Vatican City-State who wasn't afraid to confront communists and capitalists, to kiss the tarmac of almost every airport in the world and weep alongside the death wall at Auschwitz, this brave heart who confessed the Church's complicity in a parade of historic errors that included promotion of the Crusades and the Inquisition and not doing enough to stop the Shoah, this 264th pope in a line of succession that dated back to the first century, was dead.

CHAPTER THREE

Vacant

The Sacredness of the Process

In the metaphorical bestiary of the Catholic Church, tradition is always the lion. And so, when papal power passes and the See of Peter is, as they say, "vacant," the keepers tend to put the lion on public display. That is, they try to follow an ancient protocol that dates from 1274. A dead pope first gets a death mask (but he is not embalmed). A dead pope is bathed and vested, just as if he were being readied to say mass. A dead pope lies in state, to be seen first by members of the papal household, diplomats from all the countries accredited to the Vatican, and kings and queens of all Christendom. A dead pope gets a wooden casket, which is later placed in a nest of two other caskets, one of lead and the other bronze. A dead pope gets nine days of funeral rites, the *novemdiales*. Four cardinals are chosen each day to pronounce the words of absolution over the pope's remains, and for each of the nine days, one of them is chosen to say a mass in Saint Peter's and, in a prepared homily, to speak well of him.

In 1996, John Paul II modified some of these provisions in a document called *Universi Dominici Gregis* ("The Lord's Universal Flock") but he insisted on retaining the nine days of ceremonies. The cardinals were to pray for him and for themselves as they took on the most solemn responsibility of their lives, to elect his successor. The pope wanted the people at large to feel they, too, had a part in the process, mainly to pray that the cardinals would be guided by the Holy Spirit, and he suggested that the cardinals over eighty who could not vote should lead the people in prayer, so the electors could "make their choice before God alone."

The tone was typical of most Vatican documents, pious in the extreme, but what the pope meant to say was clear: We may look like we are in charge, but we are not. God is running things.

Thus, there was an insistence in his order that the sacredness of the whole process be preserved, which was more likely if the cardinals couldn't gossip about it afterward. John Paul II, accordingly, set the most stringent penalty, excommunication, on those who violated his rules for an election that he wanted to be secret—forever. The election should, moreover, maintain an aura of the sacred. The voting would continue to be held in the Sistine Chapel, "where everything is conducive to an awareness of the presence of God, in whose sight each person will one day be judged."

Church historians say that papal elections are surrounded with adornments of the holy to make up for all those centuries when there was nothing holy about them. For six centuries, the clergy of Rome elected the pope and sought confirmation by the people. By the end of the first millennium, however, the papacy had become a pawn in a power game that had very little to do with the faith and much to do with the temporal power of the popes over lands and people. The people seemed willing to pay taxes that redounded to the enrichment of these popes and, often enough, for the comfort and consolation of their mistresses and illegitimate children.

Naturally enough, the papacy had become a prize. Roman nobles used everything from bribery to assassination to gain the papal throne for their own. One pope, Sergius III, who ruled from 904 to 911, came to the papacy after ordering the murder of his predecessor. Pope John XII, who became pope in 955 at the age of eighteen, died from an unfortunate fall, tossed from a bedroom window by a furious husband who had caught him with his wife in flagrante delicto. Benedict IX was elected pope three different times between the years 1032 and 1048, years that were punctuated by the assassination of three rivals.

In 1268, the cardinals gathered in Viterbo to elect a successor to Clement IV (who had died there), and they engaged in a three-year wrangle before finding the necessary two-thirds consensus. The people of Viterbo, who had been feeding and housing the cardinals for all those months, forced the issue by confining the sixteen cardinal-electors to the palace and curtailing their food supply. When the enforced fast brought no immediate action, they exposed the electors to the weather by stripping off the palace roof. Their eventual designee took the name Gregory X, and it was he who began what is now known as the conclave. His own constitution on papal elections in 1274 provided that within ten days after a pope's death, the cardinals were to gather in a common room and remain under lock and key (*cum clave* in Latin) until they chose a new pope. If three days passed without a decision, their meals would be reduced to a single dish at midday and another in the evening. If there was no result in five more days, they would be put on bread, water, and a little wine—to help them concentrate more closely on their task.

The new system hardly solved all the attendant political problems that followed, nor did it prevent outside forces from exerting their influence on the cardinal-electors over the next several centuries. France itself captured the papacy in the early 1300s. Avignon, an elegant royal city in southeastern France, served as papal headquarters from 1309 until 1378, when Gregory XI, the seventh successive French pope, died during a trip to Rome. A Roman mob forced the cardinals who had been traveling with him to name an Italian successor, and they did. That man, Urban VI, turned out to be a world-class schemer who planned to diminish the power of the French cardinals by giving the red hat to a dozen or more Italians.

But the French cardinals slipped away, one by one, and returned to Avignon, declaring the election of Urban VI invalid and promptly electing the French king's cousin, who took the name Clement VII. At that point, the Church had two popes. By 1409, a third contender was telling the world he was the pope. It took an ecumenical council, at Constance from 1415 to 1417, to put aside all three of them and elect a new man, Martin V, who proceeded to restore some prestige and power to the papacy by returning to Rome.

Martin's efforts were quickly undone, however, by his successor, Eugenius IV, the most political of all popes, who started handing out cardinals' hats to prominent members of the courts of Europe and to representative members of old Roman households as well, encouraging every important ruling family in the Italian peninsula in the belief that they were entitled to have at least one member in the College of Cardinals. Over the course of the fifteenth and sixteenth centuries, during the high Renaissance, the college came to be populated by the ruling families of Milan, Florence, Pisa, Siena, Ferrara, and Naples. The conclave that elected Rodrigo de Lançol y Borgia as Pope Alexander VI in 1492 was the most venal in history.

Borgia bought the papacy by bribing a set of cardinals that included ten nephews or great-nephews of dead popes, eight representatives of noble Italian families, four cardinals who had been nominated by foreign kings, and one teenage boy whose father had been a loyal commander in a previous pope's army. No one cared about the general welfare of the Church as much as they cared about their own wealth and power.

The wealth, as always, came from the people, through taxes and the sale of indulgences—instant salvation in the form of free passes through purgatory. The indulgence economy had been set up four hundred years before by Urban II, who, in preaching the First Crusade at Clermont in 1095 to win back the holy places in Jerusalem from the evil empire of Islam, promised plenary indulgences—full remission of all the temporal punishment due to sin—to every Crusader struck down in battle. Then, when the armorers and outfitters of the Crusades pointed out that they were as important to the war effort as were the knights on horseback, they were granted plenary indulgences, too—for their contributions. Soon, all those giving goods or money to the papal exchequer were lining up for their direct passes to heaven.

No one really complained about the arrogance of the claim that a pope or a cardinal had the power to issue tickets to heaven. That was largely a given. But the sale of indulgences seemed necessary, in any event, to finance the construction of the new Saint Peter's Basilica, which was begun in the early 1500s by Julius II, surely the most protean of the popes. Julius II not only commissioned the architect Donato Bramante to design Saint Peter's; he was also the chief patron of both Raphael and Michelangelo. (He was also a military man, who led his own army in a successful expansion of the Papal States into northern Italy, and sired three illegitimate daughters along the way.)

Julius II's successor, Leo X, in charge from 1513 to 1521, bribed his way to the papacy with a subtle set of compromises and political alliances that were made possible by his own inherited wealth (as the son of Florence's Lorenzo de' Medici, the Magnificent) and by his forcefulness and his panache. In response to a conspiracy against his life in which perhaps a majority of his cardinals were implicated, Leo X had one cardinal strangled in the dungeon near Saint Peter's called Castel Sant' Angelo, and two other conspirators hanged, drawn, and quartered. Then he diminished the relative power of the other cardinals by holding a grand consistory, nominating on a single day thirty-one new cardinals loyal to him. It was something that had never happened before and was not to be repeated again until John Paul II created forty-four new cardinals in the winter of 2001.

During the sixteenth century, most papal elections felt the weight of Spain, because of the preeminent standing in Catholic Europe of Philip II, king of Spain from 1556 to 1598. In the seventeenth century, France was a major player at the papal court, especially during the reign of Louis XIV. In the eighteenth and nineteenth centuries, popes became less and less relevant to Europe's political life. The conclaves of 1758 and 1769 turned on matters of little universal importance; the main issue was the suppression of the Jesuits, whose growing influence in Europe threatened the power of its crowned heads. The conclave of 1769 found a candidate willing to dissolve the Jesuits, and in 1773 Clement XIV suppressed the order, more than twenty-three thousand strong, and imprisoned its general, Lorenzo Ricci, in a dungeon near the Tiber, where, two years later, he died.

By the time Pius IX was elected in 1846, in the middle of numerous political and social revolutions, the barque of Peter seemed swamped in a kind of backwater. In 1864, Pius IX issued his infamous *Syllabus of Errors,* which condemned democracy, among other things. (He ruled that Italian Catholics could not participate in the political life of the new nation.) In 1870, the pope lost the Papal States to the forces of the Risorgimento, retreated to Vatican City, and took an embattled, defensive stance against the world. That hardly started changing until 1959, when John XXIII called the Second Vatican Ecumenical Council—Vatican II—in a move to update the Church and make it more relevant to the real world.

. . .

On Thursday, March 31, 2005, when the wire services were reporting that John Paul II was dying, Larry Stammer, chief religion reporter for the *Los Angeles Times,* was on the phone to Cardinal Roger Michael Mahony. Yes, Mahony told Stammer, he'd be headed to Rome as soon as he could get on a jet, and yes, Stammer could come along with him on the same flight, and no, he didn't want to be the new pope. Under other circumstances, he told Stammer, he might have expected some votes at the conclave. He didn't need to tell Stammer he was the right age (sixty-nine), that he was of Italian extraction (his orphaned father had been adopted in Vancouver, British Columbia, by Irish-Canadians named Mahony), and that after dozens of trips to Rome during the last twenty years, he spoke almost fluent Italian (as well as fluent Spanish). He was familiar with the state of Vatican finances (by reason of his membership in the Prefecture for Economic Affairs of the Holy See) and he had a comfortable relationship with many of the men in the Vatican bureaucracy. Like John Paul, he was a good people person (more than he was a scholar) and he had a firm fix on where he felt the Church should be headed in the new millennium.

But if Cardinal Mahony wasn't in the running, Stammer asked him, who was? Mahony said he wasn't sure. "Cardinals don't announce their candidacy. I don't know if anyone really wants to be pope. Not the kind of pope that John Paul has been." He reminded Stammer of John Paul's killing pace, and he recalled the pope's own description of the job: "like sitting on a low-voltage electric chair." Officially, no one wanted this post. That reluctant stance was part of the unofficial protocol. Admitting he wanted to lead the Church would say to the other voting cardinals that he was too ambitious—and therefore not exactly the kind of man the Church really needed.

One of the most interesting popes in history, Leo X, of the Medici family, was more honest. He told his brother, "Let us enjoy the papacy, because God has given it to us." By all accounts, he not only enjoyed it, he wallowed in it. His whole reign, from 1513 to 1521, was a nonstop revel: he presided over masked balls, processions led by clowns and elephants, splendid performances in the Colosseum, classic orations in the Capitol, feasts and speeches on Roman anniversaries, daily parades, and ceremonies for the arrival of ambassadors and princes with groups so large they looked like armies. He went off on hunting expeditions with falcons at his wrists, and packs of dogs, along with cardinals and their retinues, the happy poets of Rome, and a mob of barons and princes and scores of beautiful, charming, and witty courtesans.

In 2005, the papal court was still a court, full of anachronisms that were under attack even by many loyal Catholics. But this papal court was nothing like the Renaissance court of Leo X. There was little or no nepotism, and not a clown or a courtesan to be found. And so Mahony could believe in the sincerity of cardinals all over the world who were telling their local newspapers they did not want the job. What cardinal thought he had the right stuff to follow in the footsteps of Karol Wojtyla?

CHAPTER FOUR

Legacy

More Than a Pope

WHERE HAD KAROL WOJTYLA'S ENERGY come from? Some suggested it came from his countless uncertainties, perhaps because he had had to surmount so many early doubts about his own identity and his own endowments. He was born on May 18, 1920, in a small industrial town near Krakow, Poland, an only child who lost his mother when he was in the third grade, and grew up in a basement apartment in Krakow with his father, a pious, rock-solid moralist who worked in a factory after his retirement as a captain in the Fifty-sixth Infantry Regiment of the Polish army.

At eighteen, most young men feel they can do anything. When Wojtyla was eighteen, he could only watch Hitler's occupying armies march into Poland to decapitate Polish culture. The Nazis shut down all the nation's colleges and secondary schools, banned the speaking of Polish, and made it a capital offense to attend a concert or a play. They limited everyone's rations to nine hundred calories a day and made relentless war on the Church, killing off a third of the Polish clergy, either by outright execution or by banishment to German death camps. Hitler's storm troopers gave Poles in their teens or twenties a choice: deportation to a prison camp or manual labor in Poland. Wojtyla, called Lolek in those days, chose a chemical company in Krakow. He spent his first year in a quarry, breaking up limestone and shoveling it into tram cars, then three years lugging buckets of lime in the water purification unit of the plant's factory.

In the evenings, Lolek spent his time in an underground operation called the Rhapsodic Theater, where he performed secretly onstage and even wrote some plays. Some of his peers had chosen clandestine sabotage as their way of resisting tyranny. That was not Lolek's way. His biographer George Weigel wrote: "Wojtyla deliberately chose the power of resistance through culture, through the power of the word, in the conviction that the 'word' is that on which the world turns."

Wojtyla's father, bedridden for more than a year, died in February 1941, before Lolek's twenty-first birthday. Lolek saw his orphanhood pointing to a future with another family, the family of the Church. Within the year, while continuing to work in the chemical plant, Lolek entered an underground seminary in the home of Krakow's archbishop, Adam Sapieha, who noted his diligence and his piety and then, as the newly minted Cardinal Sapieha, ordained him a priest after four years of study, and sent him off to Rome in 1946 for graduate studies. (There was no doubting young Karol's quickness. In the all-boys high school he had attended in Krakow, he had been a straight-A student, and he had memorized every seminary lesson, even as he was working the night shift in the chemical factory.)

In Rome, young Wojtyla studied with the Dominicans at the Collegium Angelicum. Other European seminaries were then opening up to an expanding intellectual universe, but not the Angelicum. Students there were trained to memorize a body of exquisitely defined and immutable truths that had been more or less set in stone by Pius V in 1566, two years after the close of the Council of Trent. Students at the Angelicum took good notes on the theses of Thomistic neoscholasticism, memorized them, and regurgitated them at exam time as received.

Wojtyla did his graduate work on the theology and spirituality of Saint John of the Cross under the supervision of Reginald Garrigou-Lagrange, the undisputed modern expert on Thomas Aquinas. He defended his thesis (an oral exam in Latin) with a perfect mark, fifty points out of a possible fifty, but he had problems getting his dissertation accepted, so he returned to Poland and was awarded a doctorate by Krakow's Jagiellonian University. With only four years of seminary training (somewhat handicapped by working those factory nights) and two years of Thomism in Rome, he became a full-fledged professor.

Considering the thinness of his six-year training (by comparison, Jesuits who go on for their doctorates study for eighteen to twenty years), Wojtyla became a priestly overachiever.

He did so against the backdrop of another tyranny. While Wojtyla had been studying in Rome in 1948, Poland became a communist nation. At twenty-eight, he had come back to a place, wrote Weigel, "where the dawn knock on the door was still expected, where prisons were full and beatings many, where the secret policeman was still his brother's keeper, and where the Great Teacher was neither Christ nor Buddha but the megalomaniac son of a Georgian shoemaker through whom millions had died."

He started out in a humble country parish, teaching religion to eighth-graders and hearing the confessions of the simple faithful. In eight months, Cardinal Sapieha called him up to a large, lively city parish in Krakow, and made him a chaplain at the Jagiellonian University besides.

He became a battler for the minds of the students, besieged as they were by the official atheism of the state. He attracted young adult intellectuals, launched the first marriage preparation program in the history of Krakow, and started a study group that read its way through the *Summa Theologiae* of Saint Thomas Aquinas in the original Latin.

He took camping trips with young people, and learned to ski and paddle a kayak. He started writing essays for Krakow's independent weekly newspaper, *Tygodnik Powszechny,* run by laymen. He wrote a didactic play called *The Jeweler's Shop* that was published under a pseudonym in a secular magazine. He became a published poet. He never had a bank account, never wrote a check. He worked eighteen-hour days, he slept on the floor, he always wore an old cassock and old shoes, and as far as anyone could tell, he was absolutely uninterested in politics.

Then he was ordered to take a two-year academic sabbatical, won a second doctorate—in social ethics and phenomenology—at the Jagiellonian University, started teaching sexual ethics at the Catholic University of Lublin, and in 1958, only twelve years a priest, became auxiliary bishop of Krakow, just in time to attend the Second Vatican Ecumenical Council in Rome. During the Council's four sessions, he made some modest contributions to its work and some friends in high places. In the middle of the Council, he was named archbishop of Krakow. Three years later, he became a cardinal. He was forty-seven.

How did he move up so fast? He had become a public figure in Poland. He was young. He was gregarious. He was writing a book on Vatican II. All of this was noted and reported to the pope by the papal nuncio in Poland. Sooner or later, a red hat was obvious. Pope Paul VI, getting older and seeing the end, made it sooner.

For ten years, Wojtyla continued to write and to publish, and he soon discovered a new outlet for his congeniality. He got himself named to four consecutive synods of bishops in Rome, one-month meetings where he had time to charm any number of prelates from around the world—who invited him to come and visit them. He traveled to Australia and to the United States, and he persuaded a good many cardinals to come see him in Krakow.

In the conclave of August 1978, he and his fellow cardinals chose a rather frail Albino Luciani, the patriarch of Venice, to take the place of Pope Paul VI. But the man who had wanted to honor the two popes before him by taking the name of John Paul I only lasted thirty-three days.

When the cardinals returned to Rome in October for another conclave (at great expense to the Vatican), they were determined to pick a vigorous, younger man, and they quickly settled on the hearty, down-to-earth Pole, the first non-Italian pope in 455 years. After fifteen years of a vacillating Paul VI, they wanted a man who was sure of himself. And that is exactly the kind of pope Wojtyla became, unafraid to assert his power, with the bluster of a man who had always had private doubts about himself.

From his high school days and through his priestly training, Wojtyla had overworked himself like a stray from the wrong side of town who had something extra to prove. He did not have a first-class education, and his scholarly work in a branch of philosophy called phenomenology drew virtually no attention. His best academic work, *The Acting Person,* sold eighteen copies in English.

But he believed in a kind of divine providence that allowed for no accidents. And if God wanted him to be the pope, then who was he to say he couldn't do it? With God's help, he could do anything. Only a few days after his election, Karol Wojtyla told a Polish friend as they strolled in the papal garden, "I think that God raised me to be pope to do something for the world. I have to do something for the good of the world, and for Poland."

He had learned at the Council that a pope's first duty (and the prime historic reason for his power at all) is to be the bishop of Rome. So he made pastoral visits around the city itself, to the jails and prisons, universities, religious institutes, convents, seminaries, nursing homes, hospitals, and, little by little, to 317 of the city's 333 parishes. No modern pope had attempted such a thing, and, another first, he was the only pope to step inside Rome's one synagogue. He even presided at the wedding (in a Vatican chapel) of a street cleaner's daughter. He held frequent general audiences, usually every week, with an average attendance of fifty thousand, and there he gave long, serious lectures that began to draw the attention of the press. In the beginning, he often showed up at Saint Peter's in mufti to hear confessions in a box labeled "Polish." Like his predecessor, John Paul I, he, too, dropped the pontifical plural. He was informal with old friends and some new ones, particularly if they were Slavs, and he brought a sense of humanity to the papal apartments.

He liked to be with people. Other recent popes had dined in solitary contemplation. John Paul preferred company. Rare was the day when he didn't have a guest, or guests, for dinner, and supper, too. "But," according to one visitor, "he never looked you in the eyes when he was talking to you." A Western psychologist would say he was frightened of intimacy—with anyone, man or woman. A Polish psychologist would see no deep meaning here. Polish priests tend to keep their gaze down. Polish priests give you half a handshake—two fingers and a thumb, not palm-to-palm, American style.

Though he often had an eighteen-hour-a-day schedule, John Paul II found time to stay fit by taking frequent walks in his rooftop gardens, and swimming daily laps in the pool he had built inside his summer palace. (An aide wondered why the pope wanted to spend so much money on a swimming pool. The pope snapped at the man because he didn't seem to understand that the pool would help keep him healthy. "The pool will be cheaper," he said, "than the cost of another conclave.")

But if he could be a good pastor in Rome, why, the pope thought, should he not be Christ's vicar everywhere else? And so, John Paul II traveled. Pope John XXIII had taken one short trip as pope, to Assisi. Pope Paul VI, the first modern pope to go on any long journeys, took ten trips in fifteen years. During Wojtyla's twenty-six years in office, he jetted to 129 nations (some more than once), and he spoke to millions of men, women, and children. "No human being in the history of the world," wrote Weigel, "has ever spoken to so many people."

Other modern popes had only toyed with television. John XXIII made a momentary appearance on the world's first geosynchronous satellite, Telstar I, in 1962, but after that, he did nothing more. Paul VI once appeared on a special broadcast for ABC television news when John Kennedy was assassinated. But he either did not understand the power of television or was too modest a man to make himself into a television star.

John Paul II, ever the actor, liked being a star. He was the first pope to use television as a worldwide bully pulpit. The notion probably came to him as some kind of instant revelation in those first moments after his election, when he stepped onto the center balcony of Saint Peter's and saw at least seven television cameras trained on him. He was no doubt surprised. Surprise quickly gave way to surmise. Those cameras told him he had the one thing that every maximum leader needs to realize ultimate visibility (whether he be a dictator or a democrat). He had the mass media in his pocket. The fact that he had it in the pocket of a white soutane made his image absolutely unique. In 1979, moreover, television was just beginning to understand the commercial value of stars who had a high recognition quotient. The North American public, at least, and most of Western Europe didn't need a last name to identify Elvis or Cher or Frank or the Beatles, or Marilyn, even years after her death. Or John Paul II. He became the same kind of cultural icon.

Within ninety days, television's program directors knew they had a new superstar who could raise their ratings. They were stunned by the live crowds he could command—massive, chanting, passionate crowds that they'd only seen before on old newsreel footage of the throngs that gathered to cheer and salute Hitler, Stalin, and Mussolini. In fact, John Paul II would outdraw all of the twentieth century's leaders combined. Over the course of his reign, he crisscrossed the planet to visit places both probable and improbable.

In June 1979, he celebrated mass before a million Poles near the Auschwitz II extermination camp at Birkenau. In May 1980, he gave fifty talks in ten days before almost the entire population of six African nations. In Ivory Coast, he dedicated the cornerstone of a new vanity cathedral (taller and longer than Saint Peter's) erected in the hometown of the country's Catholic president, Félix Houphouët-Boigny. In February 1981, when he jetted into icy Anchorage to celebrate an outdoor mass, he gave his blessing to a hundred thousand people, the biggest congregation ever assembled in Alaska.

Papa Wojtyla drew ever-increasing numbers. A million souls turned out to see him one sunny morning in Mexico City. In Santiago, Chile, 2 million. In Manila, at least 5 million, perhaps the largest crowd ever gathered in one spot in human history.

One local journalist explained the pope's attraction in Nigeria: "To many of our people, the pope is a spiritual figure who lives in heaven and comes down to earth in Rome. Just think what it means to them to understand that he is a real person who cares enough to come to see them."

According to Jean-Marie Tillard, a ranking Dominican theologian and ecumenist, John Paul II had become the kind of man who could "satisfy the rank and file's taste for marvels." When the pope had to cancel an appearance at a Eucharistic congress in Lourdes, reported Tillard, the expected crowds simply faded away—implying that the pope could draw people while the Eucharist (the body and blood of Jesus Christ) could not. In the Philippines, a lay catechist told a television reporter that the pope's impending visit was important "because the pope is the person on whose word the whole life of the Church depends." Said Tillard: "The present Catholic vision of the papacy magnifies the office. It makes the pope more than the pope." Anyone who watched an ordinary crowd of pilgrims at a general papal audience in Saint Peter's during the Jubilee Year could second Tillard and give their own examples—of wild-eyed men and women jumping up and down and laughing and shouting and weeping with joy when the pope passed.

Had John Paul II noticed he was becoming a demigod? Maybe not. Wherever he went, he bore down relentlessly on his message, preaching Jesus Christ as the way, the truth, and the life. Simple certitudes fit this pope's style and marked him as a unique leader "in a postmodern world where," as Vaclav Havel, the Czech president and playwright, once remarked, "everything is possible and almost nothing is certain." He was a man who felt he had a special handle on the truth and he distrusted those who thought truth was subtle and sometimes difficult.

One day, meeting Ronald Modras, a professor from Saint Louis University, at the Jesuit headquarters in Rome, the pope asked him what he taught.

"Philosophy, Your Holiness."

"Oh," said the pope, in a needling tone. "Do you teach the truth?" Modras was too flabbergasted to tell the pope it may be appropriate to "teach the truth" in a seminary, but not in a university, not even in a Jesuit university. In universities, philosophy professors teach students how to think, not what to think.

John Paul II tended to tell people what to think, certain he could do so because he found his truth in prayer. Anthony Kosnik, a Polish-American priest who once spent ten days as Karol Wojtyla's houseguest in Krakow, has described the method. "He didn't read a lot, he didn't seem to have time for it. [He took] his ideas into prayer every morning, and he came out of that convinced that through that kind of process the truth is found." Once he found the truth, inspired directly by God, "he wouldn't spend any more time considering the question, completely convinced of the positions he took and held."

Possessing the truth, John Paul could pass on advice that was impolitic, but often apt. He told Israelis that the city of Jerusalem ought to be under a UN protectorate to assure "a center of harmony for the three great monotheistic religions." He suggested to directors and staff of the NATO War College in 1979 that they should find another line of work. He asked television executives to give up programming "geared to instant success and maximum audience ratings."

He was fearless before dictators from the Third World. In Haiti in 1983, he challenged Jean-Claude Duvalier to his face, telling him how shameful it was that Haitians were fleeing the country "to seek elsewhere what they ought to find at home." In 1998, he confronted Fidel Castro with a full-throated call for a reborn Cuba restored to history and to the international community. (He also criticized the long-standing American economic embargo of Cuba.) In a number of African nations, addressing African leaders who had several wives, he spoke out against polygamy.

He called down the Reagan government in 1982 for deploying new medium-range missiles in Europe. On these occasions, he was taking a political position, and if he was in the business of speaking truth to power, why shouldn't he? He vetoed political involvement by priests and nuns, but he put his own considerable political skills to the task of restoring independence to his native Poland. In this effort, he may have been more like the warrior popes of the late Middle Ages and the Crusades, a principal actor in the last big political drama of the twentieth century.

His first papal trip to Poland in June 1979 was ostensibly pastoral, but it was also intensely patriotic and, therefore, in the context of the times, political, too. The pope saw 13 million people there, half the Polish population. What was more important, they saw him, and that sight—a Polish pope!—was the catalyst for a long-brewing revolt against their communist masters in the Kremlin.

For nine straight days, the pope told them they could have what they wanted if only they would demand it. He would even help them get it, by giving vigorous advice to the revolutionary Solidarity movement, which he had helped create while he was a leader in Poland's underground Church, long before he became pope. He gave Solidarity money, too—millions of dollars—against the advice of his own secretary of state, Cardinal Agostino Casaroli, who would have preferred the pope to remain neutral.

In taking a riskier, courageous course, John Paul II was following the lead of Pope Pius XII, who tried to help a group of German army officers plotting to overthrow Hitler in the winter of 1939–40. Pius XII volunteered to serve as a conduit between the British government and the plotters. Pius XII's German Jesuit secretary, sounding much like Casaroli in 1979, said the pope was going too far.

John Paul II knew how far he wanted his words to go. He wanted them heard in the Kremlin. He was hoping communist leaders could understand that the presence in Poland of a Polish pope would galvanize public opinion and give courage to political dissenters all over Eastern Europe. As it turned out, that is exactly what was happening: a young priest in Czechoslovakia who later became a bishop explained, "The communists wanted us to be afraid. After the pope's visit to Poland, we weren't afraid anymore."

But the Kremlin's leaders didn't see that, yet. They continued to put pressure on the Poles to suppress the Solidarity movement. For three more years, the communist government in Poland tried to strangle Solidarity, clapping the country under martial law at one point, jailing its leader, Lech Walesa, and executing one of its more outspoken priests, Jerzy Popieluszko. Meanwhile, the pope himself was the prime source for a steady stream of materiel going to the people of Solidarity—mainly small printing presses, copying machines, and mini radio transmitters—to pursue their war of ideas.

In the middle of the struggle in Poland, on May 13, 1981, Mehmet Ali Agca, a twenty-three-year-old Turk, walked into Saint Peter's Square at the regular Wednesday audience and tried to kill the pope, firing two bullets into his stomach. The pope survived, despite postsurgical complications, while Italian investigators tried to determine who was behind the assassination attempt.

Agca had no financial resources, but in 1980, he had traveled extensively in Iran, Bulgaria, Switzerland, Germany, and Tunisia, then ended up in Rome in January 1981. He journeyed to Switzerland and Austria in February, went to Rome in April, moved on to Perugia and Milan, then spent two weeks in Majorca, like a well-heeled tourist, and returned to a *pensione* in Rome that had been booked by an anonymous caller.

Agca was tried in Rome but he couldn't explain why he shot the pope. (In a courtroom crowded with newsmen, he shouted that he was Jesus Christ, a piece of theater no doubt intended to get an acquittal on the grounds of insanity.) He was convicted and sentenced to life in an Italian prison after he named as accomplices three Bulgarians and six Turks, who were brought to trial—and acquitted. In 2000, Italian authorities transferred Agca to a prison in Turkey. Some lawyers close to the case maintain to this day that Agca acted alone. Others believe the KGB hired him. The pope said, "The responsible one is the devil. And whether he used the Bulgarian people or the Russian people or the Turkish people, it was diabolical."

It was clear that Pope John Paul was very much a man of his time—a time when television was learning to amplify the image of otherwise normal men (and women) and make them bigger than life. In the 1960s, television created charismatic political leaders in America (like the Kennedys and Martin Luther King) whose celebrity alone triggered sick fantasies in the emotionally unbalanced. In the early 1980s, it was no surprise to see the same sickness exported to a world stage, striking down a new celebrity pope.

After he recovered from his gunshot wounds, the pope continued as if nothing had happened, traveling, writing, presiding over a Church that was losing members in Western Europe but gaining in the third world. By the end of his papacy, Catholics numbered more than a billion. He set some records that will probably stand forever. He wrote ten more encyclicals, almost a hundred other formal letters, and thousands of other discourses. *Insegnamenti di Giovanni Paolo II,* the printed record of his pronouncements, covered twenty-seven linear feet of shelf space at the Gregorian University in Rome. He promulgated two new codes of canon law and a new six-hundred-page *Catechism of the Catholic Church.* He also published a slim little volume on the virtue of hope that sold millions of copies in twenty languages. It was a simple, loving essay understood by all who read it, but it was in marked contrast to most of his other stern, uncompromising manifestos. These were drafted for him by dozens of speechwriters, then translated into Polish for his amendments, then usually turned into Italian, still the working language of the Vatican, and finally into the Church's official language, Latin.

In some cases, his declarations were easy to understand. In 1994, he called for "the boldness of brotherhood" that would transcend the clan wars making such a murderous mess among Serbs and Bosnians, Hutu and Tutsi, Armenians and Azeri. When he heard that priests were involved in ethnic massacres in Rwanda, he said, "The Catholic Church cannot accept such a vision of things." Some disagreed with his strictures against birth control, and his insistence that the Church needed to keep the law of priestly celibacy and had no right to ordain women. But most people gave him passing marks for having the courage of his convictions, and for his boldness in facing up to and remarking upon every moral issue of the day. To him, every issue was a moral issue.

By the time the pope delivered his rousing opening to the third millennium on New Year's Eve 1999, he was an almost unique model of moral credibility, at a time when many of the world's secular leaders had revealed themselves as liars and frauds. On March 12, 2000, during the same week that *Time*'s European edition did a cover story on lying (illustrated by a generic politician who was sporting a nose like Pinocchio), the pope spoke in a solemn liturgy with unprecedented candor, begging God's forgiveness for all the Church's sins of the past thousand years.

For centuries, the official Church had never admitted error of any kind. Some Catholic scholars wrote about the Crusades or the Inquisition, but the official Church took no blame for these horrors. It pretended to be unchanging and unchangeable through time, always holy, no matter what, simply by definition. John Paul saw things differently. In November 1994, he had signaled his intentions to make a public confession during the Jubilee Year 2000. He said he wanted the Church to recall all those times when its people "departed from the spirit of Christ and his gospel and, instead of offering to the world the witness of a life inspired by the values of faith, indulged in ways of thinking and acting which were truly forms of counterwitness and scandal." A "purification of memory" would be one way of starting the new millennium with a clean slate, an enterprise in keeping with the spirit of jubilee years in the Old Testament. This Holy Year would be "a year of the Lord's favor," a year of forgiveness, reconciliation, and conversion.

The pope's advisers in the Roman Curia were perplexed by this. But in classic curial fashion, they worked on a white paper that would, ostensibly, give some theological justification for what the pope wanted to do, while their real intention was to blunt his confession. This became clear just five days before the pope's scheduled mea culpa on March 12, 2000, when Cardinal Joseph Ratzinger appeared at a news conference and gave the press a woolly treatise that would put a confusing spin on the pope's revolutionary move. Think of the American secretary of state calling a news conference before the president's state of the union address to tell the world that the president couldn't really mean what he was going to say.

In nineteen thousand well-chosen words, Ratzinger's white paper, "Memory and Reconciliation: The Church and the Mistakes of the Past," tried to explain (or, better, to explain away) the pope's upcoming mea culpa. Ratzinger said that the pope couldn't admit any sins on behalf of the Church, but only for those sins committed by "the sons and daughters of the Church." In effect, he said, there are two churches: (1) the hierarchical Church, which is holy, without spot or wrinkle, and (2) the sons and daughters of the Church, who are sinners.

This was a self-serving proposition. The pope, bishops, priests, laymen, and laywomen—everybody—are sons and daughters of the Church, sinners all. The other Church was a total abstraction. But Ratzinger and the Roman Curia claimed to be in charge of this abstraction, handing out orders, telling others what to believe and what not to believe, and never failing to note—they were acting as spokesmen for the "hierarchical" Church—the "rule-by-the-holy" Church. Thus, the Ratzinger Church derived its infallible power and its infallible authority from its self-styled holiness. Its power, therefore, depended on its inability, by definition, to err. Even when the pope wasn't speaking ex cathedra—that is, infallibly—Ratzinger claimed that the pope's teachings, and by extension the teachings of his cabinet, were part of the Church's "universal and ordinary magisterium"—that is to say, its infallible teaching authority. How, they asked, can we maintain our magisterium over the sons and daughters of the Church if we admit now that we have made mistakes in the past? How can we give any assurances that we are not making them now?

Pope John Paul ignored their argument. For several years, he had been asking forgiveness for the historic faults, not of its so-called sons and daughters, but of the Church's supreme authority. It was Pope Urban II who had called for the First Crusade. Pope Eugenius III, Pope Clement III, Pope Celestine III, and Pope Innocent III mandated other Crusades. Pope Gregory IX established the Roman Inquisition, and Pope Innocent IV ordered up torture as part of the inquisitorial process. Pope Paul IV and Pope Pius V locked the Jews of Rome into their ghetto. The execution of Jan Hus, the Czech priest, patriot, and poet, was put in motion by those attending an ecumenical council at Constance, Switzerland, in 1415. That council did not condemn Hus because of some special heresy, or deviation from the faith, as Catholics had been led to believe for centuries, but because Hus criticized the pope and the bishops for bringing a caravan of Rome's most charming courtesans with them to Constance. In retaliation, they had Hus burned at the stake, an action that helped radicalize much of northern and central Europe. One hundred years later, when an Augustinian monk named Martin Luther was ready to bolt from Rome, those who remembered Hus were only too ready to follow Luther into schism. In December 1999, John Paul revisited that history, met with Hus scholars in Rome, and apologized for what the Church had done to Hus.

Now, with the new millennium, the pope felt it was a fitting time for the Church to own up to its past in a more systematic way. And so, he all but ignored Ratzinger's nineteen-thousand-word document (which had recalled sins of past history, but none in time present), and presided over a liturgy that did not bother to note the logical distinction between the Church and its people. "We have all sinned," he said in his homily. And then, following the homily, seven representatives of the Roman Curia made their confessions on behalf of the Church for sins against unity; for sins against the people of Israel; for sins committed in actions against love, peace, and the rights of peoples; and for sins against the dignity of women.

Ratzinger himself, the man in charge of the modern Inquisition, was one of those whom the pope had asked to rise and implore those inside Saint Peter's, and the huge crowd watching on TV monitors outside in Saint Peter's Square, to pray with him.

> Let us pray that each one of us, looking to the Lord Jesus, meek and humble of heart, will recognize that even men of the Church, in the name of faith and morals, have sometimes used methods not in keeping with the gospel in the solemn duty of defending the truth.

Ratzinger, looking more gaunt than usual, the wolverine rings under his eyes blacker than ever, raced through his text in a monotone, and then the pope launched into a prayer that placed the blame for the excesses of the Inquisition on the Church itself. It was as much a warning for Ratzinger and the men in his office as it was a prayer asking God's pardon for the sins of past Inquisitions.

> Lord, God of all men and women, in certain periods of history Christians have at times given in to intolerance and have not been faithful to the great commandment of love, sullying in this way the face of the Church, your spouse.
>
> Have mercy on your sinful children and accept our resolve to seek and promote truth in the gentleness of charity, in the firm knowledge that truth can prevail only in virtue of truth itself.

The pope had taken a huge step, owning up to the many ways in which the Church had failed to live up to the gospel. And at the end of the two-hour liturgy, he gave a ringing peroration:

> No more contradictions against charity in the service of truth.
> No more actions against Church unity.
> No more offenses against peoples.
> No more recourse to the logic of violence.
> No more discrimination, exclusion, oppression, contempt for the poor and downtrodden.

According to George Weigel, John Paul II hoped this was only the beginning of an ongoing project, a radical reevaluation of public policy by (and for) all men and women of goodwill. But some misunderstood the pope. An op-ed piece in the *New York Times* claimed that John Paul II couldn't have criticized past popes "on basic doctrinal matters" because that would have put him in the position of questioning the doctrine of papal infallibility. "This the pope was not prepared to do."

Curiously enough, it seemed that with his mea culpa, John Paul II had done exactly that. He hadn't questioned what past popes had taught, but he had put into play a whole new attitude about the Church's fallibility by turning the focus on what some past popes had done, and done wrong, or at least done in ways that "departed from the spirit of Christ and his gospel."

Vittorio Messori, a veteran Italian journalist who had collaborated on a book with Ratzinger, saw the implications of John Paul's move. "If we can say that past popes have erred," he wrote, "how can we be certain that this pope isn't erring, too? Who can assure me that his successor will not beg pardon for John Paul's begging pardon? And what will the Church be like tomorrow if today we honor as prophets those who are opposed to the teachings of even saintly popes? Are human rights and pluralism and dialogue the unique overriding criteria for the faith?"

Messori was speaking for some inside the Curia who could not openly criticize what the pope had done. But they were worried, because, as John Navone, a veteran Jesuit professor at the Gregorian University in Rome, observed, "Paradoxically, this pope has just destroyed the kind of superpapacy that he had labored for years to build."

Indeed, for this pope, his mea culpa was out of character, but something that his severest critics on the Catholic left were now ready to applaud. The pope's begging pardon for the Church's sins—from God, but with the whole world watching—raised the pope's credibility for Catholics who had felt for years that the pope had betrayed the charter elaborated at Vatican II. Maybe this was his last stab at greatness—to tell those who only knew him as a man who was too sure of himself and of his Church's claims that, in the end, he was not so sure. And that he could admit it.

He was considerably more sure that the Church hadn't done enough about the Holocaust, and in a further move toward a reconciliation with the Jewish people and in the same spirit that motivated his recent apologies, he demonstrated his feelings two weeks later by traveling to Israel and Jordan, and making his confession even more explicit to the men and women of Israel and to the world at large. More than two thousand journalists made the journey with him to Jerusalem, and an international television feed chronicled most of his activities there.

For three days he visited Christians, Muslims, and Jews in their respective sacred places. He also paid a visit to the Western Wall to place there his own printed regrets for the Church's sins against the Jewish people. But the moment of highest drama came when he made his halting, painful way into the Yad Vashem Holocaust memorial in Jerusalem on the fourth day of his visit, an event that lasted eighty minutes and was carried on television in Israel (as it was all over the world). Entering slowly with the aid of a cane, he came face-to-face with death camp survivors and other elderly European Jews, some of whom wept in his presence. The pope paused to look at the names of twenty death camps engraved on the black tile floor, then pulled a lever at the eternal flame that intensified the fire in front of a bier filled with ashes of those killed in the Shoah. He stood quietly before that flame, his face reflecting the orange glow. A cantor sang a prayer for the souls of martyrs, then John Paul greeted six survivors—each one meant to represent a million Jews who died in the Nazi gas chambers and crematories.

Before John Paul II's visit to Israel, Jews everywhere were asking him to apologize for Pope Pius XII's silence during the Holocaust. But when he finally spoke in a mostly darkened room illuminated by a single spike of light on the podium, he said that silence was his first and most appropriate response to the enormity of the evil commemorated there at Yad Vashem. "Silence in which to remember. Silence in which to try to make some sense of the memories which come flooding back. Silence because there are no words strong enough to deplore the terrible tragedy of the Shoah."

But he did find some words. He remembered his Jewish friends and neighbors in Poland, some who perished and others who survived. And he paid homage to the millions of Jewish people who were murdered in the Holocaust.

If the pope wished to remember, he wanted to do so for a purpose, "namely to ensure that never again will evil prevail, as it did for the millions of innocent victims of Nazism." He noted that Yad Vashem had honored some gentiles who had "acted heroically to save Jews, sometimes to the point of giving their own lives. Not even in the darkest hour is every light extinguished."

If anyone had doubts about the depths of the pope's sincerity, they were dispelled on this day. The pope continued:

> As bishop of Rome and successor of the apostle Peter, I assure the Jewish people that the Catholic Church, motivated by the gospel law of truth and love and by no political considerations, is deeply saddened by the hatred, acts of persecution, and displays of anti-Semitism directed against the Jews by Christians at any time and

> in any place. The Church rejects racism in any form as a denial of the image of the Creator inherent in every human being.

Afterward, the pope's host, Prime Minister Ehud Barak, whose maternal grandparents were killed by the Nazis at the Treblinka death camp, told the pope, "You have done more than anyone else to bring about the historic change in the attitude of the Church toward the Jewish people, and to dress the gaping wounds that festered over many bitter centuries."

It was a weary triumph for John Paul, who at the end of his trip looked like he had just finished running a ten-thousand-meter race. When his helicopter had delivered him to Israel a few days before, he had been startled by a large graffito on the landing pad: a Christian cross, an equals sign, and a swastika. But maybe, for a headline-loving pope, the run was worth it. He received huge laudatory banners in the Jewish newspapers. To many in Jerusalem he was now a hero.

It wasn't only a Catholic vision that magnified the office (and hence the man). Even Jews went gaga over him. Haim Ramon, a senior officer of the government of Israel, said at a news conference in Rome on March 10, 2000, less than two weeks before Pope John Paul's trip to the Holy Land, "This visit is the most significant event in the history of Israel." His government had spent more than $7 million on "infrastructure" to get ready for the pope, and it had assigned some five thousand police and members of the Israeli secret service to take care of his security. Why was the visit so significant to the Israelis? Ramon implied it meant so much to them because "there will be anywhere from a half billion to two billion people watching the pope on worldwide television." Ramon's government was like every government in the world: in thrall to television. Television was a twenty-first-century key to power.

POPE JOHN PAUL II left his mark on the world. He helped end the Cold War. He helped make communism falter in Poland, even before communism all over Eastern Europe fell of its own ideological weight.

He tried to reconcile the tension that had always dogged the Church, which needed to be in the world but not of the world, but in doing so, he got caught up in contradictions. Critics had accused Paul VI of being a Hamlet. It appeared that John Paul had a little of the Hamlet in him, too. He had a hunger for power, but he also wanted to be loved. He didn't seem to know that leaders cannot seek love and power simultaneously, for love comes only to those leaders willing to surrender power.

Constitutionally and culturally, John Paul had a hard time doing that. He did accept Vatican II's affirmation of religious liberty—which, less than a century before, Pius IX had called perfidious, venomous, pernicious, and contaminating. As a participant in Vatican II, Karol Wojtyla had seen how hard the majority had to fight for that switch—from condemnation to acceptance of modernity itself. And so he did not reverse this historic change, but confirmed it by asserting the dignity of every human person, a notion that undergirded his advocacy for human rights around the world and gave substance to his campaign for social justice and the rights of workers.

He did this most notably in areas of the world where Catholics held minority status or suffered persecution. In Cuba, he made his most forceful defense of democracy ("the political project best in keeping with human nature"), but democracy was a model he could not bless in his own Church. In receiving the ambassador of Taiwan and addressing himself to the shakiness of religion in China, he pointed up the right to religious freedom, insisting that it "be enshrined in law and be given effective protection." But in countries where Catholicism was the official state religion, he soft-pedaled religious liberty. He never permitted the Holy See to sign the Council of Europe's Declaration on Human Rights. The Vatican was still an absolute monarchy, with its leader exercising all three roles that help guarantee human and civil rights in most civilized nations. He made all the laws, he executed all the laws, he interpreted all the laws—and tried to silence some Church scholars who disagreed with him.

John Paul advocated dialogue with the world's religions, and twice invited their leaders to meet with him in Assisi. But there was little evidence that he engaged them theologically with their concerns. He was still a traditional missionary preaching the one true faith. In November 1999, some Asian bishops told him during his visit to New Delhi that exclusive language about salvation was offensive to Asia's dominant religions—Buddhism, Hinduism, and Islam—and provoked violence against Catholic missionaries there. Little more than a year later, he approved a haughty declaration by the Holy Office insisting that the Roman Catholic Church is the only portal to salvation and that other religions were deficient. Like many powerful men, he didn't hear what he didn't want to hear. His words tended to be more pronouncement than pedagogy, and taken as a whole, they came across as a pietistic hum that tended to overwhelm and finally bore even the most faithful of the faithful.

On the night of August 19, 2000, he faced 2 million young people gathered for World Youth Day in a field outside Rome called Tor Vergata. He spoke for almost half an hour about the virtue of chastity, and then the crowd started to chant and clap in rhythm. The pope seemed surprised and said, "Are you trying to tell me that I am speaking too long here?" They continued to clap, as if to say, "Yes, you are." But the pope went back to his text. It looked like he had only two or three more pages to go.

Again they started to clap and chant in English, "John Paul Two, we love you." The pope was piqued. It was obvious they didn't want to hear him out, but he went back to his speech anyway. They interrupted again.

Finally, the pope said—with sarcasm—*Grazie per il dialogo*—"Thanks for the dialogue." He repeated the line five more times over the next couple of minutes. It may have been the closest thing to a dialogue he had had in quite some time, but he didn't really hear what the young crowd was telling him. He kept returning to his text, and the kids kept interrupting. He couldn't understand. He had faced some of his biggest crowds at the World Youth Days in Manila, Denver, and Paris; they proved to him that the young people loved him, and he, of course, wanted their love. It was startling to hear the chants at Tor Vergata, and know those cries were mocking him.

Thoroughly nettled, the pope left the podium, his speech unfinished, and soared off with a great roar in his helicopter, shaking his head because the young people didn't want to hear him talk about chastity. Meanwhile, back on the vast field at Tor Vergata, many young people stayed the night, sharing the same sleeping bags. The *International Her-*

ald Tribune guessed that in nine months a good many babies would be born named "Jubilee."

John Paul II was a good father who really loved his children. But like many good, possessive fathers, he loved them too much, nagging them with too many preachments, not trusting them to do the right thing, and setting narrow limits to their growing up. He made unrealistic demands on their parents, too, by clinging to his own private, rather monkish interpretation of married love.

Increasingly, toward the last few years of his papacy, John Paul was acting more and more like a crusty old corporate CEO than a successor of the humble apostle Peter, who died never knowing that he was a pope. He treated most of his bishops like branch managers when they were summoned to Rome every five years to hand him written reports (and a sizable check, or an envelope full of dollars or euros). Then he would tell them what was on his mind. When they compared notes, they discovered that the pope hadn't wanted to hear what was on their minds.

Reginald Foster, a Carmelite priest from Milwaukee, had been working in the Vatican for more than twenty years, turning the pope's words into elegant Latin on almost a daily basis. He worked not more than a hundred steps away from the pope's office, but he had had a conversation with John Paul only once, in 1982. Twenty years later, he asked his boss, Cardinal Sodano, if he could see the pope again.

Sodano said, "You can see him on television."

Even in his early years as pope, Wojtyla did not much consult with members of his own cabinet. He saw Cardinal Ratzinger, his minister of truth, every Friday without fail, except when he was off on a trip. Other cardinals who held less important posts had to take their chances. In 1982, John Paul brought Archbishop Jean Jadot to Rome from his post as chief papal diplomat to the United States to head the Vatican bureau dealing with non-Christian religions. To signal his displeasure over the too-liberal episcopal appointments that Jadot had engineered in the United States, the pope let Jadot wait two years for his first audience, and then failed to give him the red hat he had every reason to expect.

In the twilight of his papacy, the same pope who had shown on his journeys to almost every nation on earth that Catholicism is universal without being provincial seemed determined to build a wall around his "one true church," to set it apart from the rest of humanity. In more ways than one, he threatened to make the Church that had become so inclusive under John XXIII into a sect. When Catholic gays and lesbians came to Rome for a Gay Pride March on July 18, 2000, he railed at the audacity of such a demonstration in the middle of his Jubilee Year; at least half of the three hundred thousand marchers were not gay, just single people or families with children who joined the demonstration to protest the pope's attempts at city hall to stop it. He put his special blessings on a number of influential, well-funded, right-wing movements and publications that identified themselves as theologically correct, presumably in contrast to those that were not orthodox by their narrow standards; these were often represented by theologians trying to express the truths of faith in language their contemporaries could understand. The pope and his guardians of orthodoxy, including many spokesmen in his pet movements, tried to discredit, marginalize, and replace these theologians—a move that some said threatened the vitality of the Church. E. J. Dionne wrote in the *Washington Post* that the Church needed self-criticism, open inquiry, and a spirit of dialogue:

> I am fearful of a tendency I see among some Catholics who call themselves traditional or orthodox to engage in what you might call planned shrinkage of the Church, to insist that those of us who so strongly identify with its traditions, who are not grab-bag Catholics, who do worry about fidelity, should be cast as people who are really Protestants and should go off and join the churches where we are told we belong by those who think the Church should be smaller.

John Paul II was too sure of himself to listen to any such criticisms, preferring the advice of Cardinal Ratzinger, who once admitted his ideal Church would be a lot smaller—but more orthodox. Going along with Ratzinger, this pope left his Church more divided, both sides more angry than they were when he assumed leadership and more confused over their identity.

He encouraged new movements of superloyalists, and he was

absolutely implacable in face of demands from Catholic women around the world who wanted to be priests. Like Sigmund Freud, he could never quite figure out what women wanted. Many women left the Church during his papacy, and if they didn't, their daughters did.

Many other Catholics couldn't have cared less. They didn't read, or if they did, they didn't read theology. They didn't go to mass, or if they did, it was only on Christmas and Easter. They were cultural Catholics. It was almost easier to find them in Rome, the center of Christendom, than it was anywhere else. *Siamo cattolici, non fanatici,* they said: "We're Catholics, but we're not fanatics." But they still liked this pope. He was good for the economy, appearing for the tourists and the pilgrims with regularity, like the geysers in Yellowstone National Park, every Wednesday morning and every Sunday at noon (unless, of course, he was off on another jaunt). His usual and spectacular presence in Rome bolstered the number one business in Rome, tourism, worth a billion a year to the Italian economy. In the Great Jubilee Year, the businessmen and -women of Rome (even the city's street peddlers, 80 percent of them Jewish) leaped to help celebrate Jesus' two thousandth birthday, welcome an estimated influx of 40 million pilgrims, and count their profits.

John Paul II seemed more authentic when he was ignoring the cautions of his superorthodox advisers, more real when he was dealing with visitors. One day in a meeting with some of President Ronald Reagan's top advisers who had come to talk about the struggles of Solidarity in Poland, John Paul turned to one of the American legates to the Holy See and pointed to Reagan's national security adviser, the rather stiff Robert McFarlane. "How," he asked one of the others in the delegation, "can we get this guy to laugh?" When he fell in his bath and broke a hip, he never really mended. Given a cane, he made a joke of it, often using it as a mock pool cue, or a pretend rifle.

Some intense pope watchers argued that, while Pope John Paul II spoke glowingly of Vatican II, his actions belied the spirit of Vatican II. His best encyclical celebrated the necessary link between faith and reason, and he wrote tellingly about the need for freedom in every human society, but he often refused to let reason work in his own Church or let freedom ring there. He marginalized many theologians, and disciplined more of them than we will know, because he ordered them not to tell others about it. In June 1999, he could exclaim at the Jagiellonian University in Poland, *Vivat academia! Vivat professores!*—"Long live the college! Long live the professors!"—even as his people in the Roman Curia were insisting that professors in Catholic universities around the world take a loyalty oath, a move that told the professors the pope did not trust them.

But John Paul II was cordial to the Dalai Lama and other visiting Buddhists. He never told them he didn't trust them, or that their faith was deficient. Nor did he utter a similar word to any of the 150 leaders of the world's great religions who met him in Assisi in October 1986 and September 2000 "to be together and pray." He came across as most human and most genuine when he was delivering his own mea culpa inside Saint Peter's, or hobbling into that spike of light at Vad Yashem.

CHAPTER FIVE

Cardinal Roger Mahony

Clericalism Still Rules

HOW MANY TIMES HAD ROGER MAHONY jetted into Rome? He'd made a few trips as a priest, more as an auxiliary bishop in Fresno, more still as the bishop of Stockton, many more as the archbishop of Los Angeles, and many, many more as a member of the College of Cardinals. Most trips, he had taken Alitalia's grucling, twelve-hour-long flight 400 out of Los Angeles International Airport. Now, on Saturday, April 2, 2005, after getting word that John Paul II was surely dying, he and his public relations man Tod Tamberg were buckling into their seats, 1A and 1B on British Airways flight 268 to Heathrow Airport, with a connection on BA flight 558, scheduled to land in Rome at 9:30 p.m.

Now things were different. Now Mahony and his fellow cardinals would elect a new pope, the 265th in an unbroken line of succession (or maybe broken just a few times). As his flight made its great circle route over Canada, Mahony couldn't help thinking about how the Church could win people over to the faith—or even keep the faithful from bolting.

Mahony was a postconciliar Catholic and a postconciliar cardinal. He believed that Vatican II had given the people of God a new mandate, to realize their full potential by taking charge of themselves and seizing their adulthood in a new kind of Church, and then turning their newfound power to the task of creating a society of justice and peace.

Some among the Church's traditionalists didn't much like that new emphasis. In a famous interview with Vittorio Messori, Cardinal Ratzinger had spoken scornfully about the so-called people of God, "busily engaged in translating the gospel into an action program with social, political, and cultural objectives."

For his part, Mahony rather wished, after Vatican II, that he could have seen people doing more translating of the Jesus message into action. For him, the people of God were not committed nearly enough to social and political reform, and to help change those elements in the culture that made men and women less free and less human. For a while, Catholics had seemed energized by the Council to grow up as Catholics and, as citizens, to play a much larger role in making their own communities better. But now, almost forty years after the conclusion of Vatican II, that program seemed stalled in many parts of the Catholic world. The Council seemed long ago and far away.

What had gone wrong? One American who had run for president of the United States, Patrick Buchanan, complained that Vatican II had been "an unrelieved disaster for Roman Catholicism." He blamed Pope John XXIII for opening the windows of the Church to let in "all the poisonous vapors of modernity, along with the devil himself." Those who had loved John XXIII said that many Catholics never understood the meaning of the conciliar reforms. If they had only known the Council Fathers intended to give the Church back to the people, they might have gotten more involved in a Church that was theirs.

But now, on the eve of this conclave, all that kerfuffle over Vatican II seemed terribly abstract. What concerned Mahony's people (and indeed most American Catholics) was the state of the priesthood, which was dwindling, dying, and in many places corrupt. Parishes in Los Angeles that used to have from three to a half dozen priests now had only one. And worse, in 2005, Mahony didn't know how long he could continue to supply even one priest to each of the 304 parishes in the archdiocese of Los Angeles.

Mahony tried to put the best face on things. He hadn't lamented the priest shortage. He preferred saying it was "a sign of God's deep love for the Church," an invitation to get more of the faithful involved. He said, "Even if our seminaries were packed, we'd need to cultivate, develop, and sustain lay ministers."

During the 1990s, when it became clear that great numbers of young men were not entering the priesthood, Mahony and his pastors and parish administrators signed up thousands of laypeople, professionals and volunteers, to engage in various vital ministries, each according to his or her own talents. These laymen and laywomen ran the buzzing archdiocesan offices. They taught in Catholic schools, now lucky if they had at least one aging nun in charge. They ran religion classes for children and adults. They fed the hungry from parish food pantries. They visited the sick and the elderly and brought them Communion. They ran marriage preparation classes. They engaged in ecumenical dialogues in their neighborhoods with people of other faiths. They managed literacy programs for immigrants. They had their own charismatic prayer groups. They ran retreats, and they presided over communities of former drug abusers involved in twelve-step programs. In short, they started doing everything short of celebrating mass.

But that was part of the problem. Catholics are a Eucharistic people. For them, the Eucharist is the core, continuation, and culmination of daily existence, and a memorial of Christ's Last Supper, of his life, sacrificial death, and resurrection. It brings the faithful together around the altar with all their labors, sufferings, and joys, and in praise and thanksgiving unites them and their efforts to the redemptive acts of God in Jesus. Which is why Catholics want their masses, no matter who presides. And this need was one of the things Mahony was carrying to the conclave.

In preconclave Rome, Mahony knew seventeen, perhaps eighteen other cardinals who shared his vision of a people's Church: Martini of Milan, Danneels of Brussels, Turcotte of Montreal, Lehmann of Mainz, Darmaatmadja of Jakarta, Kasper from the Vatican's Council for Promoting Christian Unity, and Rodríguez Maradiaga of Tegucigalpa, Honduras—and among the new cardinals created in October 2003, Tauran, Marchisano, and Hamao of the Roman Curia, O'Brien of Edinburgh, Antonelli of Florence, Turkson of Cape Coast, Ghana, Toppo of Ranchi, India, Bozanić of Zagreb, Quezada Toruño of Guatemala City, Barbarin of Lyons, and possibly Erdö of Budapest. They would be arrayed against perhaps dozens of others who had a different, more clerical take on the future of the Church. He would soon know whether his group could make any converts.

There was so much more the Church could do, should do, to turn the ideals of the Council into action, and if Mahony had any regrets about the postconciliar years, it was that some of those who did understand what the Council was asking of the Church had finally quit the priesthood or their convents in frustration because their superiors had thrown cold water on every creative plan. Even before the priest sex scandal, new vocations to the priesthood and to the religious life were lagging. Interested teenagers could not see a future for themselves working in an ecclesiastical bureaucracy, a system that was forcing adult men and women to remain compliant adolescents into their sixties. They were living in a different world than the one Mahony had grown up in.

Mahony had made the most of that world. His rise up the ecclesiastical ladder demonstrated how a young aspiring priest from a humble background can do well as he does good. Some say Mahony's quick ascension—he was a cardinal at age fifty-five—was the result of canny calculation. But what kind of calculation made him ask on the eve of his ordination in Los Angeles for a transfer to the diocese of Fresno, claiming he aspired to a ministry among the farmworkers in the middle of California's fertile Central Valley? "If Roger were the ambitious sort," said an old seminary classmate, "he never would have asked to leave the archdiocese of Los Angeles and go to Fresno. Fresno doesn't get you anywhere."

Except that in Mahony's case, Fresno got him somewhere, and fast. After six years in the diocese, he was named its top administrator, and then, five years later, he became an auxiliary bishop there. Five years after that, he had a diocese of his own, just a bit farther up the San Joaquin Valley, in Stockton.

On the way up, the harder he worked, the luckier he got. Mahony threw himself into the work in Stockton, and he also extended himself at national meetings of the National Conference of Catholic Bishops in Washington, D.C., and started to help make Church policy at the national level. The country was having terrific domestic problems with race and poverty, yet President Reagan had doubled the arms budget, was spending billions on a weapons program in outer space called Star Wars, and was giving the whole world a case of nuclear jitters. So the bishops wrote a pastoral letter opposing nuclear deterrence as a means of keeping the peace, and calling for a halt to the production and deployment of any nuclear weapons. Mahony was one of the principal authors of that pastoral.

In his talks about that document, Mahony added his own twist: he said that no Catholic could support or cooperate with policies that contemplated the use of nuclear weapons, "even in a defensive posture." His statement went a bit beyond the American bishops' position, but he was only repeating words that had already been delivered by Pope John Paul II. The assertion—from an American bishop, no less—seemed to add some extra credibility to the pope's notion. So it was no surprise when, in 1985, John Paul II appointed Mahony as the new archbishop of the most populous Catholic city in the United States, Los Angeles. Now he would almost automatically get a red hat.

Mahony rewarded the pope's confidence in him. He moved decisively to take control of an archdiocesan corporation (twelve thousand employees and an annual budget of $295 million) that was still serving 4.3 million Catholics with a management style set in the 1950s. Mahony hired a team of consultants, brought in a financial planning board, took priests out of administrative positions and replaced them with lay professionals, appointed women to high staff positions, introduced computers throughout the archdiocese, and started publishing annual financial reports. He asked the pope if he could have five new auxiliary bishops, to help him manage his sprawling archdiocese. He got what he asked for.

Mahony looked like nothing so much as the CEO of a major corporation, but he was just a priest making $500 a month, plus room and board at the rectory of ancient Saint Vibiana's Cathedral, just a few blocks from L.A.'s Skid Row. He lived a Spartan life, sharing the quarters with two priests on his staff and his gray cat, Miguel, and working out three mornings a week on a cross-country ski machine. He often took his turn cooking in the rectory kitchen, or ordering takeout chicken from the Original Texas Barbecue King near the *Los Angeles Times*. "That chicken," he said, "is to die for."

This was a very unlikely prince of the Church. He laundered his own underwear. He bused his own dishes. He made his own bed. Arriving at his cabin in the Sierras, he walked around wearing a carpenter's belt, fixing fans and opening drains. When a workman did a sloppy job on a fire alarm in Saint Vibiana's rectory, he pulled out a screwdriver and rewired it himself.

He was soon piloting his own $395,000 blue-and-white Hughes 500D, a four-passenger jet helicopter given him by a consortium of wealthy Catholics who wanted to help Mahony after they heard the cardinal had gotten stuck in one too many freeway gridlocks. But Mahony did not forget his own humble beginnings, shoveling manure on his father's chicken ranch in the San Fernando Valley, and turned immediately to the city's booming Hispanic community. He helped resettle thousands of refugees from Central America, and set up five regional offices to help the homeless find jobs and provide them with legal counseling. He stipulated that all of his seminarians learn the Hispanic culture and the Spanish language. He founded a weekly Spanish-language newspaper, set up a $100 million scholarship fund for Hispanic children going to Catholic schools, and appointed a number of Hispanics to key posts in the archdiocese. One of them said, "Mexicans have never been asked to participate in this way before." Mahony told a reporter, "I haven't done nearly enough for the Hispanics. But stay tuned."

Richard Riordan, a Los Angeles lawyer who would later become mayor of the city, said Mahony was doing entirely too much for the Hispanics. He recalls going to see Mahony with Stafford Grady, a prominent Los Angeles banker, and telling the cardinal that "rich people have souls, too." Riordan told Mahony he had to "pay a little attention to us." Riordan said he understood that Mahony had refused an invitation that very week to the Catholic debutantes' ball. Riordan felt he should have been there. When Riordan and Grady left his office, Mahony phoned the chairperson of the debutantes' ball and asked if the ball committee would consider inviting him next year. Mahony was discovering, among other things, how to be the pastor of all the people.

Sometimes, Mahony consorted with rich outcasts, too. In 1998, when he heard Frank Sinatra was very sick, Mahony climbed into his 1985 Olds Cutlass Sierra and drove to the Sinatra mansion in Beverly Hills unannounced. He knocked on the door, introduced himself to the maid, and said, "I would like to see Frank Sinatra." The maid gave the cardinal a seat in the living room and disappeared. A few minutes later, Mahony was standing at Sinatra's bedside. Sinatra stared at the cardinal with his cool blue eyes. Mahony said, "I think it's time you made your peace with God, Frank."

"Sit down, Your Eminence," said Sinatra. America's favorite bad boy crooner for the past fifty years was a Catholic who hadn't been to church since his boyhood in Hoboken, New Jersey, and he'd met very few cardinals in the course of his colorful life. But he was touched by Mahony's directness. They talked for half an hour or so. Sinatra asked him to come back, and Mahony did, three times. And when Sinatra died on May 14, 1998, Cardinal Mahony took over the sanctuary of the Church of the Good Shepherd in Beverly Hills (it was filled with a thousand gardenias), presided over the mass of Christian burial, and gave a simple homily that moved to tears many of those who were lucky enough to get a seat in the jammed church.

Mahony was learning to charm some of the most creative people on the face of the earth, many of them members of his own flock in Hollywood's film community, but it took a while. In a speech at the Los Angeles Press Club in 1991, he suggested Hollywood tighten its own rules and censor the sex and violence that was becoming more and more a staple in the industry. Some in the film guilds disliked his talk, and vented their feelings in the *Los Angeles Times,* whose editors hated censorship almost as much as they hated Bible-thumping evangelicals. The *Times* said so in print.

And so Mahony set his sails on a different tack. With help from Catholics in the industry, he tried to emphasize the positive. He crafted a pastoral letter that encouraged writers and producers "to use the great power of film and television to communicate values, form consciences, provide role models, and motivate human behavior." The cardinal's letter was a model of forward thinking about television and cinema and their potential power for good or evil. No previous archbishop of Los Angeles had ever dreamed of saying how much religion and art had in common. "We are a storytelling religion," he wrote. "The essence of our faith is the story of God's passionate love for every member of the human family and of our ambivalent, on-again, off-again, response to that love."

Mahony's tentative success at winning friends in Hollywood helped kick-start the fulfillment of another idea, that the Church ought to be making more effective use of the mass media. In his last year as a student at Saint John's Seminary in Camarillo, California, in 1961, Mahony had helped organize a panel discussion on the subject for his fellow seminarians. His presentation emphasized the potential outreach of "the secular media," where, he said, "we can reach millions if only we can learn." Now that he was in charge, he could put his theories into practice, in one of the biggest media centers in the world.

Mahony began to make himself available to editors at the city's newspapers and broadcast stations, who were delighted they finally had an archbishop in town who wasn't afraid of the press. Mahony told me about his two predecessors. "Cardinal McIntyre," he said, "was almost adversarial. Cardinal Manning didn't like public attention. I think they missed many opportunities. I don't mind picking up a phone and talking to an editor."

He didn't mind facing a bank of television cameras either, but not to satisfy some desperate need for attention. He went on television only when he had something arresting to say, and then he delivered messages that were not pious claptrap, but serious straight talk, usually on peace and justice issues that concerned everyone in the community, not only Catholics. No one was surprised in August 2000 to see him open the Democratic National Convention in Los Angeles. He liked to be where the cameras were.

Mahony pushed in the press for an American nuclear freeze, lobbied the state government in Sacramento on behalf of migrant farmworkers, and advocated giving amnesty to refugees from Central America who were fleeing for their lives while the United States Immigration and Naturalization Service was trying to deport as many of them as it could. He used local media to get out the word that the Church of Los Angeles would help thousands of undocumented aliens fill out their paperwork under the amnesty program of the INS. After six social-action Jesuits were killed by military goons in El Salvador in November 1989, he had television crews at Burbank airport to document the takeoff of a plane loaded with forty thousand pounds of food and medical supplies—his own relief effort for El Salvador. He flew along with the goods to appeal for peace in El Salvador and to make sure the supplies were actually delivered to the people there.

Mahony also used his high press visibility to reiterate some basic Catholic doctrine. For one thing, he took a strong pro-life stand and came out against capital punishment at the same time. "We follow magisterial teaching that is in the time-honored tradition," Mahony said. "And abortion clearly falls into that category. The teaching of the Church here goes back to the year one hundred and six. If there has ever been an issue on which we never had a different position, it is this one." He instructed his priests to tell women faced with unwanted pregnancies not to compound the problem by making a new problem for themselves, "the guilt and the anguish that you will never get over." He urged that unwed mothers put their babies up for adoption. While they were waiting to deliver, the Church in Los Angeles would pay their hospital bills, even their room and board if necessary.

In May 2000, he gave a speech before the National Press Club in Washington, D.C., to open a public dialogue that he hoped would ultimately bring a permanent end to state executions. He noted that California then had 565 inmates on death row, the most in the nation, and they were predominantly black and Hispanic.

Some cardinals use their office as bully pulpits that enhance their own public image. Mahony's style was different. He was beginning to understand that he didn't have to do everything himself, and that the art of leadership consists in inspiring others. Mahony sold his helicopter, and he began to look for ways to get many others involved. His call for lay ministers was one example of that. His citywide synod was another.

So was his annual education congress at the Anaheim Convention Center, a combination trade show and tent revival meeting that drew forty thousand teachers and catechists every year, some from as far away as Alaska, to attend hundreds of workshops presented by some of the American Church's most inspiring witnesses to a new kind of upbeat, joyful American Catholicism. The congress had become, in the cardinal's words, "the greatest event of its kind in the world." He could be proud without a touch of vainglory, because it wasn't his show, it was Sister Edith Prendergast's. Sister Edith was a tall, sturdy Irish nun who came to Southern California for a visit in 1986 and stayed on when Mahony gave her the job of planning the yearly congress. "If I could," Mahony told me, "I'd ordain Sister Edith tomorrow."

It was a racy remark for a cardinal who was then serving on the cabinet of a pope who had forbidden any discussion at all concerning the ordination of women. But Mahony was a Hollywood cardinal, literally and figuratively. (In fact, John Paul II called him "Hollywood.") He not only knew how to talk the American idiom; he gave it an informal, free-swinging West Coast overlay, different in both style and substance from the careful, almost pompous formality of the Eastern clergy.

If an archbishop hasn't inherited a cathedral, he wants to build one. This is what archbishops have done since the Middle Ages, and this is what Mahony did in Los Angeles in the late 1990s, when he raised $193 million to pay for a temple designed by Spanish architect José Rafael Moneo. Mahony thought that his cathedral, made of Los Angeles concrete and Carrara marble and set down on the edge of the famed Hollywood Freeway, "summed up two thousand years of Church history and reinvented it for the next millennium."

Some criticized Mahony for building a cathedral at all. Jeff Dietrich and his wife, Catherine Morris, directors of an organization called the Catholic Worker, asked, "How can the Church of Los Angeles lavish its substance on mere brick and mortar and alabaster windows when there are empty bellies to feed and naked bodies to clothe?" The Dietrichs spoke out of a prophetic tradition. But a Catholic archbishop comes out of another tradition—the priestly tradition. Normally, a priest doesn't speak out against the existing order of things. He blesses that order and makes it holy. He doesn't tear down, he builds up. And as Mahony saw it, Los Angeles was long overdue for some building up. He quoted Mayor Riordan: "If not now, when?" What Riordan meant was that Los Angeles at the turn of the millennium was riding the crest of an unprecedented financial boom of the kind most famously enjoyed by the Medici of Renaissance Florence. If the Medici of Los Angeles did not build their own duomo, the angels would weep for them.

The angels did not weep and Mahony got his cathedral. But his big plans for a huge cathedral dedication in September 2002 were derailed by the priest sex scandal that struck Boston and soon spread to other parts of the United States, including Southern California. Mahony made the grand opening of his cathedral a little less grand while he himself became a little less available to the local press, which wanted him to talk about the priest-predators he had been hiding.

At first, it looked like Cardinal Mahony understood the situation in a way that other American bishops did not. When he talked about the scandal at all, he said he had not known about the few of his priests now being named as pedophiles and vowed that his Church would pursue a policy of total transparency. For the next three years, however, Mahony was no better than most of the American bishops, who were trying to cover things up "for the good of the Church"—meaning, of course, the institutional Church. Mahony spent more than $3 million in legal fees, paying a team of Los Angeles's highest-priced lawyers, led by J. Michael Hennigan, to help him fight off the efforts of Steve Cooley, the district attorney in Los Angeles, to obtain information on his priest-malefactors, in some cases dating back decades before Mahony took over as archbishop.

Mahony's refusal to come clean went counter to his rhetoric, and it came as a surprise to many who had considered him the most progressive of the American cardinals. Not long before, the *National Catholic Reporter* had said in an editorial that Mahony was "a leader interested in developing consensus rather than imposing decisions by fiat—a leader, in other words, who realizes the tired phrase 'the church is not a democracy' does not mean it must therefore be an autocracy." Now suddenly Mahony was acting like an autocrat. The people of Los Angeles now knew what they had always suspected, that clerics, even their dashing cardinal-archbishop, believed they had special legal privileges that the rest of humankind did not share.

Mahony said he had to save the confidentiality of his dealings with his own priests. And as for the charge that he had been protecting his pedophile priests from prosecution, he said he had simply been following sound medical advice by sending them off for treatment. But he knew that the recidivism rate for pedophilia is second only to that of exhibitionism. He knew that pedophilia was and is a felony in every state. An attorney for one of the victims asked, "Just what was it that Mahony didn't know?"

After a meeting of the American bishops in Dallas in May 2002 that drew huge media coverage, Mahony made a big to-do about pushing the bishops into a new policy, which he called "zero tolerance." That meant that one misstep in this area by any priest and he was out of the active ministry. Mahony enforced the rule selectively, as he should have. Bishops who applied it woodenly were suspending priests with no due process and creating a huge morale problem among many good priests. But he also stonewalled criminal prosecutors in Los Angeles who were demanding he turn over files on suspected priests. Perhaps Mahony was emboldened by prelates in Rome who seemed anxious to downplay the sex scandal in the United States. Archbishop Julián Herranz, a ranking member of the Roman Curia, castigated the American bishops for reporting sexual-abuse accusations to civil authorities and for turning over files to prosecuting attorneys. The Jesuit dean of canon law at the Pontifical Gregorian University wrote in *La Civiltà Cattolica*, a Jesuit monthly in Rome that vetted all its articles with the Vatican before publication, that bishops are not morally or legally responsible for what priests do, should not make them take psychological tests, should not report accusations to civil authorities, and should not inform parishes when an abusive priest is reassigned.

This should have told the American Church not to wait for Rome's solution to the problem. Many were beginning to see that Rome *was* the problem. Andrew Greeley, the famed priest-sociologist-novelist wrote in one of his syndicated columns, "Rome doesn't have a clue about American Catholicism. These Curialists don't know anything about American society, culture and law, or about American Catholics. They don't grasp that whatever the faults of the tort system of Anglo-Saxon law and of the American media, these two institutions have brought the sexual abuse out into the open where the Church can no longer cover it up and permit it to continue."

In public, Mahony seemed to go along with Greeley's sentiments. He wrote a pastoral letter on sex abuse that looked like a tough assault on the malefactors. "Let me state very clearly," it said, "the Archdiocese of Los Angeles will not knowingly assign or retain a priest, deacon, religious, or lay person to serve in its parishes, schools, pastoral ministries or any other assignment when such an individual is determined to have previously engaged in the sexual abuse of a minor." The implicit message was that other Catholic bishops might appear flatfooted in the face of the worst scandal to rock the Church in centuries, but that Roger Mahony was the man with a plan.

The plan amounted to little more than a public relations campaign designed by Sitrick and Company, the Enron Corporation's former public relations firm that Mahony had hired to advise him in this crisis. The Sitrick people recommended Mahony appoint a lay advisory group to oversee personnel matters, and so he did, a Clergy Misconduct Oversight Board that Mahony said represented "another chapter in the efforts of the archdiocese, to make certain all churches are safe for children and young people." It did nothing of the sort. This board had no authority, as Mahony admitted when pressed. He said he could not surrender that authority "because only bishops are empowered under canon law to make personnel decisions about priests."

Blaming canon law seemed like an easy out for Mahony, and it showed Mahony's true colors: he would defer to Rome, no matter what common sense seemed to dictate. Some reputable canon lawyers said he should have found a way to finesse canon law. In a white paper written for the Association for the Rights of Catholics in the Church, James Coriden, a former president of the Canon Law Society of America, explained:

> Church laws have a different purpose than civil laws. They serve to keep good order and protect personal rights, but their ultimate aim is the spiritual good of the members, mutual love among them, and, indeed, their eternal salvation. Rules within the Church have a different kind of reality and effectiveness. Actions which are taken in contravention of canonical rules still very often achieve their basic religious purposes.

Mahony didn't even come close to doing that. He fell back on a thousand-year-old misunderstanding about episcopal authority in the Church, now embedded in a canon law that claimed absolute powers for a bishop to "teach, sanctify, and rule" that were never contemplated by any of the apostles. Acording to scripture, the apostles were sent by Jesus to carry the Good News to all nations, not rule over them, much less rule absolutely with the kind of power that corrupts absolutely.

Church historians tell us the Church veered into its absolutism in the early Middle Ages, when the popes and their advisers, anxious to protect Church property, began asserting their immunity from judgments in secular courts. Their warrant was a set of forgeries called the Pseudo-Isidorian Decretals citing historical evidence that popes and bishops had always had an absolute, divine right to rule absolutely. "The first decretals in the collection," wrote Ken Pennington, a professor of Church history at the Catholic University of America, "were attributed to Popes Clement I (c. 92–101 A.D.) and Anacletus (c. 79–c. 91). For later canonists, the existence of these letters was a powerful and convincing argument that the bishop of Rome had been the primate of the Church since Apostolic times."

Gregory VII (1073–1085) made liberal use of the forgeries to claim papal primacy, an absolute authority that Richard McBrien says "covered not only the whole Church, but kings and their kingdoms as well," creating a new ecclesiology unknown in the Church for a thousand years. In 1142, a monk named Gratian codified the reforms of Gregory VII in his *Decretum*, a compilation of approximately 3,800 texts (inluding some forgeries) from patristic writers, conciliar canons, and papal letters, and, to a more limited extent, borrowings from Roman law. It was the Western Church's rule book until 1917, when Pope Benedict XV promulgated a new code of canon law, to the delight of some Church lawyers, who, for centuries, had been trying, with a great deal of success, to turn the Church from a Church of love into a Church of laws. Vatican II attempted to get rid of this legalistic overlay, but John Paul II, as part of his efforts to restore the Church to its preconciliar clarity, published an updated code in 1983.

Given their knowledge of canon law's shady antecedents and its development as an instrument of a papal power grab, American bishops had every reason to ignore canon law. In October 2003, Francis G. Morrissey, an Oblate priest in Ottawa, suggested to fellow members of the Canon Law Society of Canada that Roman law is not an absolute. "Perhaps the day is gone when a universal law suffices for the entire Latin Church. Situations are just so different." Ladislas Orsy, a distinguished Jesuit canonist at Georgetown University, wrote a long paper for the Canon Law Society of America asserting that the Church had "outgrown its structural and organizational framework." In the spring of 2002, fifteen members of the board of the Catholic Theological Society of America reviewed the depth and breadth of the sex scandal and asked the American bishops to address the structural issues that made the scandals possible.

The scholars got no response from the bishops. Indeed, any talk of structural change in the American Church frightened them, and many proceeded to condemn reformist groups in the United States, like the Voice of the Faithful, a grassroots organization with chapters in all of the fifty states, whose members wore badges to their meetings affirming their determination to "Keep the Faith, Change the Church."

Leonard Swidler, a longtime Catholic theologian from Temple University and the founder of the Association for the Rights of Catholics in the Church, told VOTF members meeting in San Francisco in March 2004 that American Catholics could have created a more accountable Church at three crucial moments early in American history by melding their Catholicism with their Americanism.

The first moment came in 1785, when John Carroll insisted that the first bishop in the United States should be elected by a vote of the nation's priests; in fact, those priests elected Carroll, and, later, they elected two more coadjutor bishops as well. Carroll had a top priority, governance by consensus, as befitted both the new American democracy and the traditions of the most ancient religious orders, who had been electing their own leaders since before the Middle Ages. Unfortunately, the Vatican saw little value in governance by consensus. After John Carroll's death in 1815, American bishops became creations of Rome; the American Church's first potentially democratizing moment had passed.

The second moment occurred when John England came to the United States as an emigrant bishop from Cork County, Ireland, in 1820, and took over as bishop of Charleston, South Carolina. England was a quick study. Soon after he became a United States citizen, he started to write a constitution for his own sprawling diocese, an attempt to make the Catholic Church more American. His constitution turned the governance of his Church over to elected laymen, and he kept his people informed about their Church by starting the country's first Catholic newspaper, the *Catholic Miscellany*. Never a shy man, England gave a two-hour oration to a joint session of Congress in 1826 attended by President

John Quincy Adams and the members of the United States Supreme Court. They heard England give his rationales for religious liberty, separation of church and state, freedom of speech, and freedom of the press—all of which would be condemned by Pope Gregory XVI some six years later in his encyclical *Mirari Vos*.

England told them, "I would not allow to the pope, or to any bishop of our Church outside this Union, the smallest interference with the humblest vote at our most insignificant balloting box. He has no rights to such interference." And in a letter to Pope Gregory XVI, he wrote that the American people "ought to be consulted in all important matters, including Church matters. The American people are a law-abiding people, and the laws are respected so long as the voice of the people is heard in their making."

The trouble is that the American bishops who surrounded England (and followed him) took another path. They made it a point not to write constitutions for their dioceses, preferring accountability to Rome rather than to their own people. If they would follow any law, it was to be the Church's canon law, which, incidentally, gave them something very close to absolute power in their dioceses. They proceeded to set up a hierarchical, even monarchical, model for the American Church. That was the end of the second potential democratizing moment in the history of the American Church.

The third moment came late in the nineteenth century, when Bishop John Ireland of Minneapolis-St. Paul and a group of other American bishops were working to democratize the Catholic Church in America. Pope Leo XIII sided with those loyal to Rome among the American hierarchy to slap Ireland down in 1899, for a heresy he labeled "Americanism."

Now, said Swidler, perhaps a fourth moment has come—an opportunity to make the Church less Roman and more catholic. And more American. Such a Church could work toward consensus on the questions that vex American Catholics—and not only questions about the sex-abuse crisis. The American Church could serve its people better, he said, even bring back millions of disaffected Catholics, if it could help give them a sense of ownership in the Church.

"I have been pushing this for the past thirty years," said Swidler. He argued the need for a Catholic constitution in the United States, with an executive branch, a bicameral legislature (a House of Bishops and a People's House, all of them elected by the people), and a judicial branch appointed with the advice and consent of both houses. "That," he said, "would give people a sense of ownership." Elect our own bishops? "Why not?" he said. "That would make the bishops accountable—and give us a sense of our citizenship, too."

EVEN AS HE HEADED TO THE CONCLAVE, Mahony knew Steve Cooley still had him under criminal investigation, and he wasn't faring very well in civil court either, with 544 lawsuits filed by abuse victims, at an estimated settlement cost of more than $1 billion, still in limbo. Nor was Mahony getting along too well with the press, which had begun to see through his continuing efforts to spin things his way. At the Vatican, he was nonetheless a cardinal-elector in good standing, still determined to play a leading role in the conclave. And why not? Other cardinals from around the world had been faced with similar legal and media problems. Cardinal Pell had himself been accused of tampering with a young man, and he was exonerated in an Australian court. Cardinal Bernard Law was at the conclave, too. He was the deposed and disgraced archbishop of Boston, where hundreds of priest-pedophiles that he had been shielding and covering up for were exposed in 2002 and 2003, but he'd been given a sinecure in Rome, and was still a papal elector, filled with pride that he, too, would help pick the next pope. The cardinal from Naples, Michele Giordano, was tainted with Mafia connections. They had all risen to their high rank by remaining loyal (indeed, vowed in their loyalty) to the Church as institution. If they ever admitted to themselves that they had a dark side, well, they had only to ask forgiveness for their sins, do penance, and get on with their lives. Right now, they had to pick a next pope they could look up to.

"I'M QUITE SURE THE CONCLAVE will not pick an American," Mahony told Larry Stammer. They had settled into the VIP lounge at Heathrow to wait for their connecting flight to Rome, and Mahony was engaged in one of his favorite pastimes, talking to the press about

Church politics. Among some cardinals, he told Stammer, an American pope would be regarded with suspicion. It sounded silly, but more than one Vatican monsignor had told Mahony with some seriousness, "Who could swear, Your Eminence, that you are not a tool of the CIA, or of Wall Street?" As far-fetched as that statement was, Mahony knew that few would think of an American pope after the American Church's sorry handling of its priest-pedophiles. That was ironic. The American cardinals had been trying to protect the institution headed by the pope. Now that precluded the possibility that any of them could become pope.

EXCURSION I

Priesthood

No Kind of Magic

POPE JOHN PAUL II never allowed himself to think seriously about reform of the priesthood. He said the very prospect reminded him of a song: "It's a long way to Tipperary." Too daunting, even for a pope who prided himself on being one of the most proactive popes of all time. To map out the future of the priesthood, one first had to deal with its long, twisted past, a past that was immensely complicated by a clerical misogyny—the fear and hatred of women—that goes back to the fourth century. Consider the writings, for example, of certain Fathers and Doctors of the Church on women, marriage, love, and sexuality.

For Saint Jerome, woman was "the devil's gateway, a dangerous species, a scorpion's dart." To Saint John Damascene, woman was "a sicked she-ass, a hideous tapeworm, the advanced post of hell." Saint Francis de Sales wrote that married couples should not think of the act they might have to perform at night. Saint Thomas Aquinas believed "woman is misbegotten and defective." Pope Saint Gregory the Great said that woman's "use" is twofold: harlotry or maternity.

This is the kind of nonsense produced by men who are not graced by the abiding warmth and wonder of good women. Even today, many priests will admit they suffer from what a Council Father at Vatican II had once called "a celibate psychosis," a malady that has kept the official Church from doing serious thinking about the future of the priesthood. (The people's Church knows what to do. Public opinion polls in the United States say that 80 percent or more of the Catholic population believe priest celibacy should be optional.)

For years, bishops from the Pacific Islands, where the people see a priest every two years or so, have been asking for Rome's permission to ordain married men. John Paul said no, God would provide. In the pope's cultural cosmos, that meant God would provide sufficient celibate males. As a result of John Paul's policy, in 2005 one-half of the parishes in the world had no priest in residence. The pope ended up choosing celibacy over easy access to the central mystery of the faith, the Eucharist, and triggering a priest shortage that he himself denied.

After Vatican II, many young men who might have aspired to the priesthood a generation before were not signing up for the seminary. The Council had made it clear that men could be first-rate Catholics, could serve the Church in one special capacity or another, even if they married. As a result, the pool of potential priests was getting shallow; bishops and religious superiors were forced to accept what candidates best described as "bottom of the pond." Many other outstanding candidates had a homosexual orientation. Years before, gay candidates wouldn't have passed through a normal screening process and were asked to leave the seminary if they did get through and were found out. Now they were being welcomed as long as they could affirm they had not been sexually active for the past three years, and promised to remain chaste in the future.

By 2005, however, it was easy to see where this policy was leading. Except in some third world countries, where the seminaries were full of eager young candidates seeking to serve God (and obtain a free education as well), the number of priests had dwindled to roughly half of what it had been a generation before, and they were trying to serve twice as many Catholics. A good many of them were only nominally celibate. There were different reasons for this, in different places. In Latin America and Africa, where, particularly in rural villages, a man was suspect if he didn't have a wife, many parish priests lived in open concubinage. In the United States, some experts estimated that at any given time at least half of the Catholic clergy had an active, clandestine sex life—with women, with other men, with boys. One young priest in Phoenix told an older pastor he intended to leave the priesthood because he wanted a woman. "My dear boy," said the pastor, "you don't have to leave. You can have almost any woman in town." One homosexual Jesuit rationalized his long-standing affair with a young man on the grounds that he was faithful to that young man, just as a chaste husband is faithful to his wife. So how was he violating his vow of chastity?

Many clerics knew what was going on and said nothing. Members of the same exclusive club, they winked and looked the other way. So, in fact, did the Vatican itself. One day in 2000, a Vatican official approached the superior general of a major religious order in Rome asking him to assign one of his men to become bishop of a vacant diocese in Latin America. There were fifty-three diocesan priests there with the training needed to become a bishop. But all of them had common-law wives—and children.

Order priests take a vow of chastity, which means they may not have sex, ever. Diocesan priests do not take such a vow; they make a promise of celibacy, which means, strictly speaking, they may not marry. In theory, there is really no difference between a Franciscan's vow of chastity and a diocesan priest's promise of celibacy. In practice, however, a promise of celibacy may help a diocesan priest rationalize sleeping with his housekeeper. In Latin America and in many parts of Africa, one can guess where concubinage is countenanced by checking successive volumes of the *Annuario Pontificio,* the Vatican yearbook, which gives statistics on every one of the more than forty-six hundred dioceses in the world. A number of dioceses have Jesuits, Dominicans, Franciscans, or Salesians serving as bishops. One suspects these bishops have a good many diocesan priests living in common-law marriages. They have "solved" the celibacy problem, de facto if not de jure—and the Vatican knows it, which amounts to tacit permission for priests to marry, as long as they don't do it legally.

Someday, a pope will write an encyclical telling the world the Church has always had two kinds of priests, order priests who take lifelong vows of chastity, and parish priests who marry. The letter will begin, as most encyclicals do, with two Latin words: *Sicut semper*—"As always." The current situation—which gives priests some comfort but ordinarily leaves their common-law wives with no legal rights when they die—would be unnecessary if the modern Church stopped trying to follow rules for priestly celibacy that were codified in the twelfth century. Those rules were made by men. Men could unmake them.

John Paul II never agreed with that view. When in 1986 he was preparing his encyclical letter on the priesthood, *Pastores Dabo Vobis*, "I Will Give You Shepherds," it took his ghostwriters much of one day to persuade him that celibacy is not essential to the priesthood. They had to remind him that twenty Eastern Rite churches in union with Rome, some of them more ancient than the Roman Rite, have had married priests from the beginning, and that some of the original twelve apostles were married. They also pointed out that many priests in the Roman Rite were married until 1078, when Pope Gregory VII, borrowing the discipline of celibacy from the monks of the fourth century to impress the people with the Church's holiness, finally mandated celibacy in the Latin West. Historians say the pope did this to stop priests' families from inheriting the patrimony of the Church.

John Paul II seemed most nettled when he heard of anyone suggesting the Church could meet the priest shortage by ordaining women. Early in his pontificate, at a public meeting in the fall of 1979 inside the cathedral at Washington, D.C., John Paul rebuked Sister of Mercy Theresa Kane, president of the U.S. Leadership Conference of Women Religious. She was dressed in a business suit and she certainly didn't look much like the Polish nuns that came to Rome with Karol Wojtyla to wash and iron his shirts and cook for him. When her turn came to address the pope, she told him that women had to be included in all the ministries of the Church, including the priesthood.

The pope had been prepared for this. He responded with a scripted answer out of a history that was not history. He said that American nuns should model themselves on the Blessed Virgin Mary, "who was never part of the hierarchy of the Church, but made all hierarchy possible because she gave to the world the shepherd and bishop of our souls." Sister Kane was not permitted to give the pope the answer he deserved, that, in Mary's time (and for a good long time thereafter), there was no such thing as "a hierarchy." And that Jesus was never a bishop, much less a priest.

During John Paul's papacy, thousands of modern women, many with impressive theological credentials, were still clamoring for the priesthood. Why, they wondered, are there seven sacraments for men in the Church, and only six for women? For them, ordination was a matter of justice, but John Paul II denied that. "The priesthood is not a right," he wrote, "but a privilege." In two papal documents, he tried to explain why women had no right to priestly ordination, and why he had no right to authorize it for them. And he forbade any further discussion, for *he* had already considered all the cultural, sociological, and historical arguments and, because they were not persuasive, rejected them in favor of his own theology of the priesthood. At mass, he said, the priest must act *in persona Christi*—in the person of Christ. The pope explained what this meant: a priest should have "a natural resemblance" to Christ. To Peter Steinfels, a columnist for the *New York Times* and author of a best-selling book on the state of the Church, this was an obvious circumlocution:

> Does a chubby, bald, blue-eyed, red-faced, bibulous, weak-willed, and irritable seventy-year-old man display more of such a "natural resemblance" than a fit, dark-haired, brown-eyed, olive-skinned, strong-minded, eloquent, and compassionate woman of thirty-five? If so it may be crude but unavoidable to ask, isn't "natural resemblance" just a euphemistic way of saying "possessing a penis"?

The Vatican proved how serious its position was by taking steps in 2003 to defrock a priest who had undergone a sex-change operation.

John Paul II wouldn't hear talk about a far less radical step than making women priests—the ordination of married men. At lunch in the papal apartments with Canadian bishops during a regular every-five-year visit in 1994, John Paul II pointedly ignored a suggestion from Bishop Remi De Roo of Victoria, British Columbia, who told the pope, "We should talk about the ordination of married men." Later in the lunch, thinking the pope hadn't heard him the first time, De Roo brought up the subject again. The pope reddened and, still clutching his knife and fork, banged his fists on the table and said, *Deus providebit! Deus providebit!*—"God will provide! God will provide!" So far, God has not provided the kind of priests the pope had in mind.

There was no shortage of new (and wildly differing) ideas about solving the priest shortage. In June 2005, Dean Hoge, a highly respected sociologist at the Catholic University of America, told a Boston College conference on the priesthood that making celibacy optional would raise seminary enrollments 400 percent. With that, he said, "the priest shortage would be over."

In the fall of 2005, however, the Vatican didn't seem concerned about a priest shortage. Instead, it launched an investigation to root homosexuals out of American seminaries, a move that could drive out many gay priests as well. The Vatican seemed ready to take that chance because mandatory celibacy has been a fundamental part of Church doctrine for almost a thousand years, a tradition that has long defined holiness as sexlessness. If celibacy was made optional, church leaders felt, every pillar of Catholic teaching could be called into question. That could not be allowed to happen. Moreover, married priests (or a married pope!) would reverse what A. W. Richard Sipe called in his book *Sex, Priests and Power* "the Augustinian equation: sex = pleasure = women = evil." After quoting Gandhi about the value of celibacy as "a treasure to be fostered by those who possess its disposition," Sipe writes that celibacy is not the problem, but rather "a power system using celibacy for the domination and control of others."

The wonder is that the people lived in awe of the Church's power for so long. They were awed, no doubt, when they beheld the sacrifice of the men who seemed to give so generously of their manhood "for the sake of the Kingdom." Then came the priest sex scandal of 2002 and beyond, which destroyed any remaining illusion that all Catholics were being well served by a holy priesthood. It wasn't only the spectacle of priest pedophiles and priest ephebophiles facing justice in the courts. Catholics now had confirmation that priests and bishops had covered up for their colleagues. Had they remained silent because they didn't want their own private sex lives revealed?

A gay Jesuit in Rome once told me, "Everyone has a sex life." Perhaps that is an exaggeration. I know many good priests who sublimate their sex drive "for the sake of the Kingdom." But if Dr. Sipe is right that no more than 10 percent of the clerics he knows are doing that, then we have to conclude that priests are living double lives, trying to serve their people by day and coming to terms with their sexuality by night. They have learned that ordination is no kind of magic. The dishonesty—on the part of men who are billed as "other Christs"—is appalling.

Until a new kind of pope is ready to dismantle the entire hierarchical system, I believe priestless communities are likely to fall back on the example of the early Church, where, in the first two centuries of its existence, it had no priestly, celibate caste at all, and a Eucharist celebrated in household churches, often enough by women (St. Paul gives us some names: Phoebe, Priscilla, Prisca). Today, in many parts of the world, women are celebrating mass without the presence of a priest, saying the age-old formulas in unison, and receiving communion, sincerely believing that Christ is sacramentally present.

When that practice becomes the rule rather than the exception, we can expect the Vatican to take notice. The hierarchy might be well-advised even now to create a commission to study the issue, much as Pope Paul VI proceeded with regard to birth control. Independent scholars from a variety of disciplines and some married Catholic couples should be brought together to study the celibate system. A fearless pope would call for a Church-wide discussion of this issue, letting the people decide whether they want to be served by honest men (and women) who glory in the fact that God has given them wondrous ways of loving one another, or by eunuchs who use their power to dominate, not to serve.

CHAPTER SIX

Cardinal Cormac Murphy-O'Connor

People of Other Faiths?

CORMAC MURPHY-O'CONNOR'S MOTHER likes to tell the story of his reply at age four to a visitor who wondered what he wanted to be when he grew up. "Doctor," he announced, with a glance at his father, a surgeon in Cork at the time. He thought a moment, remembering he had three uncles who were priests, and added, "Or pope."

On the eve of the conclave, Murphy-O'Connor, archbishop of Westminster, in London, and soon to cast his vote for a successor to John Paul II, could tell that story on himself because he knew he didn't have any hope of being the next pope. But he was a fine figure of a cardinal who represented the most earnest wishes of millions of Catholics around the world that all the Christian churches would get together—soon. If there was any message that the cardinals in conclave needed to hear, it was that ecumenism, the push to Christian unity, which was in a backwater during the last years of John Paul's reign, isn't dead.

At the same time, Cardinal Achille Silvestrini of the Roman Curia, once considered a *papabile* himself, was telling his friends in the press, "Don't count out the Englishman." That was an original, imaginative call. None of the Vatican watchers had seen Murphy-O'Connor as a potential pope. But Silvestrini's speculation was only one more indication that many believed (at least at that time) that this was going to be a wide-open conclave. With a smile, Silvestrini recalled the words of John XXIII after his election in 1958: "Anybody can be pope. The proof of this is that I have become one."

An English pope? There hadn't been one in 851 years, not since Nicholas Breakspear, an Augustinian monk, became Pope Adrian IV in

1154. Adrian IV was not a distinguished pope and the history books say he spent a great deal of his time negotiating treaties with kings and princes to nail down his feudal sovereignty.

The very name of Adrian IV was a reminder, however, that Catholic Christianity had a long history in England, and that England is still a Catholic country in a sense. Anglicans who are members of the United Kingdom's official Church of England are not Protestants. They are Catholics—English Catholics, but Catholics nonetheless—who profess the same creed that Catholics do, and have the same sacraments, including the Eucharist.

For eight years, Cormac Murphy-O'Connor chaired the Anglican–Roman Catholic International Commission (ARCIC), a high-level panel that hammered out language embodying this understanding. This experience made Murphy-O'Connor feel closer to the conclave's most ecumenically minded cardinals, and his presence at the conclave could only remind other cardinals that they had a duty to keep the ecumenical spirit alive. They could do this by electing a man who was committed to doing that.

Silvestrini did not think Murphy-O'Connor's ecumenical credentials alone would win him many votes in the conclave. "But a big part of any conclave is talking together. Cormac will be chatting people up in the hallways." (He noted that Murphy-O'Connor was part of the conclave's largest bloc, men who spoke English as either their first or second language.) "And in a long conclave, who knows? He may start picking up some votes. People like him."

People like Murphy-O'Connor because he is an affable, friendly sort, a tall, lean, handsome fellow, with a head of distinguished gray hair and a jowly, ruddy Irish face that is more ready to break into laughter than a frown. When he wasn't laughing, he was listening with a quizzical smile that seemed to imply, I think I know what you're trying to say. Go on.

Many of the cardinals remembered Murphy-O'Connor's proposal at their consistory of May 2001, when he suggested the Church promote a pan-Christian gathering that would draw up its own agenda for bringing all the Christian Churches together under a pope who would preside "not in terms of jurisdiction, but of love." The notion hadn't created much of a stir in Rome. But it won approval in England, where people were happy to see that Murphy-O'Connor was following in the footsteps of the late Cardinal Basil Hume, who got on so famously with the Anglicans. On January 13, 2002, Cormac preached before the queen in a service at Sandringham House, the first Catholic prelate asked to assist at a royal service since the Reformation. And the last time Rowan Williams, the Anglican archbishop of Canterbury, came to Rome, he and his wife stayed at the English College as Cormac's guests.

So this was another plus on Murphy-O'Connor's résumé: he was a major player in the ecumenical movement. The word "ecumenical" (from the Greek *oikoumenikos,* meaning "worldwide") was first used at a meeting in London in 1910 by Protestant missionaries who understood, far sooner than most Catholics, that the rips and tears in the seamless robe of Christ were a shock and a scandal to people everywhere. ("See those Christians, how they hate one another.") World War I, a conflict in which American soldiers wearing Saint Christopher medals were killing (and being killed by) German soldiers wearing belt buckles stamped with the legend *Gott mit uns,* "God with us," only made talks about a joint Christian witness against war that much more important.

Grieved in the aftermath of that war, Belgium's Cardinal Désiré Joseph Mercier hosted a series of meetings in his ancient cathedral town of Mechelen, with a select number of forward-thinking Anglican scholars (led by E. F. L. Wood, Lord Halifax, who had helped see England through the war) and some equally open Catholic theologians. Those meetings in 1922, 1923, and 1924, called the Malines Conversations, reached a startling peak with a talk in 1925 called "United Not Absorbed" (given by Mercier but ghosted by a pioneering Benedictine monk named Lambert Beauduin) that actually proposed a creative way of bringing English Catholics and Roman Catholics into full communion.

Mercier suggested that the Anglican Communion could model itself on the autochthonous Eastern Rite Churches of the Middle East. Then Anglicans could retain their ancient seventh- and eighth-century liturgy in English, their own married clergy, and their own unbroken line of apostolic succession. Their archbishop of Canterbury would reassume his role as the primate of England, to preside over a Church that would keep most of its English character—as reflected, for instance, in the Book of Common Prayer.

Few Anglicans ever heard about Mercier's proposal, but Rome did, and Rome was upset. Rome had banished these people from the kingdom centuries ago, and Mercier was proposing to let them back in? Pope Pius XI closed down the Malines Conversations, sent Dom Lambert Beauduin into exile from his monastery, and ordered him not to write about interfaith issues. In 1928, after hearing of two ecumenical conferences (in Stockholm and Lausanne) featuring Orthodox and Protestant theologians talking about the need for Christians to get back together, Pius wrote an encyclical that stigmatized these conferences as part of a new heresy he called "pan-Christianism." He forbade Catholics to participate in any of them, and this policy was the order of the day inside the Vatican until Vatican II, when John XXIII and the Council Fathers put their blessings on the ecumenical movement, setting a new, friendlier tone for all of Christendom, a tone that would pervade the ministry of Pope Paul VI and John Paul II.

Both of these popes encouraged separate, bilateral conversations on an international and national scale between Catholics and a wide variety of other Christian bodies—most notably the Anglicans, the Lutherans, and the Orthodox. Historians mark the day when Michael Ramsey, the archbishop of Canterbury, came to visit Paul VI in 1966, the first time since the Reformation that Canterbury and Rome had come together. Ramsey and the pope gave a jump start to an official dialogue between Anglicans and Roman Catholics by issuing a common declaration—to promote the development of "respect, esteem, and fraternal love" between the two communions in the hope of achieving "that unity in truth for which Christ prayed" and the ultimate restoration of a "complete communion of faith and sacramental life." It was something they hoped would contribute to "a strengthening of peace in the world." The two of them asked that the dialogue be founded on the gospels and on the ancient traditions that preceded the split, emphasizing what the two churches had in common, and set up a body of carefully chosen Catholics and Anglicans that came to be known as the Anglican–Roman Catholic International Commission (ARCIC) to follow where the new spirit led, rather than reopen old controversies.

The members of ARCIC met for the first time in 1970, encouraged by the pope

> to go behind the habit of thought and expression born and nourished in enmity and controversy, to scrutinize together the great

> common treasure, to clothe it in language at once traditional and expressive of the insights of an age which no longer glories in strife but seeks to come together in listening to the quiet voice of the Spirit.

For ten years, the group (mostly pastors and theologians) conferred, refining and honing their statements, and ended up producing a number of position papers on how their people understood core elements of the faith—often with contributions from other pastors and theologians around the world.

ARCIC's editors issued a final report in 1981 that outlined their "substantial agreement" on core, but historically controverted issues like the Eucharist, ministry and ordination, and authority in the Church, to generally good reviews. On November 15, 1982, the American bishops, for example, noted with approval that members of ARCIC had not evaded "the historic difficulties between the two communions." But they did avoid the "controversial language" of the past, choosing instead to use "imagery and concepts which were the exclusive legacy of neither of the two churches but in which each would hopefully be able to recognize its own faith." ARCIC even came up with a formulation on transubstantiation that both Anglicans and Catholics could live with. The *ultimate* change intended by God in the Eucharist, they said, is not the changing of the elements of bread and wine into the Lord's body and blood, but the transformation of human beings into the likeness of Christ.

Cardinal Ratzinger, just beginning his job as prefect of the Holy Office, reviewed ARCIC's final report. He didn't think it was clear enough. He said that any statement coming out of ARCIC had to have "consonance" with the definitions of all the ecumenical councils (including the formulations of the Council of Trent) and all the binding papal declarations since Trent. He also insisted on "the removal of all possible ambiguity" in future statements.

Ratzinger's demurrer prompted Edward Yarnold, the Jesuit cochairman of ARCIC, to lodge a bitter complaint against Ratzinger's office, which, he said, had ignored the important admonitions of both Paul VI and John Paul II to move ahead toward unity by going beyond formulations of the past. To Yarnold, the old formulas may have been all too clear, dealing as they did with God's intentions for the world, a matter still fraught with mystery. "The truth about God," said Yarnold, "and his gracious dealings with the human race, is too vast to be captured in any single theological formula or system. Any statement about God that is not trivial is likely to be capable of more than one interpretation." Yarnold, the first Catholic priest to win a doctor of divinity degree at Oxford in more than four hundred years, went on:

> Since terms acquire new associations when they are used in new cultural contexts and translated into different languages, it will be impossible to ensure that ideas from one theological tradition are grasped in the identical sense by another tradition. A certain ambiguity is therefore of the nature of ecumenical agreements. It is harmful only if it conceals fundamental differences; it is benign if it allows each side to bring its characteristic religious experience to the interpretations of the same fundamental faith.

Ratzinger met that criticism with one of the Vatican's most effective weapons, silence, but that didn't stop the English ecumenists from creeping ahead. In 2002, they refounded ARCIC with new Catholic and Anglican members (under the protection of Cardinal Walter Kasper, president of the Vatican's Council for Promoting Christian Unity) and gave themselves a new name, the International Anglican–Roman Catholic Commission for Unity and Mission. In its brief existence, IARCCUM has done little. Kasper and Ratzinger clashed, and Kasper was loath to excite the Holy Office by launching Catholic-Anglican dialogues on anything but the safest subjects.

On the eve of the conclave, IARCCUM was ready to publish a study on devotion to the Blessed Virgin Mary as seen by Anglican authors of the seventeenth century. It concluded that Anglicans could now reasonably consider that two Catholic teachings on Mary, the Immaculate Conception and the Assumption, are warranted by scripture. Since Anglicans had long believed that the very definition of these dogmas by the popes, not to mention their content, was questionable, this was a positive step toward the full communion that Pope Paul VI and Michael

Ramsey had talked about in 1966. But it was a very small step. There were other, far more important issues that impacted on the faith sharing of Catholics and Anglicans the world over, issues that IARCCUM was avoiding, simply because of one man, Cardinal Joseph Ratzinger.

To some Vatican watchers, it seemed that those Catholics seeking unity with the Anglicans would have to stick with topics that didn't challenge Ratzinger's orthodox criteria.

"This may be time for a pause," Cardinal Cormac Murphy-O'Connor told me on April 2002 in a meeting in his office at the elegant Archbishop's House on Ambrosden Avenue. "ARCIC was only a beginning." It was a good beginning, he said, because ARCIC focused on the principal stumbling block toward unity, the authority of the pope. But Rome failed to deal with ARCIC's challenge, that the institutional Church had to start paying more attention to the people's Church. ARCIC articulated that challenge in a 1998 document called "The Gift of Authority." It said, in part:

> The Second Vatican Council has reminded Roman Catholics of how the gifts of God are present in the people of God. It has also taught the collegiality of the episcopate in its communion with the Bishop of Rome, head of the college. However, is there at all levels effective participation of clergy as well as lay people in emerging synodal bodies? Has the teaching of the Second Vatican Council regarding the collegiality of bishops been implemented sufficiently? Do the actions of bishops reflect sufficient awareness of the extent of the authority they receive through ordination for governing the local church? Has enough provision been made to ensure consultation between the Bishop of Rome and the local churches prior to the making of important decisions affecting either a local church or the whole Church? How is the variety of theological opinion taken into account when such decisions are made? In supporting the Bishop of Rome in his work of promoting communion among the churches, do the structure and procedures of the Roman Curia adequately respect the exercise of *episcope* at other levels? Above all, how will the Roman Catholic Church address the question of universal pri-

> macy as it emerges from "the patient and fraternal dialogue" about the exercise of the office of the Bishop of Rome to which John Paul II has invited Church leaders and their theologians?

ARCIC had asked politely, but Rome responded with silence, even though the Anglican members of ARCIC seemed ready to accept the bishop of Rome as "the only one who can help maintain visible unity." Now, looking back on the work of ARCIC, Murphy-O'Connor admitted there were a good many people—laypeople and clergy as well—who didn't understand what the organization was up to, both in its general push toward unity and in some of the particular formulations that it had worked on so laboriously over the years. And what critics didn't understand, they feared. As the document on authority put it:

> Anglicans sometimes fear the prospect of overcentralization, Roman Catholics the prospect of doctrinal incoherence. Faith, banishing fear, might see simply the prospect of the right balance between a primacy serving the unity and a conciliarity maintaining the just diversity . . . of all the churches.

Recent actions by both Anglicans and Roman Catholics had more than justified each side's fear of the other. The Anglicans had taken the extraordinary step, for instance, of ordaining women, in spite of warnings from Rome that doing so would put a cloud over their hoped-for union with the Catholic Church. The Catholic Church, in turn, had become more centralized and less collegial, particularly in the last days of John Paul's reign. The pope not only opposed the ordination of women, but commanded an end to any discussion about it. Anglicans could take heart in the fact that the Romans were clearly split on the issue; a good many Catholic theologians ignored the pope's order by continuing to talk and write about women's ordination and arguing with those in the Vatican (it was really the pope himself!) who wanted to declare that the pope's decision against women's ordination was infallible. (To his credit, Ratzinger got John Paul II off the infallibility track.)

The members of ARCIC kept their composure. They said things would work out in time, for history operated in mysterious ways.

Pius IX condemned religious liberty; less than a hundred years later, the Fathers of Vatican II and Pope Paul VI endorsed it. Time was on the side of reform, and in a world being transformed by computers, modems, and geosynchronous communication satellites, time itself was accelerating. They cited the words of John Paul himself in his 1995 encyclical *Ut Unum Sint,* inviting leaders of other churches to engage with him in a fraternal dialogue on how the bishop of Rome might exercise his primacy in new ways.

But John Paul II's actions, as we've seen, often belied his fine words. Since 1995, he seemed to have turned his back on any notion that he was going to act collegially, in concert with the world's bishops, and he approved Ratzinger's *Dominus Iesus* at some considerable cost to the interfaith dialogue that many of these bishops had been pursuing in their own parts of the world.

Murphy-O'Connor said he was undaunted by *Dominus Iesus.* He knew he had to keep "pursuing the dialogue" with other Christians, and non-Christians, too. He also had to run his archdiocese—with the help of 501,900 Catholics, 962 priests, and 1,322 nuns—and try to find more creative ways of promoting the faith, which he once confessed was "almost vanquished" in England. He said he had been immensely heartened by the effectiveness of the small faith communities he first encountered when he was a young priest in Portsmouth. "People met in different houses to pray, to read a passage of scripture, and to reflect on the circumstances of their daily lives. It was my first lesson in the value of a basic Christian community."

In his next parish assignment, Murphy-O'Connor helped to form ten of these basic communities, and before long, out of a parish of a thousand or so practicing Catholics, about two hundred people were meeting regularly. In those faith clusters, a whole mix of people—married, unmarried, young and old—discovered a new and deeper experience of faith through prayer, scripture, community, and service to others. "I watched it all happen," said Murphy-O'Connor. "The groups themselves—evangelical, missionary, lay communities, communities of women—were all fired by the Holy Spirit as were the earliest Church communities described in the second chapter of Acts, which devoted themselves to the apostles' teaching, and to fellowship, to the breaking of bread and to prayers."

Murphy-O'Connor saw people in these small groups encourage one another "to go further and deeper on their journey of faith than they might otherwise. People began to discover, and then to share more openly, their relationship with God, with each other, with the whole of creation. Out of these kinds of reflection they went on to put their faith into action, and place more urgency and meaning into justice and peace issues. They had a heightened sense of belonging and being accepted. I have seen the radical change that occurs in their lives."

He wasn't sure whether he could promote a big-city version of these small communities in London, far different from a small English village, and though the faith of the half million Catholics in London was strong, it could be stronger. "We've always had to struggle. But I know one thing: the Church of the future will look very different from the Church we know today." And he was convinced that the ecumenical moves that had been made by Catholics and Anglicans would lead to a unified Catholic Church in England—in the words of Cardinal Mercier, "united not absorbed." The only question was when.

UNTIL DARK-SKINNED IMMIGRANTS (many of them Catholic) began flooding into England from all over the Commonwealth, there were two kinds of Catholics in England: the descendants of the old recusant families who refused to knuckle under to Henry VIII and Queen Elizabeth I, and people who had fled Ireland in the early twentieth century to find better economic opportunities in London, Liverpool, Manchester, and Leeds. The Murphy-O'Connor family was in the latter group, the Irish-English (who had a great deal in common with Irish-Americans). Cormac's mother, Ellen Theresa Cuddigan, and his father, George Patrick Murphy-O'Connor, were devout Catholics. His father attended daily mass before he went off to work every morning at the local hospital in Reading, County Berkshire, about halfway between London and Oxford. (Reading was once famous for its beer, biscuits, and bacon. Microsoft, Digital, Hewlett-Packard, and Oracle now have offices there.)

At age eighteen, Cormac began training for the priesthood at the Venerable English College in Rome, where his six-foot-four-inch frame came in handy when he joined the unofficial Vatican rugby team. He was also a thespian, a lad who most enjoyed his parts in the Gilbert and Sullivan operettas staged at the college. A classmate recalls, "Cormac was very much the romantic Irish tenor." After seven years at the Roman College and a degree in philosophy and theology, Murphy-O'Connor was ordained in 1956 and returned to England to serve in parishes near Portsmouth.

He spent four years as the secretary to Derek Worlock, then bishop of Portsmouth, who was the English Church's leading liberal of the time and a powerful figure among the English bishops. In 1971 Murphy-O'Connor was sent back to Rome to serve for almost seven years as rector of his alma mater, where he threw fine parties that became famous for their easy conviviality—and for Cormac's favorite concoction: potent Negroni cocktails (one ounce each of gin, sweet vermouth, and Campari).

After six years at the English College, he returned to England as bishop of Arundel and Brighton, an upscale diocese that covers much of Sussex and Surrey, where his sociability won new friends. Among them was the country's most eminent Catholic layman, the duke of Norfolk, who took an immediate shine to Cormac.

His fellow priests liked Murphy-O'Connor, too, but some said he was a bit disorganized. One aide reported, "Cormac is well known for starting things and not finishing them." A Dominican said, "I think that in many ways Cormac would be an excellent pope. He has an open spirit, and an open heart, and that would bring fresh air. He is a man of enormous goodness, and I regard him as a friend of mine. I am not sure that clarity of thought is his greatest attribute. He can be a bit woolly! But this can be an advantage for bishops, when they do not wish to be pinned down. I think he would need good advisers to bring clarity when necessary."

Could Cormac help hasten the day when Anglicans and Roman Catholics finally come together? The Dominican said, "I think it would take a lot more than Cormac to persuade the Anglicans to join us, since however nicely it is presented, there are some nitty-gritty claims that are part of our faith that many Anglicans would find impossible to accept. I think that it will take a lot of evolution on both sides to get to unity."

That was an understatement, considering the long history of the break with Rome, which was set off more by a cultural revolution called the Renaissance than by a silly argument over King Henry's VIII's desire to shed his wife for a mistress who could give him a male heir. Contrary to popular opinion, Henry VIII was never excommunicated. He died in 1547, while English theologians were still claiming they had rescued the primitive Catholic and apostolic faith from the accretions of Rome. Then the pope became impatient. Compelled by power politics and driven by a certain obtuseness, Pius V excommunicated Henry's daughter Queen Elizabeth I some twelve years after her accession to the English throne in 1558.

On the Continent, kings and princes had learned to regard excommunications with a cavalier attitude; they were often levied by cranky popes who were preoccupied with their own power, and usually over issues that were less doctrinal than political. Who's in charge here? became the key question—meaning, of course, who gets control of the lands and the taxes? But this excommunication of Elizabeth by Pope Pius V not only put the queen outside the faith, it also claimed to liberate Englishmen from their obedience to her. That made the pope and every Catholic who paid fealty to the pope an enemy of the state. When the Spanish Armada came sailing up the English Channel to restore the unity of Christendom by conquest, the pope of Rome—to the common Englishman, at least—was a political and military enemy and a threat to the English nation.

For Richard McBrien, Pius V's excommunication of the English queen—and the consequent splitting of the Church in England—was one of those "tragic and unforgivable mistakes" that marked the monarchical papacy of the fourteenth, fifteenth, and sixteenth centuries, which, as McBrien would have it, was "a bloated bureaucracy wallowing in the lust for money and power." It took almost four centuries of enmity and horrible behavior on both sides for Anglicans and Catholics to start reconsidering the split, and to ask one another what they could do to heal it.

In the fall of 2002, Murphy-O'Connor would soon be embroiled in the scandal of the century, the priest sex-abuse crisis. He was far less culpable than Cardinal Law in Boston. He had had a priest under his charge in Arundel and Brighton, Michael Hill, who was jailed for five years in 1997 for a series of sexual encounters with children, most of them altar boys. Parents claimed they had complained to Murphy-O'Connor as early as 1978, but that Hill was merely moved from one Surrey parish to another, where he found other victims. Murphy-O'Connor said that when "allegations of a more specific and serious nature" were made in 1983, he removed Hill from his parish and made sure he received "professional assessment and later therapy."

Eighteen months after he had withdrawn Hill's license to work in a parish, Murphy-O'Connor believed the priest had been rehabilitated and appointed him chaplain at Gatwick Airport—where he abused at least one other boy. In November 2002, Hill was sentenced to another five years in prison.

Murphy-O'Connor was embarrassed by the Hill affair, and he took steps to make sure that the Church handled all such cases according to norms laid down in Britain's Nolan Report. Murphy-O'Connor was no Bernard Law; he didn't hide out from the press; he tried to talk to reporters and editors and, unlike Law, was defended by most of his priests and his people, who suspected the press continued to hound their cardinal because he took a position in the fall of 2002 against Great Britain joining forces with the United States to wage war on Iraq. Murphy-O'Connor made his reasons clear in a signed piece in *The Times* of London on September 5, 2002. It said in part:

> A war in Iraq would cause great destruction and suffering. It would also entail grave consequences for our own country and for the world. There is reason to be concerned that military intervention would set the Arab world against the West, and undermine efforts directed at peace between Israel and the Palestinian people.
>
> The Prime Minister has now promised to publish evidence to support his growing conviction that the threat posed by Iraq is both grave and imminent, and that the regime must change itself or be changed. Without persuasive, preferably incontrovertible, evidence of this kind it is difficult to see how concerns in this country and abroad about this course of action could be allayed.

Murphy-O'Connor's warning came more than six months before the United States and Great Britain invaded Iraq. In light of the war's sorry aftermath, his words in the fall of 2002 were prophetic: "Head-on confrontation is liable to create as many problems as it solves."

The press retaliated by dredging up the case of Michael Hill all over again, and coming up with other undocumented charges of other priest perfidy on Murphy-O'Connor's watch. Murphy-O'Connor answered in a news conference, and in a letter to *The Times,* but it didn't seem to matter now what the truth was: the British press was in full pursuit. A columnist in *The Independent* wondered in print when Murphy-O'Connor was going to resign. A columnist for *The Times* grumbled that "there is something about the Church's response that leaves us wondering whether, at heart, it is truly penitent. Apology and self-recrimination come hard to an organization which regards itself as the one true Church, its authority as solid as the apostolic rock on which it was founded." True enough, but that had nothing to do with Murphy O'Connor's recent handling of the priest sex-abuse cases in Westminister.

I met Murphy-O'Connor a half dozen times after he had received his red hat. I always saw a man doing his best to bridge the ancient gap in the Church—between the people on one side and pomposity on the other. In public, and even more in private, O'Connor came off as an unassuming, thoroughly modest fellow. To those attending an award ceremony at a Catholic academy, he confessed that he had received only one prize in all his days at school. "Third place, for religion."

During the weeklong events of World Youth Day 2002 in Toronto, attended by some 173,000 young people from around the world (half of them from North America) who had come to see the pope, Murphy-O'Connor took his place along with several dozen cardinals and bishops to represent the Church in a series of sessions that were billed by the organizers as "catechesis." One morning, Francis Arinze, the curial cardinal from Nigeria, regaled some ten thousand youngsters with a chat on the sacrament of reconciliation (once called the sacrament of penance, or confession) that was filled with anecdotes and wisecracks. Organizers had scheduled Arinze in a big hall at the Youth Day's headquarters in Exhibition Park because, they were told (and they told the kids), "He may be the next pope."

No one told the young people gathered at the Nativity of Our Lord Parish far out in a western suburb of Toronto that Cardinal Murphy-

O'Connor might be the next pope. Less than five hundred youngsters gathered there to meet him, and many weren't even sure who that man was, that man standing up in the sanctuary wearing a simple black cassock with just a bit of red piping on it. "By the way," he said to introduce himself, "I am Cardinal Murphy-O'Connor, from England." He was thoroughly at ease with them, as he reminded them they were called to be "the salt of the earth."

"From salt," he said, "we get our word 'salary.' You have to think of salt, then, as your livelihood, your freshness, your life. Jesus has called you to a saltness." He talked about salt that has lost its freshness, and then he called upon his listeners to join him in the work of "keeping the salt fresh."

After his talk, he took an hour's worth of questions. A young woman asked, "How long before we see the conversion of England?" Cormac blinked and said, "I don't know. I am not an optimist. I am not a pessimist. I am hopeful. Am I comfortable in that hope? Yes. But I don't know how England will change. These are difficult times to be a Christian. But I think we should follow the lead of Mother Teresa, who was once asked how she could help save 'all of these people.' She said, 'One by one.'"

"How do we deal with people of other faiths?" asked another young man. "We talk to them," said the cardinal. "We see the values in their faith. Sure, we say Jesus is the revelation of God. But God does work with people of other faiths. And we dialogue with them because we have so much to discover."

Someone said she found herself defending the Church "more and more these days in the middle of the priest sex scandal."

O'Connor said, "Of course, we try to defend the Church. But we have to be realistic. There were times in history when the Church was corrupt. It reformed. It must always be reformed, because, really, it is always going to be composed of saints and sinners. Most of us are sinners. But we try to go on quietly about our business, praying and serving the poor. We needn't feel we have to do this all alone. We find support in one another, and in the Holy Spirit. Reform in the Church will come not because the pope says so, but because of the fire within us. The faith, the hope, and the charity that will lead to unity among

Christians cannot be imposed from the top down. We need a real conversion of heart, a new spirituality that ends with our reaching out to the world, that makes our Church a Church for the world."

ON MARCH 9, 2005, Murphy-O'Connor was in Rome for a meeting at the Vatican on liturgy. The pope was fading. We talked about the next pope. When I asked if he thought the cardinals would pick a pope who might exercise a collegial style of governance that would let the bishops be bishops, he said, "Yes, but that will only work if the bishops are collegial with their own people."

He felt very certain the next pope would not be a carbon copy of John Paul II. "Every pope I ever knew had a different style. We should expect the next pope to be himself, and, therefore, he would have to be different. No one can emulate Pope John Paul II. No one should even try. Seven years ago, I wouldn't have said this. Now, I hear a good many cardinals saying the next pope will have to be far less imposing, far more of a listening pope."

CHAPTER SEVEN

Cardinal Oscar Rodríguez Maradiaga

The Gospel in Every Culture

THE WORLD DIDN'T PAY MUCH ATTENTION to Oscar Andrés Rodríguez Maradiaga, archbishop of Tegucigalpa, Honduras, until February 21, 2001. That was the day he appeared in Saint Peter's Square, together with forty-three other newly named cardinals. Most of them had supporters there to applaud them as, one by one, they approached the pope's golden throne. But when Rodríguez rose to make his way forward, a roar came from a loggia off to the pope's right, from some eight hundred men and women standing in front of a huge banner emblazoned with the name "Juan Pablo III," and another name on another banner in big red block letters: "Rodríguez Maradiaga." The well-dressed enthusiasts had come all the way from Honduras, full of obvious pride that their small country had its first cardinal. Or was their adulation more than a case of local pride?

Rodríguez did seem like something special. He had a kind of star quality lacking in most of the other cardinals. They were properly solemn, but when this man strode bareheaded to the papal presence in his new red cassock, his broad smile was as sunny as the day itself. The pope couldn't help beaming back at this man so unlike himself—with his bronzed face and high cheekbones, he was the very image of an Inca prince. Rodríguez knelt to receive the red silk biretta. The pope waved a blessing at him, then gave his arm a squeeze. Rodríguez rose from his knees and wheeled around to return to his place. Now many others in the square were smiling, too. They noted that this man had an air about him. Perhaps it was the way he wore his hat. Others set their birettas square on; Rodríguez wore his at a tilt. And he had a spring in his step.

He seemed so young. Indeed, at fifty-eight, he was young compared with his fellow cardinals, whose average age was seventy-six. "Too bad," Alessandra Stanley, Rome correspondent for the *New York Times,* told three other reporters, "that he won't be the next pope." She was allowing herself a moment of cynicism. She liked him. He was such a fine figure of a cardinal. So, almost automatically, she assumed he didn't have a chance.

Her thought was soon rebutted by Yvonne Torres, a thirty-seven-year-old lawyer from Tegucigalpa, standing there in the square when Stanley approached her and the contingent from Honduras. "This is my first trip to Rome," she told Stanley. "When our cardinal is Pope Juan Pablo III, I will come back." Later, Tomás Andrés Mauro Muldoon, the Franciscan bishop of Juticalpa, Honduras, told me, "The people of Honduras want Rodríguez to be the next pope. They won't have it any other way. Particularly the young people."

The possibility that the College of Cardinals might elect a Latin American pope took hold gradually in the press. A month before, *Il Messagero* had a page-one story analyzing the shift in cardinalatial power. Some eleven of the forty-four new cardinals just named by the pope were from Latin America. The significance was clear, to the editors *of Il Messagero* at least, who headlined their story: "A South American Pope? Why Not?" *Il Messagero* went on to feature a Q&A with Rodríguez, a prelate who had learned how to fly private planes when he was studying musicology in the United States, and had also studied in Rome and Vienna.

The day after the consistory, Paddy Agnew of the *Irish Times* was also ready to say that the next pope could come from Latin America. He mentioned the names of three good candidates: Cardinal Cláudio Hummes of São Paulo, Brazil, "the splendidly named" Oscar Andrés Rodríguez Maradiaga, and Juan Luis Cipriani Thorne, of Lima, Peru. Marco Politi went further. In a story written for his paper's weekly magazine, he made it clear that he was casting his vote for Rodríguez.

Others started climbing on the bandwagon. The *National Catholic Reporter* said that Rodríguez was "articulate and passionate on justice issues." Victor Simpson, the Associated Press's chief Vatican watcher, listed Rodríguez as one of six favorites in his papal sweepstakes. Many in the press found the Honduran attractive for many reasons, not the least of which was the fact that of all the cardinals gathered in Rome during that February consistory, Rodríguez seemed readiest to talk. A few of the new cardinals, like the confident new cardinal from New York City, Edward Egan, gave brief, breezy cobblestone interviews, on the run. Rodríguez was the only one who sat for extended interviews.

At 10 p.m. on the night of February 22, when the last receptions for the new cardinals were breaking up all over town, Rodríguez received five American reporters at Rome's Holiday Inn on the Via Aurelia. He took them to a corner of the room, sat them down, loosened his collar, and asked their names. He was relaxed, charming, and eloquent, answered every question without waffling, and was courageous enough to talk about the need for more collegiality in the Church. Knowing that "collegiality" is a problematic word in official curial circles, Rodríguez avoided using it, and substituted the word "collaboration." The Church would make more sense to everyone, he said, if it could promote more collaboration within the Church—pope with bishops, bishops with one another, bishops with their priests, and priests with the faithful.

Someone asked him how he handled unwelcome orders from Rome in his archdiocese. He said with a smile, "Between Rome and my country, there is a very wide ocean." Rodríguez had a mind of his own, and would do what he needed to do in Honduras, no matter what the Curia tried to impose upon him.

Another reporter asked Rodríguez how he felt about "enculturation," a word that sums up a number of strategies meant to encourage more pluralism in the too-monolithic Church of John Paul II's restoration. If you were for it, then you believed that (1) Catholicism could flourish in different ways in different cultures, (2) Rome's version of how things ought to be done was not necessarily the model for all the world, and (3) the gospel must grow out of every culture and take on the trappings peculiar to that culture.

Rodríguez nodded with enthusiasm. He believed that enculturation was exactly what his Church needed. Later, in a private interview in Los Angeles, Rodríguez talked further about enculturation. To him, the gospel was not born in the West. It was born in the East, then passed to the West, where it adopted expressions common to the culture of Rome and, later, of Europe. When Western missionaries brought that Romanized Christianity to China in the seventeenth and eighteenth centuries, they did not bring only the gospel; they expressed Christianity in Western categories of thought, and even in Western words. Their mass was in Latin, and their churches were built according to the architectural models they knew in Rome, Florence, and Naples.

In 1939, Pope Pius XII, twenty-five years before the moves toward enculturation that were envisioned at Vatican II, indicated that he had been thinking of ways to make the Church in China more Chinese. He told the bishops in China he was giving them permission to say mass in Chinese. Most of those bishops were French-speaking missionaries; they turned down the pope's offer, protesting that the local Christians, who could understand Latin, didn't need to be treated like second-class citizens in the Church. In fact, the French bishops could understand Latin, but most of their people could not. Most of the people of China didn't even understand who Jesus was, or why he had come, or where he wanted to lead them. They still don't.

Rodríguez said he had the highest regard for Samuel Ruiz, the bishop of Chiapas, Mexico, who once told the American journalist Gary MacEoin, "An autochthonous Church ought to be able to reflect the faith in its own cultural forms, and express it with its own values." Autochthonous, Ruiz explained, does not mean autonomous. It means homegrown, homemade. This Church, he said, "should have autochthonous bishops and autochthonous priests, so that their people can express themselves in their own ways, not in univocal formulas dictated by bureaucrats in Rome." The idea was not only Ruiz's. At a Congress of the Indigenous held in Chiapas in 1974, thousands of his people representing myriad Indian communities said they needed the kind of Church that they could identify with as their own.

In three days of discussion in four Mayan languages, with simultaneous translation organized by themselves, 1,250 delegates told Ruiz what they expected from the Church: a catechesis that would encourage the recovery of and respect for the people's historical memory, its ministries, symbols, and values, and specifically the development of an indigenous clergy. The congress proclaimed the right of the indigenous to land, education, and health, the right to organize their own cooperatives, to secure adequate transport from farm to market, and to process and commercialize their products. They were the same demands the Zapatista rebels would formulate twenty years later.

The oligarchs of Chiapas, who saw the Church as a protector of their privileged status, were outraged. It was not long before a papal nuncio teamed up with government officials to force Ruiz into early retirement. Ruiz's first successor agreed with his pastoral strategy, and he was quickly reassigned. Another successor, Bishop Felipe Arizmendi, was chastised in February 2002 by a Vatican directive ordering him to stop ordaining married Indian deacons; he seemed to be setting up "an ecclesiastical model alien to the tradition and the life of the Church." Translation: we don't want a people's Church in Chiapas.

During the waning years of John Paul II's papacy, this was the very issue—call it self-determination, call it local rule—that lay at the heart of ever-more-frequent discussions in the Church under another arcane word, "subsidiarity," which meant that a local bishop is normally more in touch with his people than a pope in Rome. A bishop of Chiapas can put a serape and sandals on the gospel and walk it up the ridge to Acteal. He can do that most effectively, of course, when he talks to his people in their own language and uses their own idioms. Otherwise, the people would look upon the gospel as an imposition from a foreign land.

In order to talk to his people using their own idioms, the bishop must first listen to them. Then, after he preaches the gospel to them, he must also listen to what they've taken from his preaching of that gospel. If he did not listen to them and to their rephrasing of his message in their own ways of thinking, how could he know he was getting the message across?

Rodríguez Maradiaga understood all this in a way many other cardinals did not. Many of his peers in the Sacred College of Cardinals came to the episcopacy by moving from the seminary to an administrative position in the office of the bishop. Or like Cardinal Egan of New York, they could seek a job in the Roman Curia, then politick their way up the ladders of preferment. By contrast, Rodríguez's first job as a priest was teaching chemistry, physics, and music in high school classrooms run by his teaching order, the Salesians. After that assignment, Rodríguez was made rector of a Salesian house of studies in Guatemala, a seminary where young men training for the priesthood studied philosophy.

Four years later, in 1978, the year that Rodríguez arrived in Tegucigalpa as an auxiliary bishop, there were fewer than one hundred priests in a country of 6 million. Under successive and repressive dictatorial regimes, many Honduran priests had been killed; others had left the country. Rodríguez was under no illusions that vocations to the priesthood would ever become plentiful again. By 2001, Rodríguez had four hundred priests working in Honduras, and 120 seminarians enrolled in the national seminary run by priests from Bogotá, Colombia, and he was heartened by this recent spike in priestly vocations. But he knew that the future of the Church and the future of a just social order in Honduras "depends on the laypeople, for they are the ones who have to build a just society."

In the last few years of John Paul II's reign, the more clerical-minded men in the papal court had argued that laypeople should work in the world, but should stay out of Church ministries. In one document promulgated in 1998, four Roman congregations ordered bishops to stop authorizing laypeople to engage in various ministries. Laypeople should not distribute Communion if priests are able and available; hospital chaplains who were not priests could not call themselves chaplains. In a document issued in April 2004, the Vatican established other norms intended to put a higher wall between priests and people during their worship.

In Honduras, however, neither the letter nor the spirit of these orders applied: laypeople had to engage in certain ministries heretofore called priestly simply because there weren't even enough priests to say mass on Sunday, particularly not in the small towns and villages of Honduras. History itself was trumping the rigid clerical control that had been a dominant feature of the Church since the reforms of Gregory VII in the eleventh century, an overkill that was only established juridically in the Council of Trent in 1534, and then frozen by a Holy See that started to seize control over the appointment of bishops in 1829. But in Honduras and elsewhere throughout the world, Rome's admonitions were empty; the people had one recourse: to start doing things themselves.

Rodríguez took some pride and pleasure in talking about the collaborative nature of his Honduran Church. He had a pastoral council, a priests' council, and a bishops' conference (there are eight bishops now in Honduras—five missionary bishops from abroad, and three Hondurans, all members of religious orders) with laypeople sitting in on all of these bodies, which are run democratically.

Rodríguez was proudest of his fifteen thousand laymen and laywomen called Delegates of the Word, who were doing everything in and for the Church—their Church—except preside at mass. His eyes lit up when he said, "They lead the liturgical celebrations on Sunday in the majority of our small villages. They're trained, they read the readings, they lead the prayers, they preach, they are ministers of Communion." They also marry people, baptize their children, and bury them when they die.

When reporters asked Rodríguez if he thought he could become pope, he laughed. "You people. That's all you people can talk about. The next pope." In fact, he said that the question was "on the periphery of our real concerns." He said he was interested in poverty, violence, and governmental corruption in Honduras (which remains one of the poorest and least developed countries in Latin America).

"We are never going to have peace as long as poverty is increasing. Violence in the cities is growing. Kidnapping is an industry in Latin America—in Guatemala, in El Salvador, in Honduras, in Colombia. It's awful." Even the poor were victims. "In Guatemala," he said, "they kidnap a baby when the mother enters the supermarket," then dicker with her for a return of the baby if she will buy them sugar and Coca-Cola.

He said that the rise of Pentecostal Christianity in Central America had not helped make society less violent. "The great majority of Pentecostals do not go into politics, because they think politics is dirty." One Pentecostal, said Rodríguez, did go into politics—President Rios Montt of Guatemala. "He invited his people to come and help him clean things up. It was a beautiful idea. Eight months later, he was deposed by citizens who found out he was a thief."

"In Latin America," Rodríguez said, "many go into politics not to work for the common good, or to gain the kind of power they need in order to do things for the common good. No. They go into politics in order to become rich, as soon as possible. They look to the state as a source of booty. Yes, they are pirates. And if they don't run for office, they will invest in the political campaigns of their friends, who will help them to the spoils. This is a sickness throughout the continent. We have to change the entire political culture, because the political culture is ill. We need something different."

The answer, he said, lay in democracy. For decades, of course, much of Latin America was ruled by dictators. Now, most nations are democracies, "but they are only very weak democracies." The problem is that "you can't have democracy without democrats. Democrats are not born, they are made, through education. But this will take time. Education has to begin in the home, with father and mother teaching that everyone has a right to speak and everyone has a right to be heard. This also has to happen in our schools, in the workplace, everywhere."

The cardinal smiled ruefully. "But this is lacking in Latin America. We have this Indian blood in our veins, the spirit of *caciquismo*. Everyone wants to be a chief."

He said that spirit would be overcome only by educating a new generation of idealists who follow Catholic social teaching. Most important was "the continuing education of people in the faith." In Honduras, he said, children's Catholic education stops when they have made their First Communion (at age seven) "and then they never again hear anything about the faith." So the best people get master's degrees in engineering, for example, but still have a second-grade education as Catholics. As a result, he said, "Life goes one way, faith stays in the temple. We need a synthesis in order to have an evangelization in politics."

The goal was life and faith together. For the cardinal, showing the relevance of the gospel, mainly in the area of peace and justice, "is the great challenge of the twenty-first century." He was worried about the systemic poverty he saw throughout Central America.

After the reporters filed their stories, Rodríguez began popping up on every papal handicapper's tip sheet. Paddy Power, the oddsmaker who ran a betting site on the Internet as well as in his Dublin digs, made Rodríguez a 6-to-1 favorite, right behind Cardinal Martini of Milan.

If the Irish bookmaker had known about the history of liberation theology in Latin America, and Rodríguez's sympathy for it, he might have made longer odds on the Honduran. Rodríguez was on the wrong side of the political divide to win many votes from cardinals opposed to change. He had been a student in Rome of one the Council's leading liberal theologians, Bernard Häring, who had called for a moral theology that relied less on a natural law ethic (which made the Church into a Church of laws rather than a Church of love) and placed morality in a broader humanistic framework that also happened to be more biblically based.

Häring's approach was an unlikely one to take for a member of the Redemptorist order. For at least a century, the Redemptorists took exactly the opposite tack; they had a rigid, rule-book mentality, and they were famous for trying to scare people into loving God by preaching hellfire and damnation. Häring's views were reflected in a number of conciliar documents. Thanks to Häring, priests and their people all over the world became less obsessed with personal sin, and more concerned with corporate sin: prayer and fasting were good; putting political pressure on a big landowner to pay living wages was better. Häring's students had fanned out across the planet with that message, to help create a new kind of theology that did not please the Church's right wing. This was the liberation theology that found its first home in Latin America, more of a movement than a concept, that tried to put the Church on the side of the poor in their struggle for justice.

John Paul II said he wanted to put the Church on the side of social justice, but his actions in Latin America, at least, said otherwise. He disciplined the liberation theologians for trying to bring to Latin America the freedoms he wanted for Poland and was even more alarmed when he heard them talking about liberation inside the Church. The Franciscan Leonardo Boff wrote a book, *Church: Charism and Power,* calling for "class struggle" inside Catholicism to redistribute authority.

Liberation theology still lives, because concern for social justice has become part of the job description for Catholic leaders everywhere. Many dioceses throughout the world have active commissions for peace and justice, run mostly by laymen and laywomen. And students of the last century's ongoing revolutions have noted that advocates of other liberations have adopted the rhetoric, and some of the arguments, of the liberation theologians of Latin America. Their inspiration comes from the twenty-fifth chapter of Matthew, where Jesus tells the disciples they would not be admitted to paradise for knowing a set of abstract truths but on the strength of their giving food, drink, clothing, and shelter to the poor.

When an ad hoc coalition of sixteen Catholic bishops from debtor and creditor nations flew to a G7 meeting in Bonn, Germany, in 1999 to demand immediate debt relief for the world's poorest nations, they gave the world "a glimpse of the liberationist legacy." Their spokesman, who turned over to Chancellor Gerhard Schroeder some 17 million signatures from around the world, was Rodríguez Maradiaga. (In July 2005, Rodríguez was still lobbying for cancellation of third world debt at the G8 conference in Scotland.)

On May 15, 2001, Cardinal Rodríguez was back in Rome for an extraordinary consistory. At an ordinary consistory, the pope creates new cardinals. Every other kind of meeting between the pope and a majority of his cardinals is extraordinary. The Italian press billed this coming together as a warm-up for the next conclave. "In other times, reigning popes would try to assign their favored successor to the right pole position," wrote Marco Politi, using a racing metaphor, "but no one ever had the idea of calling all the electors in for an open discussion. Now Wojtyla brought them here to speak freely about the platform of the next pontificate."

The agenda was loosely organized under the items that John Paul II had ticked off in his letter on the new millennium released on January 6, 2001. That letter outlined the pope's surprisingly open and wide-ranging agenda, urging the Church to find new ways for its missionary outreach in the new century. Under that charge, Rodríguez, who had been selected by his peers and by the pope himself to attend five Roman synods, each of them called to discuss one aspect or another of Church policy, zeroed in on the anomaly of having the synods closed to the press. The press was standing by to relay the synod's conclusions (and some of its chatter) to the world in a more effective way than the Vatican could ever do. Rodríguez urged the synod discussions be open to the press.

He got no thanks for that from Cardinal Jan Schotte, the man who had been running the synods like his own private petting zoo since 1985. Schotte did not invite the press into the next bishops' synod in October 2001, and made sure Rodríguez did not come either, by omitting him from a list of special appointees to that synod.

"It is all right," Rodríguez told me two months later. "They won't do anything significant anyway. They never do."

On the eve of the conclave, Rodríguez Maradiaga was boarding Continental Airlines flight 2324 from Tegucigalpa to Houston for the first leg of his twelve-hour flight to Rome. When a TV reporter in Houston asked him what his chances were, he laughed and said, "Zero chance."

In fact, he had the support of some of the ten other new cardinals from Latin America, but he was not a member of the inner circle of Latin American cardinals, five of whom worked in the Roman Curia. He knew they could persuade most of the twenty-two cardinals from Latin America to vote in a bloc for one of their own on the first ballot. But it was unlikely that they would pick Rodríguez to fly that trial balloon. A majority of them were from the party of no change, and Rodríguez from the party of change. In proof of that, they could cite the Honduran's suspect views on liberation theology.

As he jetted east toward Rome, Rodríguez was less concerned about his own candidacy, more worried about the machinations of those cardinals who followed the leadership of Cardinal Alfonso López Trujillo. López had hobnobbed in his native Colombia with drug traffickers, and many of those who knew him when he was the archbishop (and later cardinal) disliked him intensely. In Medellín, the second largest city in Colombia, with a population of more than 3 million, he fought against priests who had rolled up their sleeves to help the poor.

There were a thousand stories about López. He had Federico Carrasquilla, one of the most effective, zealous priests in Colombia, suspended from the priesthood because he was organizing cooperative industries on behalf of the peons. He had sent another priest, Jaime Restrepo, to his death by reassigning him to a town he had been run out of by plantation owners and cattle ranchers who were infuriated by his attempts to teach the children of their *jornaleros,* or day workers, how to read and write. Restrepo was gunned down on January 17, 1988, on his way to celebrate mass. At his funeral, sad and furious crowds blamed López for sending Restrepo back to an area where López knew he was in serious danger. López had also scolded one missionary community, the priests of the Society of the Divine Word, who had been working in

Medellín for twenty-eight years, because "they were in line with liberation theology." And he moved the Missionaries of the Consolata away from a parish they'd served for twenty-four years because he thought they were "revolutionaries."

López had long been known as "an excellent political animal." As a young priest, he landed a job in the archbishop's office, became a bishop at thirty-five, and was cardinal archbishop of Medellín at forty-seven. He had made it a habit to fly off to Rome once a month, to nourish a private devotion that he claimed he could perform only at a particular shrine in the city of Rome. "His real reason for going to Rome," a Colombian Jesuit told me, "was to politick his way to the top, and to spike the chances of anyone who didn't see things his way. He made it a special point to block the advancement of priests in Brazil who didn't agree with his agenda to rebuild the Church that existed before Vatican II."

On the eve of the conclave, López Trujillo was sixty-nine, but he'd been a cardinal for twenty-one of those years, the last fifteen of them as the president of the Vatican's Pontifical Council for the Family. There, he played a major role in drafting the pope's encyclical *Evangelium Vitae* ("The Gospel of Life"), which focused on abortion, euthanasia, and embryonic experiments as growing threats to humanity. The encyclical praised antiabortion groups and it said they do good "when they act resolutely, but without resorting to violence." At a news conference called to announce the encyclical, however, López referred to the 1994 murder of a Florida physician who was performing abortions and said the doctor had been "a minister of death, not an innocent person, guilty, with an immense culpability." At the May 15, 2001, consistory in Rome, Rodríguez was amused to hear López announce that he was working on a huge "dictionary of sexual terms."

Rodríguez wondered whom López would be campaigning for, or if other Latin American cardinals would have their own candidate. All of them were slick political operatives who would help bring votes to the man of their choice. But only one of them—Darío Castrillón Hoyos, prefect of the Congregation for Clergy in the Roman Curia—seemed to be a serious contender. Indeed, in one "next pope" story, the *Los Angeles Times* named Castrillón Hoyos as its prime Latin American candidate. But Castrillón lost most of the clout he had with the press when he stumbled badly at a news conference inside the Vatican on March 21, 2002. He invited reporters' questions about the priest sex scandal, then ignored the questions and read a prepared statement instead that blamed what he called "America's hedonistic culture" for what "only a few priests" were doing.

EXCURSION II

Liberation

All They Can Be

LIBERATION THEOLOGY CAME ALIVE when the bishops and theologians of Latin America returned from Vatican II and took a hard look at the history of a Church that had always sided with the 1 percent of the population that owned 99 percent of the land. That traditional Church counseled the poor to be satisfied with their lot, and to join their suffering with that of their crucified Lord and Savior Jesus Christ. If they were good, and said their prayers, and paid their pastors to say masses for their dear departed loved ones, they would find salvation in the next life.

By the early 1970s, many of those priests and bishops had been radicalized—by a serious change in Latin American society, and by an equally serious change in the Church.

In the 1950s and 1960s rapid industrial development in Latin America led to benefits for the wealthy and the middle class, but it was a development that had thrown most of the peasants into deeper poverty. Millions of them moved into shantytowns on the margins of cities like Rio de Janeiro, São Paulo, Buenos Aires, and Santiago. Soon they were demanding fundamental changes in Latin American society, even calling for revolution. To keep them in line, leaders of the oligarchy used their power to replace their democracies with military governments, even military dictatorships, which sometimes controlled the people in the extreme, by killing them or making them "disappear."

Then came Vatican II, with a new theology that told the people that, yes, they would find salvation in the next life, but Jesus had also come to bring them salvation now, in the form of a new awareness that the world was good—in fact, redeemed. Now they had a vocation, as followers of Jesus, to make the world better, by bringing it under a reign of justice and peace. Soon, priests and nuns were fanning over the continent urging the little people to organize for their share of this world's goods. The priests and nuns, many of them from Germany, the United States, and Canada, taught people to read and vote, to modernize their fields, to form marketing co-ops and labor unions. They set up small Christian "base communities" that prayed together and read stories of liberation from the book of Exodus. They sang the words sung by Mary when she learned she was to become the mother of Jesus, the Magnificat, giving them a liberationist interpretation that their mothers never thought of.

My soul magnifies the Lord
and my spirit rejoices in God my savior.
Because . . . he has put down the mighty from their seat
and he has exalted the humble.
He has filled the hungry with good things;
and the rich he has sent empty away.

Soon, a small group of Latin American theologians who had done postgraduate work in Europe were reflecting on the faith they saw manifesting itself in these new ways. Gustavo Gutiérrez had studied in Louvain, Lyons, and Rome. Luis Segundo had been at Louvain and Paris. Jon Sobrino took his theology courses in Frankfurt. Leonardo Boff, a Franciscan from Brazil, learned at the feet of Karl Rahner in Munich. They had all analyzed the Council's most revolutionary document, *Gaudium et Spes,* which had addressed itself in an opening paragraph to the poor and the afflicted of a world that was freed by Christ, "a world that might be fashioned anew according to God's design and reach its fulfillment."

In 1968, three years after the Council, the bishops of Latin America met at Medellín and endorsed the radical notion that the Church should side with the rich and the powerful no longer. They said the rich and the powerful had no stake in change. And the continent needed some profound changes. They were led by Sergio Méndez Arceo, the bishop of

Cuernavaca, Mexico; Samuel Ruiz, the bishop of Chiapas, Mexico; Cardinal Landazuri Ricketts of Lima; Cardinals Paulo Evaristo Arns and Aloisio Lorscheider, both Franciscans from Brazil; and by Dom Hélder Câmara, the birdlike, ascetic archbishop of Recife, Brazil, known as the Red Bishop after he had famously urged the bishops of Vatican II to sell all their emerald rings and their diamond-and-ruby-encrusted chalices and give the proceeds to the poor.

And why shouldn't these bishops have sided with the poor? Almost half of the world's Catholics were Latin Americans, and most of them were living in poverty. Why shouldn't the bishops encourage the creation of a social order that better reflected gospel values? Grinding poverty was not accidental. It was the result of carefully constructed social arrangements of benefit to the few at the expense of the many. Why shouldn't the little people try to alter those arrangements? Why shouldn't they become more aware that Christ had called them to be all they could be? ("Conscientization" was the difficult word coined by a Brazilian educator named Paolo Freire to describe this process of becoming more aware.)

Gustavo Gutiérrez had a better, simpler word: "liberation." In December 1971, he published his seminal work, *Teología de la liberación*. In May 1971, Hugo Assmann had conducted a symposium in Montevideo—"Oppression-Liberation: The Challenge to Christians"—and shortly thereafter Leonardo Boff had published a series of articles under the title *Jesús Cristo libertador*. A movement had begun, something, more over, that caught the imagination of Catholics around the world who had been wondering what effect the Council might have on the Church. Latin America was now giving them an answer.

The movement wasn't all talk. Theologians had become pastors, militant agents of inspiration for the life of the Church at its root. A theologian would deliver a paper at a weekend congress, then return to his community to conduct a class in community organizing, resolve a labor dispute, or fix a broken water main. The Boff brothers, Leonardo and Clodovis, worked to build plumbing systems and durable housing for the homeless of Petrópolis, near Rio de Janeiro, once the imperial capital of Brazil. They also helped convert a vast rubbish dump into a recycling center.

What they were doing was recognizably right. Two international synods of bishops meeting in Rome, in 1971 and again in 1974, took positive notice of the new theology of liberation, because it confirmed what had been done at Vatican II. Pope Paul VI assigned Archbishop Karol Wojtyla of Krakow to write the final report of the 1974 synod of bishops, but was so disappointed with his draft that he put it aside and handed over the entire record of the synod to the Jesuit editor of *Civiltà Cattolica,* Roberto Tucci, who had also been an editor of *Gaudium et Spes.* Tucci produced a text for the pope that historians have hailed as one of the finest documents of Paul VI's papacy, the apostolic exhortation *Evangelii Nuntiandi* ("Proclaiming the Gospel"). That document devoted fifteen central paragraphs to a discussion of the relationship between evangelization and liberation.

When the world's largest religious order, the Jesuits, met in Rome in 1974 for their thirty-second general congregation, they emphasized the idea that Christ had come to bring salvation not only in the next life, but in this one, too. Indeed, in the Lord's Prayer, Christians had been praying from the beginning, "Thy kingdom come, thy will be done, on earth. . . ." But Christians had to do more than pray; they had to work hard, and that hard work had to include hard political action. In that meeting, which, Jesuitically thorough, went on for more than three months, the Jesuits decreed that their men in Latin America (and in other parts of the third world, particularly) get involved in helping make life more livable for everyone. They talked about "a fundamental option for the poor," a phrase that was picked up by the Latin American bishops and practically made a mantra.

Bishop Ruiz of Chiapas later pointed out, "The formulation may be recent, but the calling has been part of the Church from the beginning. The only thing that we have to answer to at the end of time is whether we have loved Christ in the poor. 'I was hungry and you fed me and gave me drink.' If we, in our Christian situation, don't love the poor, if we don't opt for them, we simply are not Christians."

The Jesuits' move was a courageous one, nonetheless, and their father general, Pedro Arrupe, knew what it portended. He said, "If we live out this decree, then we will have martyrs."

Arrupe was right. In the next two decades, scores of Jesuits were harassed, beaten, and murdered by military and paramilitary goons, many of them trained in counterrevolutionary tactics under the aegis of the United States Army at Fort Benning's School of the Americas. Thousands of others, ordinary citizens whose sympathies lay in the kind of changes that would right the inequities in most Latin American societies, were beginning to disappear. Indeed, the word "disappear," an intransitive verb in English, became transitive in Spanish, *desaparecer,* "to make disappear." The noun for "those who have been made to disappear" is *los desaparecidos.* They were the ones who were grabbed out of their beds in the middle of the night, tortured, and then loaded into helicopters and dropped from great heights into jungle and ocean. *Los desaparecidos* were the ghostly symbols of more than a decade of terror. Only the Church had the political power to stop the terror, and it might have done so, but in 1979, something happened to throw the Latin American Church into a tizzy.

The organization of Latin American bishops (called CELAM) met in Puebla, eighty miles from Mexico City, to put their blessings on the theology of liberation and preach the Church's "preferential option for the poor." That could have helped bring on a new reign of justice and peace according to the Council's vision as expressed in *Gaudium et Spes.* But Karol Wojtyla showed up in Puebla, too, and now he was wearing a white cassock. He was the new pope, and his voyage to Puebla, one of the first foreign trips of his papacy, would give him an opportunity to tell the Latin American bishops what he thought about the new theology.

He didn't think much of it. His own nuncios in Latin America had already half convinced him that liberation theology was part of a communist plot; those nuncios, in turn, had been convinced by agents of the CIA, including characters like marine colonel Oliver North. North never gave anyone the impression that he was much interested in theology; he and his men simply wanted the Church to support right-wing governments in Latin America that were giving American corporations free rein to exploit Latin Americans and take what kickbacks they could extort.

In a meeting that was closed to the press, John Paul warned the bishops at Puebla about a view of Jesus that was espoused by some of the new theologians—"of Jesus as a revolutionary, involved in the class struggle." Said the pope: "The idea of Christ as a political figure, a revolutionary, as the subversive Man from Nazareth, does not tally with the Church's catechesis." He said he was worried that the Church was advocating violence in a class struggle that was purely political.

But then the pope reversed himself, or perhaps, as happened so very often during the rest of his papacy, he put on another hat. The very next day, in Cuilapan, he spoke to a half million Indians from Oaxaca and Chiapas, and told them about his concern for the poor, who had "to make up for lost time, often a time of prolonged suffering and unsatisfied hopes." Then he blasted the injustices that had warped the lives of the Latin American poor and lit into those responsible for the ongoing repression of the powerless. "The worker has the right to real help—which is not charity or crumbs of justice—in order that he may have access to the development that his dignity as a man and a son of God deserves. It is necessary to carry out bold changes and urgent reforms without waiting any longer."

Who was the real John Paul? The man at Puebla who worried about holy violence or the man at Cuilapan keening over the plight of indigenous peoples? Over the next few years, John Paul couldn't decide who he was, or whether liberation theology was a healthy movement or something of the devil. He commissioned one negative letter on liberation theology in 1984. He had another letter drafted in 1986 that seemed to cancel the first. He was being chivied on all sides, with the Latin American bishops pushing from the left and his own nuncios in Latin American capitals and the members of Opus Dei pulling from the right. What took place during the mysterious visits to the pope of Robert McFarlane, President Ronald Reagan's national security adviser and right-wing ideologue, has yet to be revealed, but it no doubt had an influence on the pope, coordinated as it was with envelopes full of large bills delivered to the pope's friends in Poland.

In February 1992, the *National Catholic Reporter* ran a furious editorial in reaction to a *Time* magazine cover story that detailed the clandestine alliance between the American government and the Vatican. There was nothing new about the Church entering into political alliances, said the editorial. "What appears new is the extensive nature of the clandestine operation into which the pope drew the Church and the degree to which Catholic prelates and other clergy apparently worked at the direction of the CIA." It went on:

> *NCR*, along with many other Catholics, has criticized the pope for seemingly perching Vatican foreign policy upon the narrow legs of Polish nationalist needs. We see more clearly each month the debilitating and compromising effects of that parochial mindset.
>
> Throughout the Reagan years, we reported the growing confluence of aims and policies of Pope John Paul and the White House: the common desire to end martial law in Poland, to roll back Communism in Eastern Europe, to maintain a "credible" U.S. nuclear deterrent, to keep progressive priests out of politics, to diminish the influence of liberation theology, to beat back the growing political awareness of Catholic base communities. The list goes on. Now we see it was more than confluence. It was organized collusion.

If the pope took note of the struggle between the right-wing oligarchies in Latin America and the new theologians of the left, he might have asked himself, *Cui bono?* Who had the most to gain? It was certainly not the men like Archbishop Hélder Câmara, who was worshiped in Brazil as a living saint. Neither Dom Hélder nor any of his priests were advocating violence. Was the pope ever told that, by 1980, more than eight hundred Latin American priests and nuns had been martyred, largely at the hands of army officers and paramilitary hit men?

Perhaps the pope's nuncios, the sons of privilege, were, in fact, part of the cover-up. Three of them would later go on to become cardinals in the Curia, back in Rome, where they had begun their glittering careers at an elite academy for Vatican diplomats, where admission was largely confined to young men from the aristocracy in Italy. During their hitches in Latin America, two of them played tennis with the Chilean dictator, Augusto Pinochet, and part of their job was to hobnob with the rich and the powerful. Their preferential options were certainly not with the poor. The poor were threatening the security of their friends in power.

The pope should have treated the nuncios' reports about a Marxist clergy with some skepticism, but there is no evidence that he did, and every indication that when he looked at priests like Miguel D'Escoto and Ernesto Cardenal, the priests who had become foreign minister and the minister of culture, respectively, in the Sandinista government of Nicaragua, he saw images of the communist commissars he had known in Poland. By the time he was wagging his finger at D'Escoto and Cardenal in Nicaragua in March 1983, the pope had lost much of his ambivalence about liberation theology; he was also influenced by his prefect of the Holy Office, Joseph Ratzinger, who had spent his carly teens in Bavaria as a member of the Hitler Youth. (Some of his peers refused to join.) For much of the 1980s, Ratzinger went after liberation theologians with a quiet fury.

Ratzinger began his battle with the priest who invented it, Gustavo Gutiérrez, a theologian from Peru. Instead of charging him with heresy, he played a political game. He first told the bishops of Peru (where Gutiérrez had been teaching) that they should deal appropriately with Gutiérrez, for he had been "making the Church into a partisan group, *which threatens the legitimacy of the hierarchy.*" Going to the Peruvian bishops was a mistake. They did not even censure Gutiérrez after Karl Rahner sent them a letter defending liberation theology.

> The theology of liberation that Gustavo Gutiérrez represents is entirely orthodox. It is my full conviction that a condemnation would have very negative consequences. Today there are diverse schools and it has always been thus. . . . It would be deplorable if this legitimate pluralism were to be restricted by administrative means.

After that boost from Rahner, the Peruvian bishops were proud that liberation theology had, in a way, been born on their soil. But Cardinal Ratzinger was undaunted. He went after other leaders of the movement through his own inquisitorial processes, and by issuing condemnations, mostly under the pope's signature. In the summer of 1984, he published a negative *Instruction on Liberation Theology,* and in September of that year he had Leonardo Boff come to Rome for "a colloquy" about his book *Church: Charism and Power.* Ratzinger felt that Boff had made the Church into "a purely human structure" and that liberation theology reduced the gospel to "the Jesus-project," something that "looked religious but was really atheistic."

Ratzinger sent his secretary, Joseph Clemens, in his black Mercedes to fetch Boff from a Franciscan house in Rome, and specified that Boff was to come to the Holy Office alone. Boff jokingly asked, when he climbed in the car with Clemens, if handcuffs would be necessary.

Boff's conversation with Ratzinger was amiable, if indecisive. Edward Schillebeeckx once said the most awkward moment in such an interrogation comes in trying to make small talk over coffee. In Boff's case, Ratzinger began by suggesting Boff looked good in a habit and should wear one more often, that it was a sign of witness. Boff said it could also be a symbol of power. Ratzinger smiled. When the colloquy broke up with no mention of a censure, Boff thought he might have won the day.

He was wrong. On March 11, 1985, the Congregation for the Doctrine of the Faith issued a Notification on *Church: Charism and Power.* Boff's book endangers the faith, the congregation said, in its concept of dogma, in its understanding of sacred power, and in its overemphasis on the prophetic role of the Church. The word "prophecy"—used as it was in Latin America, especially by the disciples of Paolo Freire—called upon the people to speak out, to be prophets in the biblical sense. According to a biographer of Freire, "Prophets denounce what stinks to high heaven and announce the good news." Now prophetic voices in Latin America cried out about the unpleasant odor coming from the Vatican and its unseemly alliance with the power structure in Brazil, Colombia, Venezuela, Argentina, and Peru.

Ratzinger responded on April 26 with a formal order silencing Boff. He was not to publish, teach, or speak publicly until further notice. Boff accepted the decision, and for a time declined even to take phone calls from colleagues. "I prefer to walk with the Church rather than to walk alone with my theology," he said. These were not the words of a contumacious man, but of a man who loved the Church.

Gutiérrez, now a Dominican, was better known internationally, and

Sobrino and Segundo, both Jesuits, had greater intellectual range, yet Boff was the only liberation theologian hauled to Rome for an inquisitorial process, the only one silenced, the only one whose writings were repeatedly condemned, the only one whose movements were tracked in Rome with exacting precision. Boff told of going to a remote Amazon village to participate in a religious retreat. "Three days later," he said, "word had reached the Vatican about where I was and what I was saying."

Boff drew Ratzinger's fire because he was visible and voluble: he knew how to talk to the press, which made him a dangerous man inside the Vatican, and he started doing that in the late 1980s. After he had had time to nurse the wounds he had suffered in Rome at the hands of Ratzinger, Boff started to exercise his own liberation. He called a news conference to demand the dissolution of papal sovereignty and the recall of all the world's nuncios, a move that did not endear him to the Roman Curia. The Curia had a second reason to go after Boff: he came from Brazil, the most populous Catholic nation in the world. If Ratzinger was going to make an example of anyone, who better than a Brazilian? (For the same reason, Ratzinger had gone after the American moral theologian Charles Curran on the birth control question, rather than any continental theologians like Bernard Häring and Josef Fuchs, who held the same positions as Curran and were, besides, more universally well-regarded theologians. Condemning an American, particularly on the birth control issue, would get more press attention.)

Boff was also singled out because, more than any other liberationist, he trained the conceptual tools of liberation theology on the all-too-human structures of the Church itself. Boff argued that a "clerical aristocracy" had expropriated from the people of God the means of religious production, and hence had misappropriated their right to make their own decisions. This sounded like Marxist jargon, but all Boff meant was that the Church didn't want people to grow up.

Boff was also talking about schism, a word that sounded more frightening than he intended in 1984, when he said of Catholicism's destiny: "The future of the institutional Church lies in this small seed that is the new Church, growing in the fields of the poor and the powerless. The new Church must have the courage to be disobedient to the demands of the center without anger or complaint." Americans who could compare "the demands of the center" with England's imposing a ruinous tea tax on the colonials in Boston had no difficulty recognizing the legitimacy of the revolution that Boff was calling for.

But if Boff wanted to be disobedient to the demands of the center, then he had to expect the center to retaliate. In 1992, Ratzinger gave Boff the Küng treatment. He banned him from teaching as a Catholic theologian and ordered the Franciscans to censor his writings because he had "not cleansed his ecclesiology from the elements of dissent and internal class struggle." That class struggle may have been the major issue all along, not a struggle between social and economic classes but the battle inside the Church between Rome and the people out there—with Rome, the upper class, always exerting its largely unchallenged prerogatives over the underclass. From near the top of the papal pyramid, Ratzinger could only see the poor thirsting for justice in the *favelas* of Rio (with priests like Boff at their side) as people at the margins. Ratzinger could ignore them, and where he could not ignore them, as in the case of Boff, a priest and a member of an ancient religious order, he could diminish them. In the end, Boff left the priesthood, and departed with a memorable line: "Ecclesiastical power is cruel and merciless. It forgets nothing. It forgives nothing. It demands everything."

Ratzinger could be cruel because, after all, he had a theology of history that divided the world between the good guys in the City of God and the bad guys in the City of Man. It was an us-against-them approach that gave the good guys no other choice except to do battle. "The antagonism between a world under the power of the Evil One and the disciples of Christ will never be mitigated," Ratzinger told one journalist, "but will grow ever more bitter in the course of time." As a disciple of Christ, he had his duty—to oppose the surrounding culture (which he identified with the Evil One) and enlist others to do so as well, no matter what the cost. "Today more than ever," he said, "the Christian must be aware that he belongs to a minority and that he is in opposition to everything that appears good, obvious, logical to the 'spirit of the world,' as the New Testament calls it."

Ratzinger couldn't have made his diametric opposition to Vatican II and to its signature document, *Gaudium et Spes,* any clearer than that. Those who found inspiration in that document to make a better world were, to Ratzinger, simply rebelling against their lot in life. He urged they not put their hopes in "secular political progress." They should, rather, "accept the Cross of Christ."

There was something terribly abstract about that judgment, lodged by a man who had spent his whole life behind a desk. He had seen little of the cross, while the active proponents of liberation theology got to know the cross on rather intimate terms. Thousands of them—many priests and nuns, but a good many laypeople besides—were martyred at the hands of the Latin American military. And many who were not murdered found their struggles ending in apparent failure. This, too, was part of the cross—a manifest imitation, many of those who suffered believe, of Christ himself, who didn't want to die, but accepted his death at the hands of the Romans and certain Jews for daring to speak his truth to their power.

In 1988, John Paul II told a large crowd gathered in the cathedral at Santa Cruz, Bolivia, "The pope and the whole Church, all of us, have to create a meeting point between the so-called world of the left and the so-called world of the right, because the world cannot live in continuing division, it cannot live in conflict. I want to tell you who belong to this third world that the solution for overcoming the divisions of left and right must be found right here in your human, Christian and social reality. That is my hope."

Soon John Paul II was convinced he could not trust the liberation theologians to create that meeting point between the left and the right. They were consorting with the political left. In fact, to him, they were the left, and he didn't want to speak with them any longer.

When Boff was standing in judgment at the Holy Office, Cardinal Arns came to Rome with him, but was barred from the meeting. So Arns asked to see the pope. After waiting for two weeks, Arns called the papal household and said that if he couldn't see the pope, he would head back to Brazil. The next day, Arns was received, but it was barely an audience. The pope sat in a high-backed chair. Arns was left standing. Arns spoke his piece, telling the pope that liberation theology was entirely in the spirit of the gospel as he understood it, and that the people of Latin America were no different from the people of Poland. They, too, needed and wanted freedom from the exploitation of their masters. When he had finished his defense, the pope, still wordless, reached for a button and buzzed for his secretary to take Arns away.

CHAPTER EIGHT

Cardinal Francis Arinze

Developing Local Theologies

IT MAY HAVE SEEMED IMPROBABLE in 2005 to think that the cardinal-electors would even dream of voting for a "people's candidate" for pope. True, for the Church's first six centuries, the priests of Rome had elected their own bishop—that is, the pope—and then called upon the people of Rome for their approval.

But if one could give any credence to informal preference polls taken in Rome during the years leading up to this conclave, the people of Rome seemed to favor an African. As one greengrocer on the Via Margutta put it, "The time has come for Africa." In the long history of the papacy, there had been three African popes, the last of them named Gelasius I, who was born in Rome of African parents. He served from 492 to 496. "Electing a black pope," observed a thoughtful Roman taxi driver, "would say something to the world about racism."

There were twelve eligible Africans in the College of Cardinals, but Francis Arinze of Nigeria was the only African on everyone's shortlist, probably because he was the most visible. For one thing, he worked in Rome. For another, he had headed the Pontifical Council for Interreligious Dialogue, the Vatican's official contact point with Islam, before he moved to another important post, leading the Congregation for Divine Worship. For a third, Arinze had been spending roughly half of his time outside Rome, most often in the United States, giving speeches in highly visible venues where he received good media coverage. In October 2001, students at Boston College saw Arinze as he was leaving a jam-packed campus chapel blessing the crowd with two fingers—as popes have been doing for centuries inside Saint Peter's.

In most of his talks, Arinze had been insisting, even before the terrorist attacks on September 11, 2001, that leaders of the world's religions ought to be prime promoters of peace, not war. On August 29, 2000, Arinze gave an address at the Millennium World Peace Summit of Religious and Spiritual Leaders at the United Nations in New York that called on them not to misuse religion by promoting violence. Moreover, he said, religious leaders could give greater attention to the causes of social unrest, even pressure affluent nations to help advance development among the poorer ones. He quoted Pope Paul VI, who had visited the UN in 1964: "The development of peoples is the new name for peace."

Arinze's words were all the more eloquent for their simplicity, and the greetings he brought to this meeting from Rome were also simple and clear. The pope said those attending this summit at the UN had a chance "to make it abundantly clear that the only religion worthy of the name is the religion that leads to peace and that true religion is mocked when it is tied to conflict and violence."

Since that meeting, Arinze had presided over at least three major interreligious gatherings in turn, raising his media profile. Four months after 9/11, he helped organize a huge gathering of leaders—Moslems, Hindus, Buddhists, Jews, and Catholics—in Assisi, where a similar meeting had been held a decade before. Curiously, the delegates prayed separately, because Cardinal Ratzinger had decided not to encourage joint prayer by men and women who believed in different Gods. Arinze didn't fight Ratzinger on that. Neither did the pope.

On the eve of the conclave, Arinze led the list of papal candidates on Paddy Power's Internet Web site, with odds of 11–4 (with Dionigi Tettamanzi in second place at 7–2). Because of Arinze's ascendance, even in such a dubious corner of cyberspace, the multitude of reporters who streamed into Rome on the eve of the conclave needed to describe what kind of man Arinze was, and what kind of pope he might be.

They learned that Arinze was one of five children born to an illiterate farm family of the Ibo clan in a rural farming village in Nigeria called Eziowelle; they lived in a single-story house with a tin roof, no electricity, and no running water. At the age of nine, while attending a Catholic elementary school, young Francis became a Catholic by his own choice and under what he remembered as the subtle urging of his teachers. His brothers and sisters became Catholics; so did his mother, Bernadette, and even, finally, his father.

At the age of fourteen, full of admiration for the charismatic village priest, Father Cyprian Michael Iwene Tansi, Francis enrolled in the local seminary in nearby Onitsha. So did most of his elementary school classmates, because they were all quite taken with Tansi, and because they believed a seminary education was the best education available to them. Many didn't stay the course. Young Francis did, through minor seminary (that is, at the high school level) and then through a three-year course in philosophy at the major seminary. He did so well that his bishop, an Irish Spiritan named Charles Heerey, sent him off to Rome to study theology in 1955. Arinze was just twenty-two.

In Rome, Arinze studied at the college for students from mission lands then known as Propaganda Fide. He did his thesis on the sacrifice of the mass, comparing Christ's sacrifice on the cross to the sacrifices performed in the Ibo religion. After three years at Propaganda, he was ordained a priest by Cardinal Peter Agagianian, the pro-prefect of the Congregation for the Propagation of the Faith. That same year, 1958, his mentor Tansi left Nigeria to enter a Trappist monastery in England, and died there only six years later at the age of sixty-one. (In March 1998, John Paul II traveled with Arinze to Nigeria to beatify Tansi, in a process set in motion fourteen years earlier by Arinze.)

After ordination, Arinze returned to Africa and became the first Nigerian to teach on the staff of the seminary in Onitsha. After a year there, his bishop sent him to London to study the English educational system, then put him in charge of all the schools in the diocese. Two years later, in August 1965, he was made coadjutor archbishop of Onitsha, just in time to attend the last session of Vatican II. He was thirty-two. With his flawless features and slightness of build (five feet six inches, 148 pounds) and his great teeth, he looked like (and was) the youngest bishop at the Council. He did not rise to speak at Vatican II. "I was slightly afraid," he later admitted. "I was more comfortable with what has been than with what could be."

Arinze's modesty was appropriate. Some seminarians come to Rome and, with the help of the right professors, learn to explore the frontiers of theology. Arinze had the bad luck to land the wrong professors, as did most of the third world seminarians attending Propaganda. These priests from "the missionary lands" were there to be indoctrinated in the Romanness that had been so much a part of the Western Church since the Council of Trent, then sent back home to carry Rome's version of Catholicism to the jungle or the bush.

Two of Arinze's professors, Pietro Parente and Antonio Piolanti, would soon become vociferous, angry spokesmen for the forces of the status quo at Vatican II. They taught not only at Propaganda but at the Lateran University as well, a bastion of traditionalism where the students were trained not to think so much as memorize. Parente and Piolanti were also stalwarts in the Holy Office of Cardinal Alfredo Ottaviani, the man who would complain through the four years of the Council about the "peripheral bishops" who were ruining his Church. Another of Arinze's professors, Jan Visser, a moral theologian, was made a member of the papal birth-control commission in 1964, where he aligned himself with three other traditionalists who bucked the commission majority, only to be voted down at every turn.

In 1985, Archbishop Francis Arinze was brought to Rome, given a red hat, and then put in charge of the Pontifical Council for Interreligious Dialogue (which is responsible for forging closer ties to all of the world's great religions), rising, in accordance with the Peter Principle, to the level of his incompetence. He made a good many public appearances. He dazzled one and all with his flashing smile and his soothing, rounded, rather elegant English phrases (expressed in a kind of musical Nigerian cadence). But the meetings he attended were mainly ceremonial. He was a simple, amiable man who could be counted on to do what he was told.

Still, for most of his years as a cardinal, many considered Arinze a potential pope. Whenever John Paul was indisposed, the press would dust off its lists of potential candidates and put Arinze forward as a possible choice. Some press observers believed that Arinze would be "the most qualified to continue the historical conversations initiated by John Paul II with Jews and Muslims." But that was a shallow judgment, based on nothing more than Arinze's presidency of the Vatican office for interreligious dialogue. Dozens of Roman Catholic prelates and scholars who had been engaged during the 1990s in a series of creative and peace-building encounters with Buddhists, Hindus, and Jews did not believe Arinze was interfacing well with scholars from these other religions. He tended to tie the salvation message of Jesus far too tightly to the Church he knew, the one, holy, catholic, and apostolic Church—the Roman Church. Nor had Arinze provided much leadership in the area of dialogue with the world of Islam. The Jesuit Jacques Dupuis, one of the Catholic world's experts on interreligious dialogue, observed in a 1999 issue of *Louvain Studies* that "the African churches hardly figure" in advances that have been made in the theology of religions during the past decade. "African interreligious dialogue with Islam," he wrote in 2004, "is still largely in the making."

ON THE EVENING BEFORE the cardinals would gather in the Sistine Chapel for their first vote of the conclave, Francis Arinze changed from the usual baggy white cotton sweatshirt and black pants he wore around his apartment on the north side of Saint Peter's Square to the everyday black robes and black cape with the bright red piping of a cardinal of the Catholic Church. Then he grabbed a small black bag he had packed for the conclave. In it: a few pieces of clothing, pajamas, slippers, some toilet articles, his breviary. No cell phone. No laptop computer.

Arinze left his apartment and walked a little more than a hundred yards south across Saint Peter's Square, then turned west past the Swiss Guards at the Santa Marta Gate, checked into the Casa Santa Marta, and received the key to his assigned room and a roster listing the room numbers of the other cardinals. All the voting members would be sleeping and dining here in the Casa, even those cardinals who, like Arinze, lived in Rome. If they gave a prize to the cardinal who had come the farthest, Cardinal Thomas Stafford Williams would win, after a journey of some eight thousand miles from Wellington, New Zealand. Arinze's trip was exactly 326 paces.

At supper, Arinze smiled at everyone. He always smiled at everyone, even though there were some who did not smile at him. He had a very winning smile. And he liked winning, ever since his days as a halfback on the soccer team at his high school in Nigeria. As a natural competitor, then, he must have wondered now whether any of these men, those who smiled at him and those who didn't, might vote for him on the first ballot. To be sure, he was not running for pope, but a few votes, even just one vote, would tell him that someone was thinking of Africa.

If that happened, he could be pardoned for a pinch of pride, because a vote for an African would mean that for the first time in a long while Africa was in the game. Only a year ago, his friend Anthony Okogie, archbishop of Lagos, Nigeria, had told a reporter, "It would be a credit to the developing world if an African were chosen. In the good old days, Church leaders could scarcely believe there was a God in Africa. Today, things are changing. The Church is growing."

Indeed it was. In fact, throughout Africa, Christianity in general and its Catholic branch in particular was spreading faster than at any time in the last two thousand years. Among the Ibo, the Ashanti, and the Baganda, among the Twi-speaking peoples and the thousand other tribes who occupy the world's second largest continent—fifty-four nations, 750 million people—Africans were flocking to Jesus.

Plagued by corrupt regimes, crushing poverty, pandemic AIDS, and genocidal wars, Africans found they could go to the Christian churches for healing and hope—and material assistance from more fortunate Christians in the West. As a result, for the first time since the catacombs, Christianity in Africa had become a religion mainly of the poor, the marginalized, the powerless, and the oppressed, and this was not because evangelizers were preaching old-fashioned Christian resignation, but rather a new kind of "salvation now" theology that told Africans they can and must do something to change their lives.

Protestant missionaries in Africa—mainly Pentecostals trained in the American South—had been preaching something they called "the prosperity gospel," based on a literal belief in the words of Jesus that he had come so that they would have a more abundant life—in this world, not the next. Some Catholic preachers had reason to follow their lead. Many stories in the gospel dealing with the public life of Jesus revolved around his efforts at healing and driving out devils, and so the Catholic Church in sub-Saharan Africa—still the largest body of Christians in black Africa—provided healing services to keep the people coming in its direction. Once they came, the Church could provide them with everything else: the mass, the sacraments, the music, and the hope for salvation.

The people came. According to the Vatican's Congregation for the

Evangelization of Peoples (formerly known as Propaganda Fide), there were 120 million Catholics in Africa at the end of the millennium, with an annual growth rate of 4 million. According to John Onaiyekan, archbishop of Abuja, Nigeria's capital city, the gospel had finally become "inculturated" in Africa. Christianity was no longer foreign, but African, as it was, in fact, at Christianity's beginning at Pentecost. "There were Africans at Pentecost," Onaiyekan pointed out, "and they went back home and started up their own branches of Judaism in places like Alexandria and Ethiopia. But those people who called themselves Christians simply stopped there, and did not take the message to the rest of Africa. We should have gotten our Christianity from Egypt and Ethiopia, but we didn't. And you can't say that the obstacle was the Saharan Desert, because, how come that obstacle didn't stop Islam? We didn't get our Christianity from the Christians who were contemporaries of Saint Augustine in North Africa, either. We had to wait almost fifteen centuries for the missionaries to come from Ireland and Belgium and France."

With the end of colonialism, most of the French, Belgian, and Irish missionaries left Africa, to be replaced by priests and bishops with black faces. As Peter Sarpong, the archbishop of Kumasi, Ghana, told a group of mission experts meeting in Rome during the Jubilee Year: "The problem now is not how to Christianize Africa"—the old missionary approach—"but how to Africanize Christianity."

Catholics were doing so most effectively in the Congo. There, liturgists had incorporated much of the Congolese culture, including music and dance, into the mass, prompting some to talk about a "Congolese Rite"—that is, a mass as different from the mass celebrated in Rome as the mass that is celebrated by a Melkite priest in Beirut or by a Coptic priest in Cairo.

This was another kind of missionary activity, a kind of missionizing from within. "In the old days, an Irish missionary would hit the jungle in full stride, build a church and a clinic and a school, and have half the area baptized in two years," explained Kieran O'Reilly, the superior general of the Society of African Missions (SMA). "The missionary presented the people with a new God, and the people accepted that God. But now we are in a new phase."

O'Reilly and his fellow missionaries do not talk about conversion. "Now," he said, "we are entering into dialogue with people about *their* sense of the divine. We get them to ask themselves how God has presented himself to them in the mysteriousness of their understanding of the workings of the Holy Spirit. That can take a long time. If they come to be Christians, we feel it will be God who is bringing them, and we have to be in a state of readiness and openness to them and to their history and their culture. The process will be slower, and more difficult, and we do not expect to see the mass conversions we saw in the past.

"But it is the only way. Any true missionary in this century has to use that as a starting point. Ultimately, we are the agents of a divine movement. We are only a leaf on the tree, not the branch. Yes, it is a more humble way. But there is really no other approach, given the dignity of peoples and the unique nature of cultures."

The scholars who specialize in the theology of the missions believe that Africans may be readier than the rest of the Church to adapt the gospel to their own culture, probably because the missionary bishops who came home from Vatican II gave them ready permission to do so. If the gospel was for all humankind, then the Church had to start constructing "local theologies." *Constructing Local Theologies,* was, in fact, the title of a book by the American priest-theologian Robert Schreiter. According to Schreiter, "It was becoming increasingly evident that the theologies once thought to have a universal, and even enduring or perennial, character were but regional expressions of certain cultures."

Pope John XXIII put his early blessing on this new, liberating view when, on October 11, 1962, at the opening of Vatican II, he urged the Fathers of the Council to take "a leap forward" by making the gospel relevant to the people living on the planet today. "For the substance of the faith is one thing, the way it is presented is another." The Council leadership caught on quickly, and opened many a daily session with various forms of the *Missa Luba,* a mass whose music was marked by decidedly African chanting and drums. But Africans as a whole didn't do much to develop local theologies until the African synod of 1994. There, the African bishops realized that they were no longer dominated by white missionary bishops. Almost all were now African, even Archbishop Denis Hurley, a white man who was born and bred in Durban,

South Africa, and a leading Council Father himself. Hurley was, by then, retired, but he enlisted in the effort to help make Catholicism in Africa less Roman and more catholic.

What that was supposed to mean in the future was up to the imagination of Africa's lay leaders as well as its priests, and a willingness in Rome to allow it to happen. African Catholics had no wish to write a new creed, or make the Trinity—the Father, Son, and Holy Spirit—into a Happy Couple, or deny the resurrection. They did want to revisit a good many pieces of Church discipline that were man-made. If men could make the rules, then men could unmake them. Polygamy had not only made sense in ancient Africa; it probably still made sense in some modern African cultures. But Rome wouldn't hear of it. In John Paul II's view, monogamy was the only thing God could approve, despite the fact that many biblical patriarchs, including the great King David, had many wives. This would be an issue for the new pope to address (or not). As for priestly celibacy, in some African villages priests had already taken common-law wives. What would the new pope have to say about that? (As we have already seen, John Paul II knew about it and said, and did, nothing.)

The African bishops knew that the bishops of Indonesia who came to Rome in 1998 for the Asian synod told the pope they wanted an autochthonous Church. They didn't want to secede from Rome. They wanted a Church that was more homegrown, homespun, and homemade. John Paul had never agreed to that. But what would happen if the college elected a pope from the third world who had sympathy for the idea? Would he grant autochthony to the people of Indonesia, or to the people of Austria, the United States, Australia, Africa? That kind of pope would have to be a more trusting pope, a pope of the poor. Wouldn't that signal a new direction for the Church of the twenty-first century? Would that man prevail at Casa Santa Marta? Francis Arinze, and everyone else, would soon find out.

CHAPTER NINE

Cardinal Julius Darmaatmadja

A Truly Asian Church

NORMALLY, JESUITS DO NOT BECOME BISHOPS. In fact, their constitution forbids it. John Paul II saw fit to ignore the Jesuit constitution, and over the course of his pontificate, he appointed almost a hundred Jesuit bishops. The Jesuit general, Peter-Hans Kolvenbach, a polylingual Dutchman, never protested. When he was elected general in September 1983, he had a mandate to make peace, not war, with a pope who had expressed his displeasure about the Jesuits. So the Jesuits did not oppose Julius Darmaatmadja's appointment as archbishop of Semarang, which had been the seat of Indonesia's first cardinal, Justinus Darmojuwono. Jesuits normally do not become cardinals either. In the sixteenth century, the order's founder, Ignatius Loyola, lobbied furiously with most of the crowned heads of Europe to stop Pope Paul IV from giving a cardinal's hat to the Jesuit James Lainez, the Council of Trent's most brilliant theologian. He won that battle, and made his point: he did not want his Jesuits co-opted by the pope. He wanted to keep them free "to exercise a prophetic role in the Church," that is, free to criticize even a pope, when necessary.

But they stoned prophets in ancient Israel, so the Jesuits shouldn't have been surprised when another pope, Clement XIV, suppressed the order in 1773 for being *too* prophetic. In 1981, the zealous new pope, John Paul II, came close to suppressing the order again, for going too far under the charismatic general Pedro Arrupe in its efforts to promote liberation theology, for that seemed to mean getting involved in partisan political activity in Latin America. The pope delegated an eighty-year-old Italian Jesuit, Paolo Dezza, to monitor the Jesuits, and gave them two years to start seeing things his way. The Jesuits did nothing of the sort. George Weigel concluded that "the Jesuits had indeed learned some things during Father Dezza's delegacy, but the learning seemed to have had more to do with repairing broken lines of communication between the Roman Curia and the Jesuit generalate than with such matters of substance as training, theology, social activism, and way of life."

The curious thing was that John Paul's annual list of episcopal appointments always seemed to have a dozen or more Jesuits on it. He couldn't live with the Jesuits, and he couldn't live without them. In the spring of 2004, the College of Cardinals included nine Jesuits (but only three under the age of eighty, who could vote for his successor). One of them was Julius Darmaatmadja, who became a cardinal in 1994. Two years later, he moved to Jakarta, the nation's capital and largest city (population, 10.5 million).

For Darmaatmadja, as for all the cardinals in the world who ran a major see, his title was merely an honor; it conferred on him no special jurisdiction. According to Church law, the only time that his red hat mattered was now, as he prepared to join 114 other cardinals to elect the successor of John Paul II.

Well before the conclave, I visited the cardinal in Jakarta, and was startled to find the wide, palm-lined avenue leading out of Soekarno-Hatta Jakarta International Airport with almost no cars on it. My taxi driver pushed handfuls of inflationary rupees at toll collectors in five separate booths before we reached a wide freeway flanked by warrens of large, rusting corrugated iron shacks. Closer to the city, I found something more familiar along the road, huge high-rise buildings whose façades were covered with the logos of McDonald's, Century 21, Pizza Hut, Taco Bell.

The taxi careened off the freeway on to a curbless street lined with unkempt car repair shops and open-air stands selling Firestone tires. Unsmiling shabby little people watched the taxi pass. The *International Herald Tribune* had been carrying stories for days about the violence in Indonesia, and an Internet advisory from the U.S. State Department said a trip to Indonesia right now would be risky. But a Jesuit friend in Jakarta, Ignatius Ismartono, said to come ahead because "things have quieted down." They had. There was only a handful of soldiers at the airport, no burning cars by the side of the freeway, no rioting in the streets—as CNN had shown the world less than a week before.

The taxi turned into a leafy residential lane with curbs and stopped at Jalan Kemiri 15, the guesthouse for the Indonesian Bishops Conference. A woman in a white smock who didn't speak English came to the door, and led the way to room number twenty on the second floor. Presently, Father Ismartono was on the phone, to say he was dropping by at 7 p.m., but would leave shortly for an evening meeting with a coalition of religious leaders trying to draft a statement calling on Indonesia's formal and informal leadership to crack down on all the violence. Last week, bombs had been set off in Jakarta. Just this week, in a conflict on the island of Ambon, Protestants using Old Testament texts were calling on Yahweh to smite Moslems who were quoting the Quran and fighting for Allah. There were deaths on both sides. Father Ismartono took a few moments to prep me for a meeting the next morning with his boss, Cardinal Darmaatmadja.

I wanted to use Jakarta as the first stop on a tour of five Asian nations, where I could pick up the figurative tesserae I needed to put together a mosaic of Catholic Asia. Roughly half the planet's population now lived in Asia, three and a half billion souls. They defied easy analysis. John Mansford Prior, a Divine Word missionary from Indonesia, said that Asia was "pluralist to the very fiber of its being: multilinguistic, multicultural, multireligious, multiethnic, multiritual—the one continent where Christians stubbornly remain a tiny minority."

Excluding the 61 million Catholics who live in the Philippines, Catholics count for 1 percent of Asia's population. Yet there were more Catholics in India than the whole population of Australia, more Christians in Moslem Indonesia than in the country that last colonized Indonesia, the Netherlands.

The Philippines were an exception because none of the great Asian religions had yet taken hold there when the colonizing Spaniards landed in the sixteenth century, imposing their religion in the same way they had forced their faith on the peoples of Latin America. As a result, the indigenous peoples of these islands were indoctrinated in a peculiar form of Catholicism, one that Prior said was "not only patriarchal, hierarchical, and clerical but also colonialistic, capitalistic, feudal, and fundamentalist to the core." It also produced a ministry that was "dualistic, ritual-centered, and discriminatory to women."

The modernizers and mystics at Vatican II tried to change that by creating a charter for a Church that would be less like an international business conglomerate and more like a happy human family, a Church that would be less clerical and more popular—in the sense of a people's Church. The architects of Vatican II weren't proud of the Church's history of forced conversions. They did not want missionaries assessing the Church's growth by counting converts to "the one true faith," teaching, catechizing, baptizing, and building more churches in the jungle. Now they would be working for justice and peace in the world around them, to reconcile battling factions, and engage in the task of trying to understand the myriad religious beliefs they encountered in the people their predecessors had purportedly come "to save." In an address to a mission congress in Rome, Samuel Rayan, a Jesuit from India, summed up the old history:

> The churches formed under colonial auspices were replicas of Western churches. Instead of letting the Word fall in the soil of our life, religion and culture, and take root there and sprout and grow, they brought in ready-made churches, like potted plants. Everything was regulated and controlled, every detail prescribed, and all standards set for a world church by a single center, an ancient imperial capital in the West, Rome. For centuries, God only understood Latin, which the people could not follow. Pius XII justified Latin by presenting it as a sign of unity in a World Church. In truth, it represented an effective schism between the people and the clergy, a rejection of "worship in spirit and truth" in favor of ritual mechanics and of power. It was a deeply regrettable case of ecclesiastical imperialism. Theologies were imported from Western academies, royal palaces, castles and abbeys by the ruling class and for the ruling class, whose interests and designs became crystallized in those theologies. Those theologies stressed hierarchy,

power, submission, resignation and otherworldly salvation, rather than community, friendship, obedience to truth, pursuit of justice and the Reign of God on earth.

Rayan said that if you looked at Catholic liturgies in India—for the most part transplanted protocols from Rome, via Portugal—you had to conclude that "God had appeared as a stranger in our land." Rayan was hardly a maverick, just one of a great many theologians around the third world who saw, and were acting upon, what has become solid doctrine, that the gospel must be incarnated in every culture. When Pope Paul VI made his classic trip to Jerusalem in 1964 he said, "Each nation received the Apostles' preaching according to its own mentality and culture. Each local church grew according to its own personality, customs . . . without harming the unity of faith." The African bishops and the Canadian bishops raised the issue at the Council. Four separate Council documents endorsed the idea. The Latin American bishops touched on it in their famous conference at Medellín in 1968, went deeper into it at Puebla in 1979, and still deeper at Santo Domingo in 1992. (It was at Santo Domingo, at a celebration to commemorate the five hundredth anniversary of the coming of Columbus to America, that one of the bishops remarked, "Christopher Columbus didn't bring God to America in his three little boats. God was already here.")

In 1970, bishops from twenty Asian nations met in Manila to form their Federation of Asian Bishops' Conferences (FABC). Their goal was to see how they could make the gospel more Asian, and create a Church for Asians. At every one of their meetings, which have been held every five years ever since, they kept finding new ways of saying that the saving message of the gospel cannot be identified with any culture. It was a notion that some Vatican watchers predicted would have an impact on the conclave of 2005, for enculturation was one of those ideas whose time had come.

Early in his pontificate, John Paul II blessed this notion in three talks he gave in Mexico (at Oaxaca, Yucatán, and Mexico City) and he opened the synod for Asia in 1998 by noting that "Jesus was born in Asia." That drew a cheer from the 182 bishops who were in attendance, but the pope didn't like the implications of that cheer, so he quickly added, "In that part of Asia that looked out to Europe." He knew these Asian bishops hadn't been at all docile in the run-up to this 1998 synod. The Japanese bishops had completely rejected the synod agenda as prepared two years before by Cardinal Jan Schotte, and the Indonesian bishops had called for the synod to explore the possibility of an East Asian patriarchate, one that would be endowed with the autonomony enjoyed by patriarchs in the Oriental Church of the Near East.

The pope, however, did not want a runaway synod. Sensing that, the bishops at this synod were careful to affirm and reaffirm their devotion to the Holy Father. But of all the synods that were summoned by John Paul II, the Asian synod of 1998 was the most independent-minded, the one most insistent on the need for Rome to realize that the Church's outreach had to take into account local realities and local sensibilities. This emphasis on local realities would be high on the list of issues carried to the conclave of 2005 by most of the ten Asian cardinals eligible to vote for a new pope, as the Asian bishops made clear in their 1998 synod.

Before that synod began, the Vatican was telling the bishops their primary task was to proclaim the uniqueness of Jesus Christ as the one and only Savior. The bishops were saying, going in, that their people wouldn't understand this claim. A bishop from Pakistan said that making "a proclamation" like that in his country would be "committing suicide." The bishops said they preferred to make a more modest statement about Jesus and his message to humankind by reason of their service to the poor and needy (as Mother Teresa had done, becoming a heroine throughout India and, indeed, the world), and by engaging in dialogue with Asia's three great religions. They said that Hinduism, Buddhism, and Islam had been firmly established in Asia for centuries before the colonizers brought their statues of a European-looking Jesus along with them on their sailing ships.

According to Filo Hirota, a Mercedarian sister from Japan and one of the few women invited to speak at the synod, there were two synods going on in Rome. They reflected two visions of the Church: the vision of the Asian bishops and the Curia's vision. When Hirota spoke for her alloted five minutes (the bishops got eight), she called everyone's attention to the fine words of the Curia's final agenda, called the *instrumentum laboris,* which said the synod was intended "to seek a new way of being Church in Asia—new in its approaches, new in its theological expression, new in its methods, and new in its understanding of other religions."

But as often happened in Pope John Paul's Rome, the men of the Curia spoke the words of Vatican II, but then tried to mute or even erase any plans to make the words a reality. After analyzing all of the synod's 191 floor speeches, Prior concluded that "the Asian bishops, whether consciously or not, were working out an agenda for the next pontificate, perhaps even for the next ecumenical council." In his breakdown, more than three quarters of the speeches urged that the Church engage in four dialogues: (1) with other faith traditions, (2) with living cultures, so that the Church in Asia could become truly Asian, (3) with the poor and the oppressed, and (4) with its own laypeople.

Prior reported on interventions that moved him. Archbishop Fernando Capalla of Davao, in the Philippines, outlined the pioneering collaboration between Muslims and Christians in war-stricken Mindanao. The work continued, he said, in spite of the brutal murder of the Oblate bishop Benjamin de Jesus and the kidnappings of Columban father Desmond Hartford and the Dutch missionary Bernard Moes—this in spite of resistance from some of his own Christian people and from a small segment of Muslim fundamentalists.

Franciscan bishop Leo Laba Ladjar of Jayapura, Indonesia, spoke of learning to live amid the Muslim majority in his land. "We need to accept ourselves as a minority," he said. "We cannot walk alone or do big things alone while confronting the majority. Competition does not help to create peace and harmony. Whatever we do to promote human dignity we must do as an honest transparent service to humankind and not to gain strength and power for our own religious group." Bishop Bunluen Mansap of Ubon Ratchathani, Thailand, spoke of his contact with Buddhists. "I feel inspired by their simplicity of life, their openness, their humane relationships, their unassuming ways. These are values I recognize as values of the kingdom or of the gospel. Could it be that this is the good news that the Buddhist can offer us?"

Many of the bishops had wanted to bring their own theologians to this synod, but Cardinal Schotte told them they would not be welcome in Rome. At Vatican II, the private theologians brought into the Council by many of the world's bishops had won too many battles over the theologically challenged officials of the Roman Curia. And so Schotte decided that the fewer theologians who were in Rome at the service of their bishops in this synod, the better. As a result, the bishops had to craft their own speeches.

They did just fine. Some of their talks (or as they were called, interventions) openly assaulted Rome's way. Bishop Berard Oshikawa of Naha, Japan, said that all the norms for Church discipline, liturgical expression, and theological orthodoxy continue to be that of the Western Church. "The language of our theology, the rhythm and structure of our liturgies, the programs of our catechesis fail to touch the hearts of those who come searching." He concluded that the Holy See had to redefine its role, and "with prudence, flexibility, and courage mediate a new dialogue of all the Churches in the common pilgrimage to the fullness of Christ. We must move away from a single and uniform abstract norm that stifles genuine spirituality, and work for a new harmony where the gifts of the Spirit to the Churches become the new treasure of the whole Church."

Brother Anthony Rogers, a staff member of the FABC who was allowed to speak for five minutes at the synod, quoted the very first statement by Asian bishops twenty-eight years before: "The Church cannot set up islands of affluence in a sea of want and misery." Bishop Carlos Belo of East Timor, quoting popes and Vatican II, said that, "for the Church, defending human rights and the cultural dignity of the person is directly linked to its spiritual mission." From India, Archbishop Paschal Topno of Bhopal, Archbishop Telesphore Toppo of Ranchi (now a cardinal), and Archbishop Maria Callistus Soosa Pakiam of Trivandrum (Kerala) said the Church had to listen more to those Indians who had come over to Christianity from the nation's tribal religions.

Unfortunately, said Prior, none of these individual suggestions were taken up in any meaningful way in the group discussions. Nor was much attention paid to three interventions that pointed to a serious marginalization of women in the life of the Asian Churches themselves. Filo Hirota, in the name of the Japanese Religious Leadership Conference, spoke of the need for "a new prophetic way of being Church in solidarity with the cry of women everywhere." Then she spelled out practical steps to ensure greater participation of women in the Church's decision making. In all of its organizations and councils, the Church should bring women aboard, at least 30 percent of every group. All women in the Church should be justly compensated for their work. Women should be given support and opportunity to study theology. Every diocese should set up a committee to address injustices toward women and children, and encourage those committees to take effective, appropriate action. Church language should reflect the equality of men and women.

In one of the synod's working groups, someone wondered why Hirota was asking for a mere 30 percent representation by women. "Why not fifty percent?" he asked. That drew general laughter from the men, but they made no move to bring the idea to those in charge of writing up the synod summary.

Agustina Lumentut, a Protestant delegate from the Christian Conference of Asia, reported that in her country, Indonesia, women from all religions have come together to share similar experiences "that can become one of the primary sources for theological reflection. As long as Asian women find the courage to tell each other their stories and share their experiences, they have hope." Then she challenged the bishops: "Women are walking together. But is the Church walking with them?"

Not so far as anyone could notice. According to the protocol at John Paul's synods, the participants made their statements. Then the staff sifted through them for concrete suggestions (along with their stated rationales) to the working groups, where they were either sent up to be embodied in a list of propositions that were voted on toward the end of the synod, or tucked into the synod's secret files. During those working sessions, some Curia officials tried to steamroller the Asian bishops. "We came thinking the Curia would listen to us and learn something about the local Churches of Asia," one Japanese bishop reported. "We did not expect they would try to teach us." At the beginning of one working group session, he said, the curial cardinal López Trujillo harangued the members for forty-five minutes.

Invariably, reported Prior, any suggestions that would give bishops the autonomy needed to make the Church more authentically Asian were "watered down or filtered out by the synodal machine." Since the Council, many bishops had wanted to write their own liturgies. Rome has consistently vetoed their wishes, even rejecting some of the local translations of rites contained in the Roman Missal. Hirota's proposals were erased automatically, some joked, by a special program inside the synod's computer. That computer even curialized some of the popular terms. "Asian churches" became "the Catholic Church in Asia." "Other Christian churches" became "other Christian confessions." Words like "subsidiarity," "decentralization," "deregulation," and "democracy" were eliminated without discussion. All proposals to upgrade the responsibility of the bishops' conferences disappeared. One suggestion about collaboration between local Churches survived; it had to do with prayer and finance.

The Asian bishops could see that Cardinal Schotte knew what His Holiness wanted to hear, and he wasn't going to embarrass him by presenting him with any propositions that didn't fit his own bias. Schotte told one bishop he had to shelve a proposal because it was against canon law. (A Japanese bishop said that if canon law trumped the bishops' meeting in synod, why bother having them come to Rome for a whole month?)

The bishops didn't make a fuss. Prior said it was the Asian way. When Asians said yes, they often didn't mean yes. They meant they had heard you. The Japanese bishops did make a subtle, symbolic protest. At the synod's final ceremony, a solemn high mass in Saint Peter's Square, the bishops had been advised to come wearing a white chasuble and a miter, the high pointed hat that is a sign of the bishop's special status. All the Japanese bishops came to the square hatless.

Of the bishops, Prior said, "They came, they spoke, they returned home. They played the synodal game according to Rome's rules. We are, it seems, a Church in waiting." Waiting for what? Privately, the bishops said, "For a new pope." It was clear to the Asian bishops that John Paul II didn't want any sudden shifts in direction for the barque of Peter.

Then again, perhaps what happened in Rome was almost beside the point. Prior said that new visions were already taking shape in Asia, and he suggested that many bishops and theologians in Asia could enjoy "an open and honest intellectual life for the sake of the gospel" because "they think and speak and write in languages unknown in Rome." He quoted one cardinal who told him, "Yes, they have filtered out our proposals, but why become overexcited? When we return home, we shall continue to filter theirs."

Julius Darmaatmadja delivered the synod's closing statement, and to some, like Filo Hirota, his remarks were "a pleasant surprise." She said the cardinal "brought up almost all of the controversial elements in a nonconfrontational way, but he made the points very clear."

Speaking in English (a majority of the Fathers of the Synod did, for English has become the lingua franca of the Far East), the cardinal emphasized the new postcolonial theology of the postconciliar Church in Asia.

> We must make present and put into practice Christ's love, which saves people and gives them new life in him. In addition to offering hope and new life in Jesus Christ and serving directly people who are needy in so many ways, we must also take part in the task of striving to improve unjust structures, whether in the economic, political, cultural or governmental realms, as well as of building a new culture of life characterized by love, truth, honesty and justice. It is in this aspect of our Christian mission that the laity play a key role, that is, in those areas of life where they, more than the priests and religious, are living in the midst of the world and its activities. Empowerment and ongoing formation of our lay people are a must.

Darmaatmadja finessed the clash between the Curia and the bishops—the debate over proclamation versus action in concert with Asia's poor—by quoting words from the Curia's own instruction to the bishops at the beginning of the proceedings.

> As the *Instrumentum Laboris* states, the most effective and credible proclamation of the Risen Lord is the unspoken witness of a person who has undergone a deep God-experience and whose life is transformed accordingly. The credibility of an evangelizer lies in his or her being a man or woman of God more than a scholar, in being a person who lives simply but with depth. That priests, religious, and the Christian laity be known as prayerful people, who

> at the same time are active witnesses and workers, is the hope of renewal in the Church herself.

Darmaatmadja alluded to the pioneering work of Asia's theologians. The Holy Office had excommunicated Tissa Balasuriya, and issued warnings about the work of Anthony De Mello and Jacques Dupuis. Some of the bishops said they were offended at the suggestion that they discipline their own theologians. Darmaatmadja put it this way:

> We need good theologians to do careful and creative theological reflection. When there are differing views, as in other situations of disagreement, dialogue in a spirit of mutual love and mutual trust is necessary so that differences do not result in divisions but rather become a path to growth and renewal.

The cardinal spoke about the ever-present danger for many prelates, that they are often tempted to lord it over their priests and their people. He quoted a passage from the twentieth chapter of Matthew, where Jesus tells the apostles that "whoever would be great among you must be your servant . . . even as the Son of Man came not to be served but to serve." Being a bishop always brings the risk that you will be tempted to reverse that order, said Darmaatmadja. He told the bishops they could well ponder what Saint Augustine once said:

> When I am frightened by what I am to you, then I am consoled by what I am with you. For you I am bishop; with you I am a Christian. The first is an office, the second a grace. The first a danger, the second salvation.

Cardinal Darmaatmadja's waiting room had two pictures on the wall—one of Indonesia's president, Abdurrahman Wahid, his friend, and the second of the then vice president (now president) Megawati Sukarnoputri, the daughter of Indonesia's longtime leader, Achmed Sukarno. The room was furnished simply: two straight-backed chairs, one love seat, one divan upholstered with a floral print, an Oriental rug, a bowl of tiny roses, a crucifix over the calendar from the Jesuits' local Kanisius College. The clangor of Jakarta's 9 a.m. traffic rang in off the avenue called Keuskupan Agung.

When the cardinal appeared for our interview, he talked a bit about Indonesian history. "We have been proud partners in our country's asserted independence," he said. "The language is Malay/Javanese, colored with bits of Portuguese and Dutch."

The cardinal had been grieved over the bombing in Jakarta the previous Christmas Eve, right outside his cathedral's fence. "Everyone was stunned," he said. Catholics in Indonesia, though a minority, were good citizens, he said. Darmaatmadja himself was the chaplain of the Indonesian army. But if his cathedral was under attack, then, he wondered, how effective a witness was the Church in Indonesia? He said he had been assured that the bombing was no reflection on what the Church had been doing (or not doing) here. Darmaatmadja wrote an open letter to all the people of Jakarta in which he said he didn't blame the Muslims. He wanted to believe that his letter helped pacify the country. He was sure that most Muslims in Indonesia were already well disposed toward the Church. "They know we have very large hearts."

He also knew he had to assure the whole world that all was well. He did so by telling the Catholic news agency FIDES (which had clients in the secular press) that it shouldn't make any polemics over the bombing. Two days later, on December 26, he was invited by the Muslim leaders in the capital to join them in the compound of Jakarta's national monument as an honored guest for the Takbir Akbar 1421 Hijriyah—the public opening of the month of Ramadan, the Muslim month of fasting. He went in his full cardinal's regalia, and was joined by a number of Protestant leaders. "This had never happened before," he said. "The Muslims here would rather have peace. They do not want a religious war. They know as we do that we can't let ourselves be trapped to be against each other."

But back in April, mosques in the city had also been bombed, and there had been more violence. When I asked who gained by this violence, Darmaatmadja said, "We don't have investigators on our payroll. But I can smell the evil." Where did he smell this evil? "Well, maybe, in the military. As long as there's unrest, the nation needs a strong army."

And maybe the violence gave the nation an excuse not to pay its bills. Indonesia was saddled with a debt of some $600 million to the world's bankers.

So maybe even someone in the government is trying to buy time? The cardinal said, "We have information that some of the kids who fill the streets with demonstrations are getting paid—fifty thousand rupees, for a good demonstration." Later, Father Ismartono reported, "Terrorists probably get much more than fifty thousand. We think they're getting paid by the military."

The cardinal apologized for not addressing a list of questions I had sent ahead by e-mail. He had put them aside in favor of discussing a matter he was obviously more interested in: peace and justice. He believed the Church in Indonesia could make most effective progress by engaging in widespread dialogue with the Muslims, "so that any possible suspicion and tension can be reduced and minimized. I am convinced that such a dialogue is possible as well as enriching. There is a group of Muslim extremists in this country, but the majority of the Muslims are not with them. Catholics and Protestants have the same problem; there are also some extremists among us."

He was on firm ground in his own Church. He had a less firm faith that his nation would soon come to order. The next day, Ignatius Ismartono pointed to a huge map of Indonesia on the wall of his own office, with pins inserted throughout the archipelago, and white paper tabs on each pin, detailing the killings, documented by their source, usually a local newspaper: On Indonesia's main archipelago, 3,218 dead. On Timor, 34. On Sampit, 3,000. On Ambon, 1,023. Ismartono also had a book of news clippings, three inches thick, from July 1999 to March 2001, documenting the violence.

For Ismartono and his cardinal, the presence of Muslim extremists in their country loomed large. And the reason for their fears became more apparent after 9/11, when the press began to do in-depth features on the Taliban and their jihad academies throughout Asia. It wasn't entirely clear that Darmaatmadja wanted to see the Taliban routed, not if it meant that American planes would be dropping bombs on Afghanistan. But soon after the attack on the World Trade Center in New York and on the Pentagon in Washington, Darmaatmadja found himself in Rome for the international synod of bishops in October 2001. There, he told a reporter that he was calling for an immediate end to the American-led air strikes on Afghanistan. At the same time, the American bishops who were in Rome for the 2001 synod were drafting statements in support of the U.S. retaliation. As Tip O'Neill, the longtime Boston congressman, once said, "All politics is local." And in a country where Muslims made up 88 percent of the population, Darmaatmadja had to be both political and local, as did the American bishops.

But I wasn't there to talk about world politics. I wanted to know what Darmaatmadja was thinking about the upcoming conclave. "What qualities," I asked, "would you like to see in the next pope?"

Without hesitation, he said, "I will be looking for a man who knows how to listen. Someone with discretion and discernment. The process of discernment means listening, learning all the facts."

Darmaatmadja's prescription reflected what I was beginning to hear from many, including many bishops visiting Rome for their regular *ad limina* visits every five years, that John Paul II was not a great listener. Darmaatmadja, on the other hand, was trained in the art of listening. His Jesuits had always put such a high premium on superiors who could listen. This wasn't only a Jesuit virtue. The Dominican master general, Timothy Radcliffe, has written about the need for superiors to hear everyone out. And Saint Benedict, founder of one of the Church's most ancient orders, reminded his monks that good ideas in any community could come (and often did) from its lowliest members. The Benedictines had a culture of free speech long before Columbus sailed to the Americas.

To make his point about a pope's need to listen, Cardinal Darmaatmadja cited the synods, where a good deal of listening went on. "The synods are the way pointed out by Vatican II."

John Paul II's synods did not exemplify listening to a high degree, I said.

The cardinal smiled and said quietly, "The tension at the synods is necessary. It makes everyone aware of what the problems are. I like to take the long view. We will make progress, in time." As far as edicts from Rome were concerned, he said, "They are often not very relevant here." He said he had read a story on the Internet about Cardinal Rodríguez

Maradiaga, saying that between Rome and Honduras "there is a very wide ocean." And he laughed when I told him that Roger Mahony, the American cardinal from Los Angeles, had applied a "we just don't ask" strategy in many of his dealings with Rome.

At the mention of Mahony's name, Darmaatmadja said, "I think it would be a good thing to elect an American pope."

I allowed that an American cardinal, almost any American cardinal, might put a new, democratic twist to Catholicism's spinning top, and that Mahony might make a good pope if he knew where to draw the line between his Catholicism and his Americanism. But I doubted that this would be a problem. "If Mahony were elected pope, I suspect he would go to the president of the U.S. and say, 'Look, Mr. President, I won't tell you how to run the country if you don't tell me how to run my Church.'"

Darmaatmadja laughed and rose. The interview was over.

Some months later, I received an e-mail from Cardinal Darmaatmadja, a thoughtful attempt to answer a previously unanswered question. He wanted to confess how far he and his Church of Indonesia were from implementing the charter that was written for the Church at Vatican II.

> The Church is still too clerical, even though it wants to become more perfectly the Church of the people of God. One of the concerns we have among others is the feudal culture in which equality is hard to achieve because rank is often more highly valued than function. Jesus valued the function of service over hierarchy for the people of God, and Vatican II emphasized this. The Indonesian Church has chosen as a priority "the strengthening of the basic community." I have come to realize that my role as archbishop is to lead in a collegial way, so that more religious and laity will be active in decision making. Leadership such as this means listening more to the faithful at the grassroots, listening to the movements which come from there, and watching for the sign of the Spirit in myself and in those around me, all the people of God. May we see and hear the Spirit at work in the wide world of our people. To do all this, new mechanisms have to be created.

He considered the small faith community "the most promising new mechanism." (They are called base Christian communities in Latin America, among other places.) There are literally hundreds of them in Indonesia, especially in the rural areas, which see a priest only rarely. The cardinal said he hoped the base communities would strengthen the faith of his people, whether a priest was with them or not.

In January 2000, at a pastoral center twenty miles outside of Bangkok, some 160 Asian bishops and other Church leaders met for ten days to make plans for the new millennium. Their meeting came just two months after Pope John Paul II's weekend trip to New Delhi to give the bishops his response to their 1998 synod in Rome. The pope repeated an old directive—that Asian bishops must evangelize primarily by proclaiming Jesus Christ as the unique savior of the world. The Asian bishops did not openly reject the pope's exhortation, but they said they would proclaim their faith by their actions, by witnessing to the gospels and by entering into dialogue with followers of the other Asian religions. They talked about building local Churches characterized primarily by service and love. A number of bishops said openly that to proclaim Jesus as savior in Asian countries with majority Muslim populations would be an outright act of suicide.

The bishops repeatedly expressed their respect for the Holy Father and their desire to be viewed as bishops within the universal Church. But they had their own vision of how they wanted to build the Church's future in Asia.

Observers from other parts of the world were impressed. Bishop John S. Cummins of Oakland, California, the American bishops' liaison with the Churches of Asia for more than a decade, told Tom Fox of the *National Catholic Reporter,* "Asia has a grasp of the Holy Spirit that we don't have." Fox suggested Western Catholics could learn a lot from their Asian counterparts. "You can grab the hope here! The Asian bishops really exemplify hope and they keep their faith in the context of the community. There is nothing parochial about their mindset here."

At the conclave of 2005, Cardinal Darmaatmadja would have laughed if anyone asked if he were a candidate to succeed John Paul II.

He was hoping the next pope would have a truly global vision, would be someone who, above all, could launch a more effective dialogue with the leaders of Islam that might have a ripple effect throughout the Muslim world. As he checked in to the Casa Santa Marta on April 17, he hoped that his vote for that kind of man would make a difference.

In naming Pope John XXIII its Man of the Year in January 1963, *Time* reflected the world's approval of his efforts to bring the Church into modern times, making it more democratic, more free, more fun, more human, more humble in the face of history. (Time Inc./Time & Life Pictures/Getty Images)

Pope Paul VI was featured in *Time* later in 1963, after he promised the cardinals who elected him that he would bring Vatican II, the initiative launched by his predecessor, to a successful conclusion. In fact, he made only halfhearted efforts to create a more democratic Church, and he lost a good deal of authority when he issued a 1968 encyclical reaffirming the Church's condemnation of birth control. (David Lees/Time Inc./Time & Life Pictures/Getty Images)

Above: John Paul II with President and Mrs. Ronald Reagan in Miami in 1987, on one of his myriad journeys. He visited 139 nations, some more than once, far exceeding the travels of any previous pope. (Diana Walker/Time & Life Pictures/Getty Images)

Bottom left: On August 12, 1993, President Bill Clinton joined the pope at World Youth Day in Denver. Political leaders loved being photographed with John Paul II, but he often gave them stern, sometimes impolitic, advice. (Luke Frazza/AFP/Getty Images)

Bottom right: John Paul II told priests and bishops not to get involved in politics, but he never hesitated to do so himself. On January 21, 1998, he traveled to Cuba and confronted Fidel Castro with a call for a reborn Cuba's full return to the international community. (Michel Gangne/AFP/Getty Images)

Considered a post-conciliar liberal and a very able politician within the ranks of the American bishops, Cardinal Roger Mahony of Los Angeles found it difficult to politick at the conclave for a "people's pope." He may have been distracted by multimillion-dollar lawsuits back home from victims of priests' sexual abuse and rumors that he might be criminally involved in a cover-up. (David McNew/Getty Images)

)n the eve of the conclave, Nigerian Cardinal 'rancis Arinze led the list of papal candidates on 'addy Power's Internet betting site. One poll in ,ome (where Arinze had been working since)85) also made Arinze a favorite. "Electing a lack pope," said one Roman taxi driver, "would ay something to the world about racism." AFP/Getty Images)

Cardinal Oscar Rodríguez Maradiaga of Honduras is an advocate of liberation theology, which for him is a movement seeking sustenance and justice for his people. Rodríguez has had some success getting debt relief from the World Bank for countries throughout the third world. (Orlando Sierra/AFP/Getty Images)

British Cardinal Cormac Murphy-O'Connor has spent much of his life as a priest working to bring Christians closer together and is as optimistic about the Church of the future as Pope John XXIII was. He has called for "a new spirituality that ends with our reaching out to the world." (Bruno Vincent/Getty Images)

Cardinal Julius Darmaatmadja, a Jesuit from Jakarta, Indonesia, believes the Church is "too clerical," and his personal style (here, he is strolling around St. Peter's Square) accurately reflects his being a man of the people. Along with many Asian bishops, Darmaatmadja wants to create a Church that Asians can feel at home in. (Marco Longari/AFP/Getty Images)

For three days and three nights in early April 2005, more than three million people poured into Rome to view the mortal remains of Pope John Paul II lying in state. (Joe Raedle/Getty Images)

On April 6, President George W. Bush, his wife, Laura, the first President Bush, former President Clinton, and Condoleezza Rice paid their respects to the pope. It was the first time an American president attended a papal funeral. (Tim Sloan/AFP/Getty Images)

Final rites for John Paul II on April 8 were beamed by satellite TV to some three billion people around the globe, making it the most watched funeral of all time. Cardinal Ratzinger seized front and center here, and many said he looked so papal he could almost be the successor—if only he hadn't served for twenty-five years as the Church's "enforcer."(Peter McDiarmid/Getty Images)

Thomas J. Reese was the most visible of the ten thousand reporters, editors, and photographers who went to Rome for the conclave, appearing as a commentator for many of the world's major broadcast networks. He didn't know it at the time, but Cardinal Ratzinger had already demanded his resignation as editor of *America* magazine, a voice of the thinking Church in the United States. (Thomas Koller, S.J.)

On April 18, 2005, 115 cardinals gathered in the Sistine Chapel to take a series of oaths—to elect the best man, and, under pain of excommunication, to keep the secret of the conclave. Many cardinals leaked what occurred inside the conclave, but so far no one has been excommunicated for breaking the oath. (Arturo Maris/Staff/AFP/Getty Images)

Some Italian cardinals tried to put Dionigi Tettamanzi, one of their own, on the throne of Peter. Billed as a middle-of-the-road moderate, the genial archbishop of Milan won some early support, but in the end received only two votes. (Giulio Napolitano/AFP/Getty Images)

Carlo Martini, the retired Jesuit archbishop of Milan, won only nine votes in the conclave's first round while a Jesuit colleague from Brazil received ten. After Martini protested that his poor health would make it impossible for him to serve, his liberal supporters were left to founder. (Thomas Coex/AFP/Getty Images)

American cardinals Ted McCarrick and Bernard Law in a moment of high hilarity. McCarrick, of Washington, D.C., appeared frequently on television in the days before the conclave. Law avoided the media. In disgrace for his cover-up of priestly pedophilia, Law had resigned as archbishop of Boston, but John Paul II gave him a sinecure in Rome as archpriest of the Basilica of Santa Maria Maggiore. (Ed Bailey/AP)

Before the conclave, few believed Cardinal Ratzinger had more than a slight chance of becoming the next pope. As it turned out, he was the only cardinal to mount an effective campaign. He gathered eighty-four votes on the final ballot and was soon appearing on the balcony of St. Peter's as Pope Benedict XVI. (Andrew Medichini, AP)

Belgian Cardinal Godfried Danneels was so unhappy with the election of Cardinal Ratzinger that he left Pope Benedict's victory dinner at the Casa Santa Marta and repaired to a news conference at the Belgian College. Making a distinction between faith and theology, he told reporters, "We don't have to accept the pope's theology. It may change. I hope it does. I change my theology every day." (Bruno Vincent/Getty Images)

Cardinal Jorge Mario Bergoglio of Buenos Aires received all but three of the thirty-one votes withheld from Cardinal Ratzinger on the final ballot. If he were elected at the next conclave, he would be the first Latin American pope in history, the first non-European in the last nineteen centuries, and the first Jesuit. We shall see. (STF/AFP/Getty Images)

EXCURSION III

Syncretism

The Heart, Then Understanding

Syncretism . . . the amalgamation or attempted amalgamation of different religions, cultures, or schools of thought.

THE NEW OXFORD AMERICAN DICTIONARY

IN ORDER TO SEE HOW, in very concrete ways, the Church has been living out its new, postconciliar mission in Asia, I visited more than a score of Catholics in Asia and talked to a good many Asians over a five-year period in Rome. My intent: to hold a mirror up to a part of the Church that is working out a new and realistic way of being Christian on its particular piece of the planet. I hoped that the cardinals in conclave would elect the kind of pope who could put his blessings on, even give a special impetus to, this new way of "being Church."

In Jakarta, I called upon Anne O'Neill, a nun from Cleveland, Ohio, and a member of an elite order, the Society of the Sacred Heart, founded in France in the early 1800s. Like the Jesuits, these sisters have dozens of high schools and colleges sprinkled throughout the world. The empress of Japan is an alumna of one of them. Mary Robinson, former president of Ireland and the UN high commissioner for human rights, is an alumna from another. In the late 1980s, the members of her order, some thirty-five hundred strong, said they wanted to try to encounter a piece of the world that was not Christian. They were not doing this to make converts, but simply to be with people in need. "If those people ever become Catholics," said Sister Clare Pratt, the order's superior general in Rome, "they will do so on their own."

This was a piece of good, postconciliar theology, and it was also a long-standing article of Catholic teaching—that faith is a gift of God, and not something that a missionary can coax into people, much less force them to embrace. Catholic missionaries all over the world, particularly in the third world, had adopted the same stance. Pratt had suggested that Anne O'Neill could tell me how this new idea was working out in Indonesia.

I took Anne O'Neill to dinner at the poshest restaurant in Jakarta, a steak house in the Hotel Internationale. Nuns used to travel only in pairs, dressed in yards and yards of black serge, and never, never went out to dinner with anyone. Now American nuns go where they want when they want, and they dress no differently than bank executives or schoolteachers. (Some European orders are now beginning to follow their lead.) On this particular night in Jakarta, Anne wore a green silk suit and she had a direct way about her.

She said she had come on her own to Indonesia twelve years before, at the age of sixty, not knowing a word of the language. In two days, she found a job teaching English at a secular university called Atma Jaya, which means "the spirit will prevail" in the Indonesian language. Few in her classes knew she was a nun. "The kids called me Ibo Han," she said. "It means 'Mrs. Anne.'" She decided she could proclaim the gospel best without uttering a word—with her life, and with her lifestyle. So she rented an apartment in a Jakarta slum, living side by side with the poorest folks in town, eating frugally, walking to work at Atma Jaya.

Eventually, other members of her order joined her in Jakarta, and when there were enough of them, they bought a big Honda motorcycle to get them around quickly in the tremendous daily traffic. Since the machine was too big and too powerful for any of the sisters to drive, they found a man to rent it; he paid his rent by driving the sisters around town, perched behind him on his saddle.

Anne said her community of Sacred Heart sisters (now grown to seven members, from six nations) were giving shelter that very night to a dozen students from Borneo who had come to Jakarta so they could demonstrate the next day in front of the Indonesian parliament, seeking redress from the Indonesian government for the people of South Kalimantan (formerly a part of Borneo). Some of these people were Christians, some members of native religions; all of them were being forced off their native land, land rich in oil, gas, timber, and minerals, by an opportunistic group of Muslims. She was told the Muslims were using religion as a cover for their greed. Anyone could see why her community in Jakarta sympathized with these young people. It was one way the sisters had to exercise their "fundamental option for the poor."

Leaving Anne that night, I was not at all sure whether and how her order's experiment in Indonesia would work. But I thought her model might point to new ways of being Catholic and being, at the same time, accepting of everything that is human, even accepting the goodness of another religion. Anne told a story at dinner that illustrated how that might happen. One of her community of sisters was a devout Muslim, as well as a devout Catholic, something that her community discussed at length and finally decided was entirely compatible with their mission in Indonesia. This sister prayed in the mosque across the street five times a day, and kept the Ramadan fast, and one day, she will probably visit Mecca. The head of the mosque, the local imam, knows her by sight, and recently accepted her invitation to come to a post-Ramadan party at the convent. He enjoyed his visit with these charming and intelligent Catholic women. But he said he was puzzled. "Only one of them," he said, "is a Muslim." The point was that he was comfortable with the notion of a double religious identity. Wasn't everyone?

I MET SISTER MARY JOHN MANANZAN on a sunny Sunday morning in her office at Saint Scholastica's College in Manila toward the end of her two-year term there as president of the college. She was a handsome woman with flashing brown eyes, a Missionary Benedictine who had gotten a superb education at the Wilhemsuniversität in Münster, Germany, and at the Gregorian University in Rome, where she earned a Ph.D. in linguistic philosophy while minoring in systematic theology and missiology. In 1981, in New Delhi, she had taken the lead in organizing the women's commission of the Ecumenical Association of Third World Theologians (EATWOT).

"Then, and for the next twenty years," she said, "we made it known that we no longer wanted to be a token presence or fill quotas at EAT-

WOT meetings, or just be politely listened to and then ignored. We demanded that whatever EATWOT did would have to reflect the unity and equality in Christ that Christians claim. We insisted that EATWOT agendas address sexism as a theological issue if indeed the association wanted to seek a truly just world."

By January 1983, the women theologians turned out in force at the sixth international conference of EATWOT, a dialogue between the third world theologians and their colleagues in the West held in Geneva. Ten women from the third world came to the conference; so did a dozen women theologians from the West. "At this conference," Mananzan said, "everyone could see that our feminist theology was the most fully developed theology of liberation in the first world, and we created the greatest impact on the gathering with our plain talk about sexism in the Church." The women's commmission continued to meet over the years. Every five years, it ran its own international conference—in India, the Philippines, Korea, Hong Kong, and Malaysia.

"We had no trouble working out a platform," she said, handing over a sheet of paper that summarized a consultation of Asian women held in Manila in 1985. It stated some truths the women considered almost too obvious:

1. Oppression of women is sinful. This systemic sin is rooted in organized structures: economic, political, and cultural, with patriarchy as an overarching reality that oppresses women.
2. The patriarchal Churches have contributed to the subjugation and marginalization of women.
3. Theology itself, in its premises, traditions, and beliefs, has blurred the image of God.
4. The bias against women in Christian tradition buttressed the male-oriented Asian religious beliefs.

But the participants also rediscovered empowering elements in their Christian faith: Jesus' saving mission, which includes all; his supportive attitude toward women; the creative power of the Holy Spirit, which can overcome the forces of sin and death; the Magnificat, the song of the Virgin Mary in Luke 1:46–55, after her visit by the angel Gabriel, wherein she exulted in God's putting down the mighty (through her) and exalting the humble; and the command of Jesus to struggle for justice and the greater humanity of the poor and oppressed. The women renewed their commitment to the people's struggle, especially the women's movement, in confronting patriarchal structures. They called for a solidarity beyond gender and a race toward a new community of men and women characterized by justice, equality, peace, and love.

I asked her whether any men in the Church had harkened to these calls. She made a wry face. "Some have. Most haven't. Don't get me started." Of all the hard nuts to crack in the Catholic Church, she said, this was going to be the hardest. "We have to keep fighting," she said. "But we have to be patient, too. In the meantime, we are educating thousands of young women. We have a student body here at Saint Scholastica's of more than five thousand women. And there are Catholic colleges and universities all over the world that are educating women as we are. When these women go out into the world, either to marriage and/or to the marketplace, they will not be anything other than confident and self-possessed. And they will not stand for second-class citizenship in the Church."

I asked how the priests of Manila treated her. She made another wry face. "They keep their distance from us. And we from them. We don't call for priests to say mass for the community anymore. We celebrate our own community mass. Where two or three of us are gathered in Jesus' name, he is there in the midst of us. We don't ask whether Jesus is sacramentally present, much less argue about it. We know he is with us. And that is good enough."

I asked how she had come by her extraordinary spirit of independence. She said, "You ought to read the history of the Philippines. There, you will see that Filipinas have never taken a subordinate role to their men, and that pattern has persisted till now."

As I made ready to leave, she asked me who else I was going to see in Manila. I told her. She said, "They're all liberals. Don't you think you ought to talk to some of the others? I can give you the names and phone numbers of some local members of Opus Dei."

. . .

I READ ALOYSIUS PIERIS once I discovered he was Asia's leading liberation theologian, the author of *An Asian Theology of Liberation,* a work first published in German in 1988. There, he laid out a program of solidarity with Asia's great religions and with Asia's poor that will take at least a century to come to maturity. Pieris wrote that "Christian monks may lead the way. They are the ones now learning the language of *gnosis* spoken by Asia's non-Christian monastics, and also the language of *agape,* the only one that the Asian poor can really understand." In other words, for Pieris, the future of the Church in Asia will revolve around basic human communities, with Christian *and* non-Christian membership, "where mysticism and militancy meet and merge: mysticism based on voluntary poverty and militancy pitched against forced poverty."

For Pieris, liberation theology was more a process than a theology—less talking, more radical involvement with the poor and the oppressed. "We know Jesus the *truth* by following Jesus the *way,*" he wrote.

> Asian theology cannot become mere God-talk, for in our cultures God-talk in itself is sheer nonsense. As evidenced by the Buddha's refusal to talk of nirvana, all words have silence as their source and destiny. God-talk is made relative to God-experience. The word game about nature and person or the mathematics of one and three have only generated centuries of verbosity. It is wordlessness that gives every word its meaning.

I arranged to see Pieris at his home in Sri Lanka outside the capital city of Colombo after I had read a privately circulated paper on Christ that he had delivered to a group of Jesuit theologians in India. In it, he attacked the doctrine elaborated by the Council of Chalcedon in 451 (which had decreed that in Jesus Christ there is one divine person, but two natures, one human and one divine). In my seminary days, I pondered that proposition a good deal, but I could never really understand it. There were times during my Ignatian contemplations that I "watched" Jesus acting as if he didn't have any idea of his special "divine status." There were other times when he did. At his arrest on the night of his passion, he stayed the hands of those who wanted to help him resist. "Did you not know that if I asked my Father he would send me twelve legions of angels?" But a few hours later, when he was dying on the cross, he said, "My God, my God, why have you forsaken me?"

I was now delighted to find Pieris saying that the dogma hacked out at Chalcedon was "irrelevant and peripheral to anyone who was thinking at all deeply about the uniqueness of the person and the mission of Jesus."

According to Pieris, what's important for a Christian in the twenty-first century is "not a *belief* in truths revealed by God and accurately formulated by the Church but *action* in fidelity to a faithful God who had made a promise of salvation." When, years ago, I was studying Thomistic philosophy in a Jesuit house of studies, we used a formula to define what we were doing—*fides quaerens intellectum* (faith seeking understanding). Now I found Pieris scrapping that formula on the grounds that we cannot understand a good many things that have been "revealed" and shouldn't break our heads trying. Pieris suggested a better course: we should see Jesus in the poor and downtrodden of this earth, because whatever we did for the least of God's children on this earth, we did for Jesus. And then maybe we would know more. The heart comes first, then understanding. Pieris quoted 1 John 4:8: "Whoever does not love his neighbor does not know God." And he suggested that understanding is generated by "the encounter with the One who is our Love and our Salvation." He proposed a new formula to help label what Christians ought to be engaged in: *fides sperans salutem* (faith hoping for liberation), a formula that he picked up from Vatican II's Constitution on the Church: "She [Mary] stands out among the poor and the humble of the Lord who confidently await and receive salvation from him."

Pieris explained: Mary, the model of the Church, "appears quite conspicuous" among the poor and the humble who hope for and, therefore, receive salvation. The Church that is conspicuously present among the poor and the humble in a Marian fashion, hoping for salvation and receiving it, exercises a faith that unfolds itself as a theology of liberation (or salvation). And since God *is* salvation/liberation (as the name "Jesus" literally means), to "hope for salvation" is to hope for that love which God *is* in God's self and which God *speaks* as God's Word. "This is the beginning," Pieris wrote, "and the end of an authentic Christology." He added:

> Unfortunately many theologians who criticize the seminal Christologies of Asians do so from within the Chalcedonian frame of mind. One must certainly agree with what Chalcedon was *trying* to say within its own particular paradigm, namely that the divine and the human allow neither fusion nor fission in the way they constitute Jesus as one personal unity. By acknowledging this truth, we duly express our orthodoxy as well as our solidarity with the faith of the church. But *how* exactly the two natures remain distinct while being united is a question that appears soteriologically inconsequential and defies human explanation and therefore cannot be invoked as a criterion of orthodoxy.

I was intrigued by that phrase "soteriologically inconsequential." *Soter* is the Greek word for "savior." Soteriology is the study of salvation or, better, salvation history. I guessed at the meaning of the whole phrase: it doesn't make any difference if people understand *how* Jesus could have been both human and divine. What matters is that Jesus has given them a plan of action—to be all they can be. That is salvation. What a relief to find a theologian who wasn't trying to mystify the people in the pews. I was anxious to meet this man.

It was close to four in the morning when I arrived at the Tulana Center in the middle of a jungle outside Colombo, but I found Pieris waiting up for me, a diminutive, slightly graying man with a caffe latte complexion, wearing a colorful shirt and a red sarong and sandals. He shook my hand warmly, then led me to my room. After many twists and turns and steps through the fairly elaborate complex, we ended up in the center's only guest room. I was soon asleep.

I arose at ten and went to the kitchen for a breakfast of bread and jam, a cup of coffee, and a small banana while Pieris joined me for a cup of tea. We dined at a large circular table in an airy common room dominated by some stunning art. One of the pieces was a bas-relief of Jesus washing the feet of his disciples. It was created by a Buddhist monk, Sadu Janarabaya, who is now studying Catholic theology in Milan, and it may be one of the few portraits of Jesus ever done by a Buddhist monk. Pieris obtained a scholarship for Janarabaya in Italy, not to convert him to Catholicism but to help him be a better Buddhist. "I have never converted a Buddhist to Christianity," he says. "The good Buddhist doesn't need conversion. He is honest, he is generous, he is not caught up in greed or in power games."

We studied this piece by Janarabaya for a time. Then we moved over to another bas-relief, done by another Buddhist, Kingsley Gunatillaka. It was called *Jesus Lost in the Temple.* Pieris said, "I let these artists read our scripture stories, then I leave it up to them to interpret what they read. Doing it this way helps me understand how the Christ event comes across to them, and to the others I encounter here in Sri Lanka. For me, it is a form of interreligious dialogue. I think art speaks better than words."

The bas-relief *Jesus Lost in the Temple,* which was done in a kind of native sandstone, had a text in Sinhalese running down the left side. It said that Jesus, a chubby, almost cherubic figure here in the lower foreground, was "listening and questioning" the elders, whose figures and faces dominated the bas-relief. But their faces were not Semitic faces. I could descry Buddha and Krishna, Lao-tzu, Confucius, Socrates, Plato, Aristotle, and Moses. And there were two women here in this picture to remind those who behold it that women are not to be blocked out of the Jesus community. Pieris quoted Saint Paul's description of the early Church: "neither male nor female, neither slave nor free."

I could see the mother of Jesus in the lower left foreground reaching out to restrain Jesus, but he is fending her off with his left hand, while gesturing to the elders above him with his right. Pieris explained, "Mary is trying to control the Word of God, but Jesus won't let her do that. He must be about his Father's business. God's business, not the Church's business." Pieris drew a lesson here: "The Church, like Mary here, is to support, not control."

Pieris was one of the most important Catholic theologians in Asia, but almost since the day of his ordination in Naples just before Christmas in 1963, he had been ignoring efforts by Rome to control him and his theological explorations in Asia, grounded in the conviction that the gospel message was meant for all humanity, and that theologians had a duty to pass that message on in ways that all people could understand.

In a letter to Asian bishops in 1972, Pope Paul VI endorsed this new approach in these words: "The Church must make herself in her fullest expression native to your countries, your cultures, your races. Let the Church draw nourishment from the genuine values of the venerable Asian religions and cultures."

A liberal pope (as Paul VI was, for most of his fifteen years in office) could say this, but the words seemed suspect to the bureaucrats who were still running the Vatican machinery. One of the investigators in the Holy Office launched an inquiry on Pieris some years before for an essay he had written on liberation theology. Fortunately for Pieris, his Jesuit superior in Sri Lanka challenged the Vatican's competence to even understand what Pieris was saying in English, and after another exchange of letters, the Holy Office sent a note to Pieris's superior stating there was nothing "intrinsically against orthodoxy" in Pieris's writings, but that the Holy Office thought he was "confused."

Pieris is a native Sri Lankan. His country—then known as Ceylon—became a British tea colony in 1802, after successive dominations by the Dutch and the Portuguese that dated back to the seventeenth century, when Pieris's forebears became Catholic converts. Pieris is thankful they did; otherwise, he would never have received the education he did in the Jesuit order, which he joined at the age of nineteen at an international house of studies in India. He did his theology in Naples, close to the action of Vatican II during the early 1960s, when he and his classmates often entertained some of the Council's leading theologians, including the German Jesuit Karl Rahner. Pieris remembers his last encounter with Rahner and Rahner's exact words: "Vatican II is not an end, but a beginning. You have to spell out its implications for your people in the context of their life situations."

For the past thirty-five years, Pieris had been trying to do exactly that. After finishing his Jesuit training, he returned to Sri Lanka to study Buddhist philosophy at the University of Sri Lanka's Vidyodaya campus. He was the first Catholic priest ever to win a doctorate there in Buddhist philosophy. At one time, he had no aspirations to live the life of a scholar. "I was a poet and a musician," he recalled. "I wanted to write plays. I wanted to dance. And I wanted to work with the rural youth." At the time, in the late 1960s and early 1970s, revolution was in the air, and Pieris studied with the rambunctious youth in Sri Lanka's cradle of revolution, the university campus, to watch them grow from the unthinking tools of others into adult actors in their own futures. Then the Jesuit general, Pedro Arrupe, asked him to teach Buddhism at the Jesuits' Gregorian University in Rome and, during the Rome summers, at another Jesuit training ground in Manila, the East Asian Pastoral Institute.

When Pieris returned to Sri Lanka, he felt called to cross-fertilize the socialist concerns of these rural students (and others in Sri Lanka) with their Buddhist roots. In 1974, after two years of discernment, prayer, and consultation with his superiors, he founded his Tulana Center, "as a kind of laboratory where people could feel at home and deepen themselves in their own orientation." The word *tulana* comes from the Sanskrit root *tul,* which can mean to elevate, weigh, compare, lean toward more important things. In its infancy, the Tulana Center seemed anything but important.

"We started with a hundred rupees," recalled Sister Frances de Silva, who served as Pieris's bookkeeper and general factotum for twenty-five years. A few months later, Pieris opened a letter from Jean Leclercq, a French Benedictine monk who applauded what Pieris was doing. It contained a check for $240, a fortune in Sri Lanka at a time when a dollar could then buy enough groceries for a week.

Since those humble beginnings, Pieris pursued his pioneering work with two things in mind: to understand Buddhists, not to convert them, and to work with them in what he called "our common struggle for liberation." While Pieris could understand some Jesuits in other places in the world who remain Jesuit priests and also assume the mantle of Buddhist monks, particularly as Zen Buddhists, that route was not for him. "Our people would not understand this double identity," he said, "and therefore I don't claim it."

Instead, Pieris continued to deepen his own knowledge about the sources of Buddhism. Working with its prime original texts in Sinhalese, Pieris went on to publish a number of learned commentaries on Buddhism, and his Buddhist library at the Tulana Center was now a place where Buddhist scholars came to read, reflect, and confer with him.

The center had become something of a gathering place for a wide variety of people—Marxists and fallen-away Christians, Buddhists, and Asian Christians of all faiths. "People can just drop in, without an appointment," said Pieris. "They are free to stay here. We don't have many rooms for them. They generally sleep in our big communal hall, and bathe in our communal well, and they eat whatever we have to offer. If they can bring a little rice of their own, or a little coconut, all the better." Life, therefore, was simple and, by Western standards, exceedingly poor. Pieris had an aged houseboy who cooked for him, mostly vegetable curries, but he had no gas or electric stove. On my first morning at the center, I found the houseboy boiling water over an open wood fire.

Pieris scheduled occasional seminars at the center, mostly dialogues between Buddhists and Christians, where they played off each other's strengths and one another's insights. "In understanding Buddha," said Pieris, "we become better Christians. And in understanding Jesus, they become better Buddhists." An all-day seminar begins in the morning with conferences about some particular verses of the Buddhist or Christian scriptures. In the afternoon, the attendees read some contemporary literature dealing with the same subject. In the evening, after dinner, they put on their own dramas, or see a film. "We Sri Lankans love theater," says Pieris, "and dancing, too." Late at night, conferees make their way, one by one, to Pieris's office for a chat; often it is a chat that deals with each person's own individual struggles for liberation, often enough from their own fears.

One day in the early 1990s, Buddhists came to Tulana for a conference that began with a mass celebrated by Pieris. Later in the day, the pope's legate, or nuncio, in Colombo, an Italian named Nicola Rotunno, arrived at the Tulana Center to look around. He had heard that Buddhists would be attending mass, and he wondered, perhaps, if Pieris was caught up in syncretism, a bad word in the Vatican, quite ignoring the manifestations of religion throughout history, a story of creative borrowings, from one religion to another and back again. "Oh, I'm late," the nuncio said to Pieris.

"You're not late," said Pieris. "You weren't invited."

"I'm worried about you," said the nuncio. "We are colleagues. You don't know how much I care."

Pieris nodded skeptically.

The nuncio said he had to ask. "Did any of these Buddhists attend mass here today?"

"They did."

"The whole mass?"

"Yes."

"But we have the mass of the catechumens and the mass of the faithful. As you know, the catechumens must leave at the *Sanctus.*"

Pieris scoffed. "These Buddhists are not studying to become Catholics. Therefore, they are not catechumens."

The nuncio protested Pieris's attitude. Pieris wasn't cooperating. Rotunno reminded him: "I am the representative of the pope!"

Pieris snapped, "To the government, not to me." Pieris was right, but the distinction is often lost in some countries. The American bishops have always paid exaggerated deference to the pope's chief legate in Washington; as a matter of fact, the nuncio represents the Holy See to the American government, not the American bishops.

A few years later, after Archbishop Rotunno was transferred out of Sri Lanka, Pieris discovered that Rotunno had made an inquiry about Pieris at his old Jesuit house of theology in Naples, but Rome filed no charges.

"What would they charge me with?" said Pieris. "I do not call myself a Buddhist. I am critically loyal to the Church. I have a deep faith in Jesus Christ." And so, because he is so certain and so secure in that faith, Pieris hasn't worried about inquiries from Rome. "We have a great advantage here in Asia, because we work in languages that the men in the Holy Office do not understand." The situation in Sri Lanka, at least, can only get worse, from Rome's point of view. Pieris has a new generation of young lay theologians working with him, writing in their native Sinhalese. He mentioned one of them, a young man named Shirley Wijesysingha, who has a passion for biblical studies. He got one degree in scripture from the Biblical Institute in Rome, and a Ph.D. at the University of Louvain. Now in Colombo, he leads a mass movement of people studying the Bible, and his graduates are laypeople who can (and do) preach homilies at Sunday mass, and get involved in various sorts of social action. When he writes, he will write in Sinhalese, a language that will be rather impervious to inquiries by the Holy Office.

Pieris not only oversees those biblical studies. For years, with a solid assist from an order of nuns, he has financed and operated a school for the hearing-impaired who could not otherwise find an education in Colombo. He continues to write more books and many more learned articles. During my stay, I found that he rose early and worked far into the night, sometimes in searching conversations with scholars who are writing their theses on Pieris.

Pieris's most recent book was a slim self-published paperback based on private talks that Pieris gave to predominantly Jesuit audiences in 1997 and 1998. Until then, *The Christhood of Jesus and the Discipleship of Mary: An Asian Perspective* had brought down no official reprimand from Rome. This is surprising, for in the book Pieris takes up some of the very issues that led to the excommunication in 1998 of Pieris's fellow Sri Lankan theologian the Oblate of Mary Immaculate Tissa Balasuriya, an edict that was later revoked by Pope John Paul II after a worldwide outcry in defense of Balasuriya.

In this book, Pieris went right to the heart of the Ratzinger agenda with a gentle attack on the very notion of dogmatic definitions themselves—pieces of legalism, he said, that owe more to Roman law than to the loving words of Jesus and his followers in the early years of Christianity. "Faith," he wrote, "began to be judged, and the deviants condemned, entirely on the basis of one's adherence to the formula of faith" as defined by Church authorities. As a result, the Vatican has produced a set of faith propositions that need to be maintained in their doctrinal purity by something very much like George Orwell's Ministry of Truth—the Holy Office, which is run, says Pieris, by "a powerful clerical class armed with massive punitive powers."

Pieris says the Church should have known better from its own history. "The history of the Christological dogmas is not an edifying story of an innocuous development of a teaching; it is a sad story of serious misunderstandings, punctuated by political intrigues and physical violence." He cited the Council of Chalcedon, which condemned the patriarch of Alexandria in 451. Pieris told me that exactly fifteen centuries later, in 1951, Pope Pius XII revoked the condemnation with an encyclical that admitted confusion over some words in the original edict. Formulas, said Pieris, often do more harm than good, especially if those formulas are asserted as "coming from divine revelation."

In fact, said Pieris, all the Church's formulas are culturally conditioned. As human constructs, then, they are "relative, time-bound, and culturally limited expressions of faith that cannot be used as absolute norms for measuring orthodoxy." But it is precisely on this ground, relativism, that Ratzinger has condemned some Asian theologians, who tend to agree with Pieris that dogmas are not divinely revealed at all, but guiding statements that serve the believing community as practical aids "to foster and fructify our faith and hope in God who is love."

Instead of dogmas, Pieris was proposing *sutras,* which in ancient Indic philosophy were designed to summarize more copious teachings with terse clarity. They wouldn't carry the weight of some putative divine inspiration, and they wouldn't be an instrument of control, but simply "invitations to faith, hope and love."

IN 1601, after spending twenty-one years studying the language, history, and culture of China, Jesuit father Matteo Ricci landed in the court of Beijing and put his Western learning at the disposal of the emperor Wanli. For almost a decade, Ricci became the most important link between East and West, between European Renaissance culture and Chinese culture, and between the ancient Chinese civilization and the world of Europe. He was reined in by Church authorities in Rome for using secular Chinese rites to honor the dead in Catholic requiem masses. They called Ricci a syncretist.

On October 24, 2001, Ricci's memory was rehabilitated by Pope John Paul II, who hailed him as the very model of a modern missionary. The pope said Ricci brought "the Christian revelation of the mystery of God" to China in a way that "did not destroy Chinese culture" and pursued the "patient and farsighted work of enculturating the faith in China, in the constant search for a common ground of understanding with the intellectuals of that great land."

Soon after that papal reversal, I met a Jesuit named Paolo Dall'Oglio, who was following Matteo Ricci's path—not in China, but in Islam. In 1991, Dall'Oglio had founded a Christian community called Deir Mar Musa, the Community of Saint Moses the Ethiopian, high on a cliff in the Syrian desert. His goal: to further a greater rapprochement with Islam by "reinventing the positive relationship that existed between the first Muslims and the Christian monks on the borders of the Arabian deserts." He was twenty-five years into a project mandated by the visionary Jesuit general Pedro Arrupe, who saw a new world taking shape in the early 1970s. It was a world the various religions had to stop fighting over, and start fighting for. That called for new kinds of missionaries who would go forth not to convert the heathens, but to listen and learn from those often more spiritual than they.

Dall'Oglio became that kind of missionary. In 1977, Arrupe dispatched him to Lebanon to learn Arabic and Islamic culture—to begin, at age twenty-three, the kind of deep cultural transformation epitomized by the gigantic figure of Matteo Ricci.

Twenty-seven years into his mission, Dall'Oglio did not consider himself a giant. But when I found him in Rome, visiting the Jesuits' Gregorian University, he did tell me he thought of himself as a Muslim—"because Jesus loves Muslims, the same Jesus who is alive in me." He was, of course, still very much a Jesuit, a tall, animated man on the move with flashing eyes, wearing Nikes, a ski jacket, and a backpack—and coughing through a very full salt-and-pepper beard. But he had this second identity as well. "In a sense," he said, "I cannot but be a Muslim—by way of the Spirit and not the letter." He said he is a syncretist "culturally and theologically—without losing my faithfulness to the mystery of the Church of Jesus Christ," as he told a group of fellow Jesuits in a prepared talk delivered at the Jesuit headquarters in Rome called "In Praise of Syncretism."

I asked about his immersion in Islam. "As soon as I arrived in Lebanon in 1977," he explained, "I tried to start thinking in Arabic." Among other things, he learned the prayer of the heart in Arabic ("Lord Jesus Christ, be merciful to me, a sinner") and made it as habitual as his own breathing. He came back to the Gregorian for his seven years of philosophy and theology, but he spent every summer somewhere in the Arab world. And he not only learned what Islam was, he learned to love it, too, not least from the writings of the Catholic hermit Charles de Foucauld (1858–1916) and the Catholic Islamic scholar Louis Massignon (1883–1962).

Dall'Oglio wrote his doctoral dissertation in theology on "Hope in Islam." He was ordained a priest in the Syriac Catholic Rite, and then moved to his first assignment in Syria, where he eventually came upon the ruin that he made into his monastery. Dall'Oglio dug into his backpack to find a picture of Deir Mar Musa, a white, fortresslike complex built on top of a cliff. It was first constructed, he said, in the sixth century, frescoed in the eleventh century, and abandoned in the nineteenth century, then given to him by the Catholic Antiochian archbishop of Homs-Hama-Nabk in 1991. The frescoes in its chapel are priceless.

In 2005, the Community of Deir Mar Musa had a dozen monks and nuns in their thirties, as well as some lay collaborators, including two married couples, and some novices. After four years, those who are approved take perpetual vows of poverty, chastity, and obedience, and promises of contemplation, work, hospitality, and loving Islam. They wear gray woolen habits, cinched with a leather belt. They do not follow any special dietary restrictions but do not eat pork or drink wine when they have Muslim guests.

Shoeless, their heads covered with prayer shawls, kneeling on fine Oriental carpets, the community shares an hour of prayer every morning, starting at seven-thirty, followed by a talk with Dall'Oglio. After breakfast, they work until two-thirty, milking their goats, making cheese, tending their gardens, and constructing a new building for the nuns and female guests. (They have already remodeled a series of ancient caves north of the monastery for the monks and male guests.) After lunch, they take a siesta when they can, they study, and they go on the Internet, creating a virtual monastery in cyberspace at www.deirmarmusa.org. In the evening, at seven, they have an hour of silent prayer in their ancient chapel. Then they do their Eucharist.

"We practice an Abrahamitic hospitality," Dall'Oglio said. In fact, hospitality is the whole point of their existence. They want to bridge the tremendous gap between the followers of Jesus and the followers of Muhammad, and they feel they can do this best by meeting with all who come—for a day or for a week—answering their questions, inviting them to join in their prayers, building on their mountain a people's park with and for them, joining in their fasts for peace.

In the beginning, they had problems with both Muslims and Christians who did not understand Dall'Oglio's intentions. He was approached one day by a group of four middle-aged men who charged him with being a spy. "This," he recalls, "was hard to refute. The more I look okay and sound okay, the more I prove how effective a spy I really am. Finally, I tell them, 'All right. Look in my eyes. If you see something that is not sincere, you have every right to beat me. And I am honor bound to let you do it.'"

They withdrew, conferred together, then reapproached him and looked into his deep brown eyes and saw something good. They did not beat him. "Today," Dall'Oglio says, "they're among my best friends."

They have a library at Deir Mar Musa containing all the classic Christian texts ("We have to sink roots deep into our own tradition") and the Quran and some of the classic commentaries on Islam's sacred book. "Our monks and nuns know the Quran almost as well as many Moslems," said Dall'Oglio.

Dall'Oglio said he saw his work of reconciliation with Islam extending in the future toward some kind of mediation between all the warring parties in the Middle East. "This is very delicate," he says, "but everyone knows that we cannot continue to use religion as an excuse for violence of all kinds. We have to find a way to break through the infernal circle of fear that we feel, all of us." Dall'Oglio said it was clear that the people in every religion have to dig deep into their own roots to find the rationales for dealing with everyone in justice and peace. He had found those roots in both the Old and New Testaments. He had found them in the Quran. People who don't go to their roots, but follow only the letter (of whatever sacred text), he said, are the real troublemakers in this world. "Follow them and we are doomed."

In the spring of 2005, the Holy Office launched an investigation of Dall'Oglio for his views on syncretism.

CHAPTER TEN

Cardinal Joseph Ratzinger

Order in the Church

Up in the pope's apartment in the Vatican palace on the afternoon of Friday, April 1, 2005, Cardinal Joseph Ratzinger found a pope who couldn't speak, a pope whose breathing was coming with great effort. He looked to the pope's personal physician and raised an eyebrow, and the doctor confirmed his hunch. "The Holy Father's kidneys are poisoned," said Dr. Renato Buzzonetti. "His whole system is shutting down. In six hours, maybe . . ."

Ratzinger nodded, left the apartment, ramrod straight as usual, headed down to the Cortile San Damaso, looked for his chauffeur, and headed off to the Monastery of Saint Scholastica in Subiaco, a two-hour drive. He had long ago agreed to receive an award, the Premio San Benedetto, from the Benedictines, and the pope's condition was no reason to cancel the date. Besides, he had an important message to deliver about the disaster that lay ahead for Europe if it did not turn back to God. If he could return by midnight, he would still be able to move into action in the morning if the pope were to die.

When that happened, Ratzinger, like most of the other members of the pope's cabinet, would automatically lose his job, one he had held since 1981 as head of the Holy Office. But with "the Chair of Peter unoccupied" (*sede vacante* is the Latin phrase for that), he would take the leadership given him during the interregnum, as the dean of the College of Cardinals, to make all the decisions that had to be made in the absence of a pope. He would have more than a little say over the election of the successor. He might even be the successor.

. . .

Ratzinger was born at home in a Bavarian village called Marktl am Inn on April 16, 1927. When he was fourteen, he was conscripted into the Hitler Youth, and was drafted the following year into the regular German army. Toward the end of the war, he deserted, only to spend the war's final days in an Allied prison camp. On September 1, 1947, he entered the major seminary at the University of Munich and embarked on a rigorous course for those candidates aspiring to an academic career in the priesthood. He was ordained in Munich in 1951, and earned his Ph.D. in July 1953 with two doctoral dissertations, the second one on Saint Augustine. Ratzinger then taught theology at the University of Freising, where he was introduced to the aging archbishop of Cologne, Cardinal Joseph Frings. Frings named him his *peritus,* or theological expert, at the Second Vatican Council. Frings was one of the ancients leading the Council Fathers in the charge against the status quo, and young Ratzinger, then thirty-five, helped him do so. He was aggressive, intelligent, dissatisfied with the approach of the Church's traditionalist leaders. He was also a quick study, and soon he was making effective arguments against the opposition's leader, Cardinal Alfredo Ottaviani, the prefect of the Holy Office.

That Ratzinger later came to Ottaviani's old post and exceeded his zeal is a remarkable turnaround. His biographers say the revolutionary year of 1968 was the turning point for him, a shift caused by secular politics, rather than any religious insight. Ratzinger watched as a wave of student uprisings washed across Europe, currents that swirled almost as strongly in the university town of Tübingen (where he was then teaching) as they did in Berlin or Paris. Some feared communism would replace Christianity in Europe. Ratzinger heard his own students chanting, "Accursed be Jesus!" This shocked him, and helped confirm his private reservations about *Gaudium et Spes,* Vatican II's most revolutionary document, which challenged Christians to get involved in a world that was, after all, redeemed. Redeemed? To Ratzinger, it was a world that was falling apart. How ridiculous, Ratzinger later asserted, to say "yes" to that kind of world. In saying "no," Ratzinger said, he understood that such an uncompromising view could drive many away from the Church. So be it. "I am not a missionary."

In May 1977, Ratzinger was ordained as archbishop of Munich-Freising, and he was brought into the College of Cardinals by Pope Paul VI a month later, along with four others. "Ironically," observed John Allen, Ratzinger's biographer, "the pope was attracted to him because of his liberal views on a number of theological questions." That was doubtful. By this time, both Pope Paul VI and Ratzinger were leaning to the right, much to the relief of the traditionalists in Rome. It is more likely that Paul VI, a liberal except in his defense of papal absolutism, knew he could use Ratzinger to help him deal with men like the Swiss theologian Hans Küng, who had been a key figure during the Council and had risen to the top of the prestigious theological faculty of the University of Tübingen. (In fact, it was Küng who had brought Ratzinger to teach there not long after the Council.)

In 1963, the Holy Office had questioned the orthodoxy of Küng's book *Structures of the Church,* and had reopened a file on him dating back to 1957, when Küng had published his doctoral dissertation at the University of Paris on the Lutheran theologian Karl Barth's theology of justification. Justification—the question of how a man or woman is "justified," or saved—was a topic that Catholics and Lutherans had been fighting about for centuries, and Küng took Luther's side in the debate. (As it turned out, Catholics and Lutherans met at Augsburg on October 31, 1999, to sign an accord that said, thanks to Küng's seminal research, the whole justification affair had been a huge misunderstanding.) Nothing came of the official objections to *Structures of the Church,* but Küng encountered problems with the publication, in July 1970, of a thin but explosive book called *Infallible? An Inquiry,* that challenged the standard Holy Office view of papal primacy. Küng was called to Rome, but he never appeared there. He was understandably reluctant to stand trial in a place that the Redemptorist Bernard Häring had warned him about. Häring had once been Paul VI's moral theologian, but after the Council he'd been hauled to the Holy Office himself for questioning. Häring, who had served as a young priest-medic during World War II, had appeared before Hitler's courts four times, and said he much preferred those venues to the halls of the Holy Office. "Dissent upon what is a matter of opinion cannot be a crime," he said, and he suggested the Holy Office take a sabbatical for a few years:

> The Church could well go on living without such an institution. Look at the Orthodox Church which has kept its spirituality and its faith without having any similar body. Amnesty International should have a look inside the Vatican. The Holy Office is a poisoned lake where healthy fish cannot swim. It is a combination of ignorance and arrogance, run by ecclesiastics who are career terrorists.

Meanwhile, correspondence about Küng's *Infallible?* had been exchanged between Küng and the German bishops and the Holy Office in Rome, with no resolution to the charges that Küng had gone too far by questioning papal authority.

Küng wasn't opposed to the papacy. He wanted to see it reformed. In *Infallible?* Küng imagined how a new pope might effect that reform, by serving the Church's rich diversity in a most unpretentious fashion. A new pope would be

> a pope not above or outside the Church, but in the Church, with the Church, for the Church, not a solitary pope, but one who is constantly seeking and realizing anew his unity with the Church. This pope then would not be against justice, but against juridicism; not against law, but against legalism; not against order, but against immobility; not against authority, but against authoritarianism; not against unity, but against uniformity. He would be a man elected, not by a college of cardinals . . . but by a representative body of the whole Church, not because of his nationality but quite simply because of his suitability. He would be able to stimulate the missionary work of the Church in the world and to continue his efforts for peace, disarmament, and the social betterment of peoples and races, with quite a new credibility, and Rome would be a place of encounter, of dialogue, and of honest and friendly cooperation.

Küng was not satisfied with simply dreaming dreams. Toward the end of 1979, he wrote a long, critical analysis of John Paul II's first year in office that found the pope wanting on most counts. Küng's article was printed in many of the world's major newspapers.

John Paul II was furious. He proceeded to cut through the due process that had been shielding Küng for seven years, and told the Holy Office to announce that Küng no longer had a commission to teach as a Catholic theologian. The Vatican decree hardly affected Küng. He was still a priest and, undaunted, went on to publish thirteen more books. He stayed at Tübingen, teaching at his own ecumenical institute; he lectured on every continent, moderated several international conferences, and appeared with regularity as a commentator on religion for German and Swiss television. Many Catholics still considered him a hero and a prophet. But by the end of the millennium, though some deemed him "the greatest theologian of our times," Küng had become marginalized in Rome.

In the meantime, Ratzinger's career had soared. He authored or coauthored forty books in addition to writing countless journal articles, contributions to *Festschriften*, and prefaces for the works of fellow scholars. His *Introduction to Christianity*, published in 1968, was a runaway success, by far his best-known title. Although it could hardly compare with works such as Küng's *On Being a Christian* or Bernard Häring's *The Law of Christ*, books that were translated into dozens of languages and have exerted an important, lasting influence on Catholics everywhere, it served to recommend Ratzinger to Pope John Paul II as the kind of man who could subdue other adventurous theologians. He was the first theologian of stature to fill the post of prefect of the Holy Office since the Jesuit cardinal Robert Bellarmine held it in the seventeenth century.

This was a canny move by John Paul II, to appoint Ratzinger to the Holy Office shortly after he himself had settled the Küng affair. The pope would set a reconstructed liberal to catch other Küngs, and someone able enough to supply the pope with the arguments he needed to restore a Church that Vatican II had set on a new, dangerous, democratic course.

In Rome, Ratzinger remained what he had been since his days at the seminary, a priest of manifest piety who rarely dined with anyone and had few friends (other than his sister Maria, who spent most of her adult life as her brother's housekeeper and remained so until her death, in 1991). He regularly assembled his staff at the Holy Office for meditation and common prayer, and pursued a life of monkish simplicity. For eleven months a year, he lived in an apartment just outside the Vatican's Saint Anne's Gate, which was furnished with thousands of books and the bare necessities, and a grand piano, on which he played faithfully every day (mostly Mozart) from six-thirty to seven in the evening.

Ratzinger spent his August vacations in a seminary in the south Tyrol that rented out its modest rooms in the summer, mainly to older priests, whom he joined for plain meals prepared by the Tyrolese sisters who ran the house. He told an Italian journalist who went to the Tyrol for an extended interview with him in the summer of 1984 that he had a duty to correct people he believed in error, no matter who, no matter where. In 1998, Ratzinger went out of his way to write a letter to all the Austrian bishops, suggesting they exclude a liberal organization with a half million members, called We Are Church, from an upcoming conference on the future of the Church in Austria. He eventually backed off, ruing his own intrusion in the affair after his letter was leaked to the press and set off howls of protest.

Sometimes Ratzinger just couldn't help himself. The following summer, driving on the autobahn on the way to visit his brother in Regensburg, he was listening to a radio talk show and heard a Polish moral theologian named Josef Niewadomski in earnest conversation with a German host. Niewadomski's words so alarmed him that he pulled over to the side of the road and put in a call on his cell phone to the radio station, to set the bewildered priest straight on a question about the infallible teaching authority of the Church.

Ratzinger did not believe theologians had a duty to push the envelope of theological understanding on the radio, or come up with any novel explanations of scripture, or produce historical commentaries that called into question everything the papacy had done over the centuries. Their job was the same as his—to suffer. As he once said, "The place of the Church on earth can only be near the cross." Ideally, according to Ratzinger, those who truly follow Jesus should want to follow him on the cross. If this means they must do violence to themselves, they would only be imitating Christ. Ratzinger's theology of the cross seemed appropriate for a man who did not play Mozart for pleasure but for pain. Of Mozart's music, Ratzinger once said that it was "by no means just entertainment. It contains the whole tragedy of human existence."

That comment helped some theologians understand how Ratzinger saw his role inside the Vatican, where he could apply strong medicine to the symptoms of doctrinal disease or reports of miscreant behavior that streamed into the Palazzo del Sant'Ufficio, the Palace of the Holy Office. Though Ratzinger had a mandate to defend the faith, he often went far beyond that commission in two ways: first, by identifying the one faith of the Church with his own theology and then attempting to impose it on others who had the same faith, but different theologies, and second, by putting a theological label on Church issues that were better described as political.

In 1997, Ratzinger excommunicated Tissa Balasuriya, a Sri Lankan priest, for his views on original sin, Mary, and the role of Christ in salvation, as Ratzinger had read them in Balasuriya's book *Mary and Human Liberation*. That work had sold only a few hundred copies—until his case became an international cause célèbre. Many felt Ratzinger had erred by giving Balasuriya the publicity, but Ratzinger not only wanted to make an example of him. He also wanted to give the strongest kind of answer to Balasuriya's attack on the magisterium. In his eighteen-hundred-word notice of excommunication, Ratzinger wrote that the Sri Lankan theologian "distinguishes between the faith due in Christianity to what Jesus teaches and to what the churches have subsequently developed as interpretations of his teaching"—interpretations that Balasuriya maintained were influenced by "political and cultural interests."

Few theologians who pay attention to the history of theology were then teaching anything different. Politics, culture, and history often challenge what the Church teaches, and at this particular time historians seemed to be making the strongest challenges. Thus, Stephen Schloesser, a Jesuit historian at the University of San Francisco, maintains that "Catholic thought is always in a dialectical process of change. It strikes me that the best elements of Catholic teaching in Vatican II probably owed themselves to Voltaire and Marx—both rabidly condemned as bitter enemies of Catholicism in their day—and perhaps Abraham Lincoln." Who, Schloesser asked, could dispute the implications of history?

Ratzinger could. He said Balasuriya was "denying the nature of Catholic dogma, and relativizing the revealed truths contained in them." Ratzinger pointed out that Balasuriya had denied the Church's teachings on original sin and papal infallibility. In some parts of the Catholic world, that made Balasuriya an instant hero, for there were few serious Catholic scholars who believed in original sin as Saint Augustine had defined it in the fourth century, and even fewer who believed in papal infallibility as Pius IX had forced the Fathers of Vatican I to define it in the nineteenth—that the pope was "infallible in himself, but not with the consensus of the Church."

After Balasuriya's excommunication, an outcry arose on the Internet. His religious order, the Oblates of Mary Immaculate, fought for him in Rome and managed to get the notice of excommunication set aside one year and thirteen days after it had been imposed.

Jacques Gaillot, the bishop of Evreux, France, had no religious order to protect him. He was a pastoral type who insisted on reaching out to his city's homosexuals. When Ratzinger had him removed from his post in 1998, Gaillot was still technically a bishop, but without a diocese. He remained, however, the titular bishop of a ghost town in Asia Minor called Partenia, so he set up his diocese of Partenia with an Internet address in cyberspace, where he continued to exercise his ministry to those on the margins.

In attacking Balasuriya and Gaillot, Ratzinger was trying to make the same point: he had the power to discipline anyone stepping out on his own in ways that didn't accord with Ratzinger's formula for keeping order in the Church. Ratzinger thus saw his job as balancing two sets of rights: the right of scholars working in the service of the Church to freedom in the pursuit of new insight and the right of the broad mass of Catholic faithful not to have the faith distorted by overly daring speculation. When he defines his role that way—weighing the rights of a small intellectual avant-garde against 1 billion members of a world Church, most without any formal theological training—it's not difficult to predict whose interests will usually prevail.

As Ratzinger put it in a 1999 press conference in Menlo Park: "If you have other ideas, you have the freedom to hold those ideas, clearly. But you should not say this is Catholic theology." Joseph Fessio, a Jesuit and a publisher who held the English-language rights to all of Ratzinger's works, put the point even more plainly: "How long would a GM salesman last if it turned out he was really selling Fords?"

As we have already seen, Ratzinger launched his first major crusade in the early 1980s, to kill off liberation theology in Latin America, because it was entirely too left-wing for his taste. Ratzinger was putting a patina of Church doctrine on, and taking sides in, the century-long battle in the secular world between communism and capitalism.

In 1998, Ratzinger plunged into the politics of religion when he launched the second major crusade of his term at the Holy Office, this time against theologians who had been too sympathetic to other religions. In the summer of 2000, he began an official inquiry on one of the best of them, the Jesuit Jacques Dupuis, who had just written a best-selling book on interreligious dialogue. And on September 5, 2001, he presided at a news conference to announce the release of a ten-thousand-word document he had written, *Dominus Iesus*, "Lord Jesus," which said that the Roman Catholic Church is the only portal to salvation. Ratzinger said the pope approved (although he did not actually sign) *Dominus Iesus*, but since it touched on core matters of faith, it was "definitive and irrevocable."

He explained that in *Dominus Iesus* he wanted to score the kind of tolerance that "accepts everything, is not concerned with truth, and is disguised by the malformation of concepts such as democracy, dialogue, or meeting of cultures." His salvo wounded a good many innocent bystanders when he said that Catholics alone "have the fullness of the means of salvation."

Many Catholics could hardly believe what Ratzinger had done, but those were the people who had not been paying attention to his attempts for the past several years to reverse Vatican II. The *Tablet* of London said, "This is a public relations disaster. *Dominus Iesus* sounds notes of triumphalism that Pope John XXIII seemed to have dispelled forever." Hans Küng told an Italian news agency that *Dominus Iesus* was "a mixture of medieval backwardness and Vatican megalomania."

Many Protestants were disappointed, but remarkably calm. The archbishop of Canterbury, George Carey, the spiritual leader of the world's 70 million Anglicans, said *Dominus Iesus* was unacceptable because it seemed to minimize efforts that had been made since Vatican II to cement closer ties among all Christians. He said, "The idea that Anglican and other churches are not 'proper churches' seems to question the considerable ecumenical gains we have made." Carey was speaking about one of the main outcomes of Vatican II, which set a new tone for Catholics that was far removed from Christian polemics of the past four hundred years. An editorial in the *National Catholic Reporter* argued with Cardinal Ratzinger, who had written in *Dominus Iesus* that he was simply "reaffirming" constant Church teaching. Those who gave *Dominus Iesus* a close read said he had recaptured an all-too-constant preconciliar arrogance.

The American Catholic theologian Paul Knitter also objected. He noted that when John Paul II met with Muslims or Buddhists, he did not talk about the inherent superiority of Catholicism or the grave deficiencies of other religions. He made no demands for conversion, no attempt to persuade them that Jesus Christ is the only path to salvation. Instead, Knitter argued, the pope was generous and affirming, and he always underscored the great good to be found in other traditions. But these actions were not consistent with *Dominus Iesus.* "If we really believe Jews or Hindus would be better off as Christians," Knitter said, "why would we let good manners stop us from saying it to their faces?" Because, he said, even the pope recoiled from the official formulas generated by Ratzinger.

In fact, a majority of Catholics in every Western democracy polled on this issue agreed with Jacques Dupuis about salvation, a term that was undefined in *Dominus Iesus.* Dupuis said that most people will find salvation in some mysterious way, but that none of us quite knows how. Carlo Martini said as much two days after the release of *Dominus Iesus* in a pastoral letter out of Milan that many saw as an attempt to heal the hurt felt by many ecumenists from other Christian churches who had been engaged in fruitful dialogue with Catholic theologians for almost forty years. "Salvation," wrote Martini, "is possible for everyone, outside of any church, so long as they follow the will of God . . . and their own moral conscience."

For a month or more, some Vatican watchers saw and heard the pope equivocate on *Dominus Iesus.* He insisted that he had approved the document. But some dug up his numerous recent and not so recent quotes that endorsed the kind of respectful interreligious dialogue that Ratzinger's position paper condemned. Was Ratzinger simply trying to settle as many issues as he could before the pope moved on?

That is how Marco Politi analyzed the situation. He saw a connection between a whole series of backward steps in the Vatican through the summer of the Jubilee Year 2000, ending with *Dominus Iesus,* that proved Ratzinger and a few like-minded prelates in the Curia were doing everything possible to tie the hands of any possibly more liberal successor to the papacy.

To do that, Ratzinger did need allies in the Roman Curia. Two of the main men: Cardinal Giambattista Re, head of the Vatican's Congregation of Bishops, and Crescenzio Sepe, head of the Vatican office that supervised all the countries still considered "mission lands." As long as Ratzinger could count on Sepe, who had the penultimate say on new bishops in those mission territories, and Re, who vetted most of the appointments of bishops around the world, he was assured of what he needed most, a cadre of bishops who knew how to take orders.

Some might wonder why anyone but a few Church professionals should care about the appointments, promotions, and demotions of bishops. Wasn't this just a matter of "inside politics" in the Church? It was, but those power moves had grave ramifications for liberal Catholics at large, including a great many reform-minded priests who provided aid and comfort to them. Ratzinger's office had no more than thirty men employed to keep people in line; forty-six hundred bishops whose first loyalty was to Rome could pay far closer attention to those tempted to take positions in opposition to the Vatican, including even some independent-minded bishops.

Ratzinger had had a long-simmering dispute, for example, with some strong national conferences of bishops, most notably those of the United States, Brazil, and Germany. Vatican II had put its blessings on these national conferences because they were seen as an instrument for bishops to bring local credibility and local relevance to the teachings of the Church, particularly on matters of social justice, which, often as not, clashed with Ratzinger's right-wing political views. In 1995, Ratzinger prevailed upon the pope to decree that national conferences may not issue statements on any doctrinal or moral issue unless by unanimous vote, and the pope did so with an encyclical, *Apostolos Suos,* "His Apostles," in 1998. After that, both the pope and Ratzinger knew they would get far less flak from the world's bishops, from the Americans, from the bishops of England and Wales, from the Germans, too, who had given him grief over other issues, and from the bishops of the South Pacific, who had asked the pope, twice, to let them ordain married men, and twice were turned down. Theoretically, the bishops had the power to ordain any man they chose and, arguably, any woman. But when a reporter asked one bishop why he didn't ordain women, he replied: "Ratzinger would have me suspended in a New York minute. Ditto if I ordained married men." In the last four years of John Paul II's papacy, it was even less likely to find bishops with minds of their own; during that period, priests considered suitable for episcopal office were company men whose first instinct in any crisis compelled them to call Rome for advice.

By 2005, Rome had never had so much power, not during the record-breaking thirty-two-year reign of Pius IX in the nineteenth century, not during the reigns of the three Piuses of the early twentieth century. Much of the power was funneled into the suppression of free speech in the Church and of free inquiry by theologians who had felt empowered by the open charter written by the Fathers of Vatican II. Rome could encourage right-wing lay movements like Focolare, Communion and Liberation, and the Neocatechumenal Way (all three of them under the covert control of clerics) and give a great deal of grief to the most rambunctious religious orders (which didn't have to answer to local bishops, but only bucked them at their own political peril) and to organizations like Call to Action and Voice of the Faithful. Local bishops found it easy to marginalize these largely lay groups by decreeing they could not meet in Church-owned parish halls—or worse: in 1996, Bishop Fabian Bruskewitz, overly sure of himself, excommunicated members of Call to Action in his diocese of Lincoln, Nebraska.

In his twenty-four years at the Holy Office, Ratzinger could always congratulate himself for his orthodoxy. Despite the world outcry against *Dominus Iesus,* Ratzinger was quite unrepentant. He rarely allowed human emotion, or indeed any human consideration, to come between him and his stern duty to guard the faith or, as many of his targets insisted, to guard his own take on the faith. If theologians couldn't satisfy Ratzinger's own rigid, disembodied, gloomy view of the truth, they had to expect to suffer for it.

Catholic fundamentalists honored Ratzinger for his stern treatment of the Church's reform wing, even made him something of a hero (on Web sites like www.ratzingerfanclub.com, for instance) for standing firm against the worldly forces he was fighting from inside his fortress in the Palazzo del Sant'Ufficio. At the beginning of his tenure in the Holy Office, Ratzinger was battling theologians from Latin America who were expounding social change, even revolution, as some kind of gospel mandate. In the waning years of John Paul's papacy, he was turning the force of his office against a threat that was, to him, just as grave—from supposedly respected theologians willing to put the Buddha and Muhammad on almost the same level as Jesus.

And no bishop ever dared criticize. The Church—the hierarchical Church, at least—was in Ratzinger's pocket. If he had his way, the conclave would not turn its back on the perfection that he and John Paul had achieved.

CHAPTER ELEVEN

Postmortem

A Tsunami of Meaning

THEY VESTED John Paul's remains in a chasuble of deep red and placed a shepherd's crook under his left arm and a white miter on his head. The props were symbols to remind mourners this man was the shepherd of a worldwide flock and the bishop of Rome. They added another, noncanonical symbol when they slipped onto his feet the simple, slightly scuffed brown leather shoes he favored on all those trips around the earth.

Members of the papal household paid the first visit that evening during a short, solemn ceremony attended by all the cardinals who were in Rome, diplomats accredited to the Holy See, the mayor of Rome, and the president of Italy. In the Sala Clementina of the pope's palace, two Swiss Guards held stiffly in attendance, and Stanislaw Dziwisz, the pope's secretary, stood alone above the pope, a white handkerchief in his left hand. Cardinal Ratzinger knelt with his face in his hands. Cardinal Edward Szoka, a Detroiter who had held a job in the pope's cabinet, seemed close to tears. Some in the crowd fingered their rosaries.

Sunday papers all over the world published lengthy obits they'd been saving up (and rewriting and rewriting) for a decade or more. Robert D. McFadden, a veteran of forty-four years at the *New York Times,* did as well as anyone when he wrote that John Paul II was "a different kind of pope: complex, schooled in confrontation, theologically intransigent but deftly politic, full of wit and daring, energy and physically expressive love. More than outgoing, he was all-embracing—a bear-hugging, larger than life man of action."

On Monday morning, members and staff of the Roman Curia said their good-byes to John Paul II as he lay in state. "Good-bye" is a word rubbed smooth of its core meaning by overuse. "God be with ye" came across more clearly when we saw it in another language—in a ninety-six-point headline in the Rome daily *Il Messagero: "L'addio,"* "The Go with God." More than a thousand employees of Vatican City and their families stood in line later that morning to say their "Go with God's," along with members of the Vatican press corps, the public officials of Rome and their families, and even the flight captains and crews from Alitalia who had traveled so frequently and so far with the pope.

On Monday afternoon, the pope's master of ceremonies, Archbishop Piero Marini, assigned a dozen Swiss Guards in their red, yellow, and blue medieval uniforms to flank twelve pallbearers in gray tailcoats and white gloves as they made ready to bear the pope's remains out of the Sala Clementina to Saint Peter's. Marini had worked out the logistics with the directors of Vatican television to do something that had never been done before, to capture the unfolding of the rites that take place around the pope's body and broadcast them to the world in real time. This event was the first of many over the ensuing days, all calculated to enhance the sacred, solemn character of the papacy itself. They brought in seven television camera crews, who took their strategic posts to capture the solemn procession: out of the Sala Clementina, on the second floor of the Apostolic Palace; down a wide marble staircase; on to the first floor; into the Sala Ducale, and then the Sala Regia; down another staircase; through the hallway of the Constantine wing; through the bronze doors; into Saint Peter's Square; and thence into the basilica. Then they placed the pope's remains on the foot of the main altar, almost underneath the Bernini baldachino, the ten-story-high bronze canopy over the papal altar held up by four twisting bronze columns. They installed three television cameras in the basilica, and kept them running day and night for seventy-two hours, sending live images of the dead pope and the millions of mourners who were coming to see and say their good-byes. The images went out on a live feed that was picked up by Mediaset (the main private Italian network), CNN, Associated Press Television, Reuters, Sky News, and Televisa.

So everything was there, for everyone in the world to see on television. But rather than watch the show on television, it seemed that the whole world was trying to squeeze into Rome. By three in the afternoon on Monday, people were fast-walking up the Via della Conciliazione toward Saint Peter's Square, compressed between heavy metal fences, a flood of people backing up a half mile, almost to the Tiber. By nine in the evening, the river of humanity, perhaps fifty people wide, was now snaking through the Borgo, the neighborhood around the Vatican, and back up to the Piazza Risorgimento.

The authorities in Rome were prepared. Four different kinds of police kept the crowd moving. Hundreds of volunteers from the Protezione Civile Volontariato, all wearing black jumpsuits with their local affiliations splashed across their backs in yellow letters, handed out ten-ounce plastic water bottles donated by a company called Egeria. The volunteers stood along the route, which police kept changing as the crowd doubled, then tripled in size and tripled again, finally extending across the Tiber and trailing up the Corso Vittorio Emmanuele into the center of Rome.

They closed Roman airspace once they determined that President Bush was coming. Antiaircraft batteries outside the city went on alert, naval ships patrolled the Mediterranean coast, and combat jets from Italy's air force, joined by an AWACS surveillance plane deployed by NATO, guarded the city. Italian security agencies posted snipers on rooftops and elite teams of the paramilitary police called *carabinieri,* armed with automatic rifles, stood at every major intersection in Rome.

Many pilgrims came from Poland, where the airlines put on extra flights, parishes chartered buses, and a long queue formed at Warsaw's central station for those trying to buy train tickets for the twenty-two-hour journey. Many Poles drove their cars—a twenty-four-hour, nonstop drive from Warsaw to Rome.

Meanwhile, the cardinal-electors were streaming into Rome, too. The cardinals were met at Stazione Termini or at Fiumicino Airport and driven to the city's finer hotels, or to the biggest suites at the Church's national colleges. They reconnoitered as quickly as they could with their friends in the Roman Curia, and made moves to meet with their counterparts from other nations, all of them attempting to be part of the *prattiche,* the informal (and legitimate) political conversations being pursued all over Rome by cardinals and their ecclesiastical allies. Many cardinals admitted that they didn't know half of the 115 men who would enter the conclave. "At present," said Keith Michael Patrick O'Brien of Saint Andrews and Edinburgh when he arrived in Rome, "I couldn't put many names to many faces."

John Paul II's funeral was one of those moments in history—actually four days in April 2005—when the event itself overwhelmed any single attempt to describe it, much less explain it. Most funerals are exercises in memory and identity. We take the occasion to remember our loved ones; with their departure, memory is often the only thing we have left of them. The memory, in turn, helps us recall who we are—sons, daughters, grandsons, granddaughters who are proud to carry on the family name and the family traditions. Funerals of the great are a little more than that, because their memories recall earthshaking triumphs and tragedies that will be chronicled forever. John Paul II's funeral was that kind of manifestation, one for the history books.

Homer, the world's greatest epic poet, took most of the twenty-third chapter of the *Iliad* to describe the last rites for Patroclus, a fallen hero in the Trojan War whose memory sent Achilles, his friend and cowarrior, into tears and incoherent rage. Other funerals in modern times made the *Guinness Book of Records* for the number of people they drew: up to a million mourners at the funerals of Mohandas Gandhi on January 30, 1948, of Joseph Stalin on March 9, 1953, and of Mao Zedong on September 9, 1976, all political figures. A man of religion had had the record until now: perhaps 3 million people had mourned Ayatollah Khomeini's death in Iran over a period of several days in 1989 amid great disorder; eight people lay dead after that event and some ten thousand were injured.

Now Rome had a funeral that probably broke that record, with no attendant disorder, and the world's media was there to record the story. It was a story that the media itself had helped create, for few would have come at all if radio and television had not trumpeted the pope's demise.

But how could the media not report the news that the world's most visible man was gone? As soon as confirmation came from the Rome bureaus of AP, Reuters, and Agence France-Presse, broadcasters were on the air, and newspapers around the world rebuilt their front pages and pulled up obituaries that had been banked long ago. Friends told friends by e-mail and they, in turn, passed the message to their friends. A new communication tool favored mostly by the young, the cell phone text message, not only helped spread the news; it helped make the news by bringing thousands of young people to Rome. Many cell phone text messages said, in a number of different codes, in various languages: "pope dead rome bound cya st peters."

In the first twenty-four hours, at least 2 million people poured into Rome, doubling the population of the city itself. That drew more media. T. J. Jones, one of sixteen staff members at the Pontifical Council for Social Communications, reported that his office had handed out credentials to more than eight thousand still and television cameramen—including permission for five film crews being dispatched by Mel Gibson. Somehow, all the media people and all the pilgrims found a place to sleep. City officials suggested (by sending out text messages) that citizens take people into their shops and homes, to eat, to wash up, to get a drink of water. Many Poles slept on the cobblestones near the Castel Sant'Angelo. Some slept in their cars or vans. Some set up tent cities outside Rome. On the Via Flaminia, just below the Villa Borghese, many who had spent the night in their vehicles were startled on Thursday morning to find Romans waking them up with cups of coffee.

The people of Rome didn't seem alarmed. They hadn't seen the passing of a pope for almost twenty-seven years, and so, when the flood began, they smiled (after all, these invaders weren't Visigoths) and told themselves how fortunate they were to be Romans, even though, finally, they were trapped in their own city.

Guido Bertolaso, Rome's special security commissioner, finally decided to close the city. "We've got to stop the flow," he told the security chiefs, one of whom agreed vigorously. "It's impossible," he said, "to control the moods, reactions, and intentions of four million people. They are a risk to themselves." Just after midnight on Thursday, city officials banned vehicle traffic in the inner city.

"The crowds forced us to stay in our homes for almost three days," said Gerardo Terzi, a Roman living in a posh home in the Villa del Rufo, "but we didn't mind. This is part of what it means to be a Roman. We need a pope here, more than we need a prime minister or a president. And when we don't have one, we are anxious."

The headline writers for Rome's daily newspapers settled on the same word to describe the coming of so many people: they called it a tsunami, a tidal wave like the one they had seen on television news rising up in the Indian Ocean some three months before. They knew what had caused that tidal wave in Asia, a sudden shift of tectonic plates on the floor of the sea. But what shift in the course of human events brought this tidal wave of humanity to Rome?

Reporters observed that most of this impromptu horde was composed of young people, so some assumed the invasion was a spontaneous manifestation of love for John Paul II, who had made the hugely attended youth days that rallied millions of kids to himself an unforgettable marker in his papacy.

Had this crowd come for their love of this pope? Not necessarily, although that's what members of Communion and Liberation wanted everyone to think. Not twenty-fours after the death of the pope, they were out in the streets with a brochure proclaiming the last loving words of the pope just before he died: "I looked for you. Now you have come to me. And I thank you." According to Renato Buzzonetti, the pope's physician, John Paul II was unable to speak for some days before he expired. So these words were a concoction, designed to play up John Paul's greatness, even on his deathbed. Make him a ghostly presence at the conclave and you help assure the continuation of his programs and policies. The leaders of Focolare decided they could do that best by promoting a campaign for the immediate proclamation of John Paul's sainthood. They planted a banner on the set of *Porta a Porta,* Rome's most popular television talk show, that read SANTO SUBITO, "Saint Now." In the next few days, the same SANTO SUBITO banners popped up all over town.

"John Paul II is undoubtedly in heaven, which is what 'saint' means," said one Roman priest-professor at the time. "Very few people aren't. But demanding his immediate canonization at this moment is an entirely political act. I wonder who has the most to gain from this campaign?"

Some of the press people wondered, too. A good many print reporters (by now, their numbers had swollen to thirty-five hundred) tried to observe and interview some of the thousands who were standing in line to see the pope lying in state. The journalists noted immediately that not many of them were mourners in any traditional sense; they saw few sad faces, even fewer tearful ones. These people looked more like children on their way to a picnic. Some sang. Some played guitars. Practically all displayed a smiling patience that belied their discomfort as they inched their way forward for hours. Reporters' questions came naturally: Who are you? Where did you come from? Why are you here? These pilgrims replied honestly, but few of them were articulate enough to explain their presence.

"Being here in Rome," said Christian Cornelis Schouter, a twenty-three-year-old exchange student from Leiden, in the Netherlands, "I cannot afford not to be here." Schouter was very well dressed for the occasion—black suit, black shirt, gray tie. "This is a one-time opportunity. I did not witness the last papal change. Okay. So I am not going to miss this one. This is bigger than any political event." He said he was a Catholic, "but not a particularly devoted Catholic," and he had no special love for the departed pope. His presence was more about his own need and his wish to be part of what was happening than it was about any special connection with the soul of a great man who had claimed solidarity with his parents' generation and then again with his. Whether he quite realized it or not, Christian was a pilgrim in something like the medieval sense of the word because he not only came on foot without food or water, but he stayed on foot for more than six hours, on into the night. He was among the lucky ones who were the first to arrive.

James Hentges, a priest in a religious order called the Croziers, founded during the Crusades, was standing in line at midnight. He'd been inching his way ahead for six hours, and he would stand in line for another six. "It almost killed me," he said three days later, still recovering from the ordeal. "I am not sure I would ever do anything like this again, but I did it." Maybe it was the challenge. He didn't bother to drink the free bottles of water that were offered along the way. He didn't want to visit the portable toilets that the city of Rome had placed in green rows along the avenues. "I thought they'd be foul," he said. (He was right. How could they not be?)

Many came to Rome because John Paul II was a piece of their lives. Michael Novak, the American political pundit and philosopher, arrived in Rome on Air Force One with the president of the United States. He didn't have to wait in line; he entered the Basilica of Saint Peter with President and Mrs. George W. Bush and two former presidents, George H. W. Bush and Bill Clinton, through a special side door. Novak would later write of the occasion on his Web site: "What a sadness to see him lying there dead, but also a joy just to be there, to be able to say a silent goodbye. It would have been so awful not to get the chance. It was like having a big tree at the edge of the forest come down, and feeling the wind on your face. The Poles felt like that today. So did I." His sister, Mary Ann Novak, who had held high posts in the administrations of three presidents (Carter, Reagan, and Bush I) caught a commercial jet for Rome in Washington, D.C., checked into her hotel, took a shower and a quick nap, and then stood in line from 4 p.m. until 8 a.m. for a final glimpse of her beloved pope. Her brother said, "She did it, she survived sixteen hours in line, and is thrilled to death to have done it."

Francesca Shin, a slim and practically penniless graduate student from Korea with the good looks of a model, flew into Rome from London on Thursday morning, stood in line for a dozen hours to say her *addio* to John Paul II, and then couldn't quite explain what had compelled her. "I couldn't really afford the plane ticket, but I just had to be here." But she said she felt as warm and close to the pope as she did to her own father, a college professor in Korea.

Andrew Greeley, an American priest best known for his novels, tapped into his academic background (he has published eighty-eight works on sociology) to analyze the crowd. He found something arresting in the fact that many of the young people he saw being interviewed on CNN spoke of the pope as father, or even grandfather. "I have a notion," Greeley said, "that John Paul II came to fill a kind of paternity gap in many families. Families today are very mobile. That often puts children out of touch with their grandparents, even their own fathers. In Pope John Paul, I think they saw in him a grandfather figure."

The Swiss theologian Han Küng wrote in *Der Spiegel,* "Don't be fooled by the crowds. Millions have left the Catholic Church under Pope John Paul II's leadership. The Catholic Church is in dire straits." It wasn't only professional critics like Küng who made that observation. On April 7, *Corriere della Sera* had a story that carried the headline "A Full Square and Empty Churches: The Latest Italian Paradox."

Whatever the answer to that paradox, the fact was that from five in the afternoon on April 4 until three in the morning on April 8, more than 3 million men and women, boys and girls flowed into Saint Peter's Basilica for an up-close look at the deceased pontiff that lasted ten seconds. But once they finally made it inside the basilica and headed toward the main altar, they beheld a sight that will remain in their memory forever: hundreds of people ahead of them in the aisle of the gigantic church, many of them with one hand held high, snapping cell phone photos of the pope and transmitting them back home to their loved ones, hundreds of cell phone screens all reflecting the same image to those behind them: that of the dead pope, stretched out stiffly in his red chasuble and his odd hat and his scuffed brown shoes.

On the morning of the funeral itself, Friday, April 8, Letta Tayler, a reporter for Long Island's *Newsday* who had flown into Rome from Baghdad to cover this story, found four New York Jews, Nan Gerson and her husband, Larry, and their friends Jeffery and Jan Scherr, who told her they "didn't have much affinity with the pope's views" and knew they wouldn't understand the funeral service, but were determined to watch it on a giant television screen in the Piazza del Popolo, some two miles away from the Vatican. Tayler went with them, to report on the funeral through their eyes. Nan Gerson told her, "The pope made his mark on the world and even though we are Jewish we can't not recognize his greatness."

At 10 a.m. Friday morning, network television cameras showed the funeral scene from a dozen different angles—panoramic, extreme close-ups, simple, grand. A huge tabletop altar was covered with white linen; it was fronted by four giant white candles, two clumps of greenery, and a twenty-foot crucifix. In front of that, John Paul II's body rested safely in a huge, closed, almost-red cypress casket, a huge white book of the gospels lying open on top of it, and a dark, rich Persian carpet below. Before the great doors of Saint Peter's, the cardinals sat arrayed in all their mitered grandeur, flanked by the purple of many bishops sitting a level below them, and rows upon rows of dignitaries: at least 138 heads of government and heads of state (including a dozen from Muslim countries). Among the dark suits of presidents and the black mantillas worn by their wives, one could identify the *ghotras* of Arab sheikhs, the turbans of mullahs and imams, the yarmulkes of rabbis, the saffron robes of Buddhists.

Largely unseen by the multitude, some fascinating encounters were taking place among the VIPs. Zimbabwe's Robert Mugabe was shaking the hand of Tony Blair. Syria's Bashar al-Assad was reaching out to Israeli president Moshe Katsav, and Katsav, who was born in Iran and speaks Farsi, spent almost an hour afterward talking to Iranian president Mohammad Khatami. "Maybe this is going to be this pope's greatest gift, that so many people have come here and have come to admire his influence and his willingness to get along," said Tom McCarthy, a seventy-year-old priest from Portland, Oregon. "Maybe this is what we needed in the world right now, a reason to come together."

The images were beamed live around the globe, across Europe, to North and South America, the Pacific, and back to the Persian Gulf, an estimated 3 billion people watching in eighty-one countries as Cardinal Joseph Ratzinger came front and center. As dean of the College of Cardinals, he was the principal celebrant at the mass. He could have delegated anyone to give the homily. That he didn't should have been a clue that Ratzinger was intent on making his leadership known to two audiences: (1) the largest chunk of humanity that had ever watched a funeral together and (2) a tiny group of 115 cardinal-electors goggling at an unusual show of rhetoric and power on the part of a man they had always known as entirely soft-spoken and shy.

But this was a crucial time in the passing of papal power, and no time for Ratzinger to be timid. He made the most of his opportunity, not to deliver a theological reflection on heaven and hell to this very mixed audience, but to tell stories about Karol Wojtyla and his spiritual journey. He ended his narrative with a confession of his feelings for John Paul II. "Today we bury his remains in the earth as a seed of immortality. Our hearts are full of sadness, yet at the same time of joyful hope and profound gratitude."

Then he looked up to that familiar window, the third one from the left on the third floor of the Apostolic Palace, where John Paul II had so often greeted the faithful. Raising his head to that window, Ratzinger said in a high, reedy voice, "None of us can ever forget how in that last Easter Sunday of his life"—not two weeks before—"the Holy Father, marked by suffering, came once more to the window of the Apostolic Palace and one last time gave his blessing *urbi et orbi*."

It was a piece of histrionics that might have suggested (to Americans in the audience at least) Abraham Lincoln at Gettysburg. "We can be sure," Ratzinger said, "that our beloved pope is standing today at the window of the Father's house, that he sees us and blesses us." And then, in direct address to the dead pope worthy of a Demosthenes or a Pericles: "Yes, bless us, Holy Father."

Good rhetoric not only enlightens minds. It enkindles hearts. And Ratzinger became for a moment a man who set on fire all the hearts that were feeling with him. Through the whole expanse of the square, and in twenty-five of Rome's majestic piazzas where thousands assisted at the funeral as it was beamed to them on giant television screens, the multitude erupted in applause (as it had already done eleven times during the ceremony). A clattering helicopter high above (the only flying machine allowed over Rome that day) sent images all over the world, cutting from close-ups of Cardinal Ratzinger to long shots of the simple cypress coffin to shots of young men holding up the same eight-foot-long banners, all printed in the same typeface, reading SANTO SUBITO.

The three-hour service began in sunlight, but as the moment for burial grew near, a deepening layer of clouds rolled in, the air chilled, and the breeze picked up until the cardinals were forced to press their red caps to their heads and let their vestments whip in the wind. Above the pilgrims in the square a lone seagull circled, then there were two, then three, before they drifted away on the now-quickening breeze. Those same freshets picked up the flags held aloft by the pilgrims from all over the world. The red-and-white banners of Poland, the stars and stripes of the United States, the astral sphere of Brazil, the tricolor of France, and the red-and-yellow bands of Spain were all to be expected. But here was the spinning wheel of India, there the Southern Cross of Samoa. The Lebanese cedar flew, even the crescent and star of Pakistan. The air grew colder, the clouds denser, until finally the coffin of John Paul II was carried inside the basilica. Then, a brief moment of sun.

Only a couple of hours later, when all the ceremonies were over, did the rains begin.

And then the people departed whence they had come, quite content, most of them, to let the cardinals enter into an arcane process that was designed almost a thousand years ago and amended through the centuries to make it ever more mysterious, the selection of a new pope.

CHAPTER TWELVE

Conclave

One Smart Move After Another

FOR A WEEK, during the preconclave, the cardinals had been meeting on a daily basis, at first to work out the details of the papal funeral and then to prepare themselves for the conclave itself, now set for April 18. Part of the preparations was to meet one another and talk, formally and informally. But many of the new cardinals were like college freshmen on the first day of class. They stood back while the returning upperclassmen embraced one another, wanting to join in the conversations but unable to because they had a hard time understanding the Italian discourse, and unwilling to because they felt they had nothing to contribute.

Kieran O'Reilly, the superior general of the Missionaries of Africa who had two African cardinals staying at his order's headquarters on Rome's Via Nocetta during their period before the conclave, said, "They'd go off to the daily meetings and come home totally bewildered." According to O'Reilly, these cardinals, also archbishops of large cities in the third world, came unprepared because they'd been spending sixteen hours a day on the affairs of their own church at home. "They'd had no time," said O'Reilly, "for anything else. Now they had to see if they could play catch-up."

"One hundred and thirteen of us were there for the first time," said Cardinal Wilfrid Fox Napier, the Franciscan archbishop of Durban, South Africa. "I went into the conclave a complete tabula rasa. I might as well have gone in there blindfolded and picked any name off the list." Cardinal Jean-Claude Turcotte of Montreal said, "It was a little like the Tower of Babel. It wasn't always easy to understand one another. We looked for a common language. Sometimes we settled on Latin."

At first, all the daily meetings were conducted in Italian, without simultaneous translation. This lack of consideration for those who did not understand Italian may not have been a deliberate attempt to marginalize one whole bloc of electors, but that was the effect of the leadership's oversight (or, possibly, its foresight). It created an inner circle of men in the know.

The less-informed cardinals in the outer circle could, of course, try to take a knowing cardinal aside and seek his advice. During the first few days of the preconclave, many of them, in fact, made their way to the Jesuit headquarters near the Vatican each afternoon and evening to consult with Cardinal Martini in a series of meetings that finally left him exhausted. Others were more inclined to seek advice from the cardinals in the Curia, with whom they had had a good many dealings over the years, and from whom they had received considerable financial assistance. Many of these curial cardinals could and did tell them to vote for Cardinal Ratzinger.

Some cardinals sought help in learning more about potential candidates from the Internet, where they could find profiles aplenty of the so-called *papabili* on various Web sites, and from the online editions of the world's media, which was taking an unprecedented interest in this election. Since the pope's death, the Italian press, in particular, had been running as many as a dozen pages every day on the leading figures in the conclave. Some of those stories were puff pieces, intended to curry favor with the Italian prelates who didn't mind seeing their lives celebrated in print. Angelo Sodano, Crescenzio Sepe, and Gianbattista Re, all of the Roman Curia, and Camillo Ruini, the vicar of Rome, had to smile when they read stories about themselves, not only in the daily Italian press but in the larger newspapers' huge, glossy feature supplements as well. The stories were careful to say these men were not seeking the papal throne, but rather that the Church was seeking *them*. None of these cardinals were credible candidates who could conceivably win seventy-seven votes, which is what it would take to equal the necessary, winning two-thirds majority of the college.

It was a fiction to think that, since half the Catholics in the world lived in Latin America, the cardinals might elect a pope to represent that vast constituency. The papacy isn't a gift to be bestowed. It is a responsibility given to men of purpose who have the political skills to marshal support. In 2005, not every cardinal had these skills, and some of those with those skills didn't want to be pope. To get the job, you had to want the job.

All those other *papabili* were simply names on an ephemeral honor roll. Two Brazilians made the list: Cláudio Hummes of São Paulo and Geraldo Majella Agnelo of São Salvador da Bahia. So did a Jesuit from Argentina, Jorge Mario Bergoglio, the ascetic archbishop of Buenos Aires. Darío Castrillón Hoyos, a Colombian in the Roman Curia, got a mention, as did Rodríguez Maradiaga, Jaime Lucas Ortega y Alamino of Havana, Cuba, and Norberto Rivera Carrera of Mexico City.

But the Latin American cardinals made no effort to pool votes for one of their own. In fact, according to Alejandro Bermúdez, the editor of the Lima-based *ACI Prensa,* a man who was close to Lima's Cardinal Juan Luis Cipriani Thorne, most of the region's twenty cardinals were satisfied that John Paul II had placed Latin Americans in powerful bastions of a Rome bureaucracy once dominated by Italians. "The Latin Americans do not feel neglected. Having a Latin American pope was simply not a priority for them."

The French press put two antique cardinals on their honor roll: Jean-Marie Lustiger, who was seventy-eight, the recently retired archbishop of Paris, born of a Jewish family in Poland and adopted by French Catholics during World War II, and eighty-two-year-old Roger Etchegaray, once the archbishop of Marseilles, and then a prominent and eloquent curial cardinal, who not only had presided at any of a number of Church meetings over the past few years but had also made two highly publicized trips to China to explore the possibilities of establishing diplomatic relations with Beijing. Other European magazines and news agencies profiled Godfried Danneels of Belgium (who had just returned from his own trip to Beijing), Karl Lehmann of Mainz, and Christoph von Schönborn of Austria.

These cardinals had no chance of being pope because they had not done the kind of serious precampaigning needed to win a majority in a quick conclave. And because of perceived media pressure, those managing this affair wanted a quick one. Francis Arinze, the smiling black cardinal from Nigeria, had done some discreet campaigning; he spent the last five years traveling in pursuit of connections, and he actually thought the college, to prove it was not racist, might turn to him. When, early in 2005, Ratzinger told the German newspaper *Die Welt* he would personally consider an African pope "a good sign for the whole of Christianity," Ratzinger was simply exercising his own political charm; some read it as a subtle pitch for a dozen African votes in the conclave—for himself.

It still seemed unlikely that the conclave would make Ratzinger the next pope. Only once, in 1566, had a man who led the Holy Office been elected pope, when the Dominican friar Antonio Ghislieri, a harsh anti-Semite, became Pius V. The editor of *America,* Tom Reese, said the cardinals—75 percent of them from outside the Roman Curia—would not elect someone from inside the Curia. But Ratzinger's public image as grand inquisitor didn't bother many of his fellows. Many of those who had met Ratzinger in private over the past few years (those visiting Rome usually make it a point to stop at the Holy Office) found him a gentle listener, a gracious, soft-spoken-in-five-languages scholar. They were, morever, already inclined to like the thrust of his leadership, so much in line with that of the pope who had created their own eminence.

According to the most popular cliché of the preconclave period, no one could fill the gigantic shoes of John Paul II. The fact was that no one could fill those shoes simply because Ratzinger was already in them. Increasingly over the past four years, he had become a virtual incumbent, making most of the papal decisions, writing many of the papal speeches, acting behind the scenes in ways the pope could not.

In January 2004, for example, he was doing something the pope should have done long before, and hadn't. He had a meeting in Rome with Anne Burke, an appellate court justice in Illinois who was appointed to chair the American bishops' review board to oversee how the American Church was dealing with its priest-pedophiles. Burke told Ratzinger and several of his aides that one uncooperative American bishop after another had stonewalled the board's investigations, quite sure they had the Vatican's backing to soft-pedal the scandal. After spending nearly three hours in Ratzinger's office, she came away convinced she had gotten through to him. "I don't know if he was misled, all I know is that we had a different story to tell him," she told members of the American press when she returned home. "I think he was surprised at what we had to tell him."

A month later, the pope had a new script for the American bishops. Reading from a text that was almost certainly written in Ratzinger's office, the pope told a group of five bishops from Pennsylvania and New Jersey who were in Rome for their *ad limina* visit that they needed to be open to their people so as "not to run the risk of distancing the pastor from the members of his flock," whom they should involve by creating "better structures of participation, consultation, and shared responsibility."

Lest no one think the Vatican was endorsing democracy in the Church, Ratzinger had fed the pope a dose of double-talk: no one should understand moves of this kind "as a concession to a secular 'democratic' model of governance, but as a necessary means of strengthening their episcopal authority."

Ratzinger didn't like democracy in the Church. But in the fall of 2004, he involved himself in one of the institutions of American democracy, the presidential election campaign. He was egged on, shamefully so, by six bishops who didn't think John Kerry, a Boston Catholic, was fit for the presidency. They were the kind of bishops whose first instinct in any difficulty was to call Rome. Significantly, they went to Ratzinger, not to the pope—and asked him for an opinion on John Kerry, whom they said was "pro-abortion." Ratzinger wrote a letter that said Catholic candidates who supported abortion could well be denied communion. That led to a dispute among the American bishops, many of whom felt they shouldn't use the Eucharist as a political tool. Ratzinger's intent may have been a worthy one, but his action in writing the letter (it implied that Kerry wasn't a very good Catholic) effectively won the November election for George W. Bush.

For a man who eschewed politics, Ratzinger had begun, over the past twelve months, to look and talk like he was running for something. He had rarely spoken to the press, but now his own byline began appearing in newspapers all over Europe, and he started giving interviews to reporters he had long ignored. In August 2004, he told *Le Figaro* of Paris that the European Union would make a huge mistake if it admitted Turkey to EU membership, because a Muslim country did not belong in a Christian Europe. "The entrance of Turkey into this community would also imply that God has nothing to do with public life and with the basis of the state." His remark implied that God is present to Christian nations, but not to a Muslim nation.

In an editorial, the *New York Times* pointed out that Turkey was a determinedly secular republic of 70 million people trying to emulate the American model of church-state separation. The *Times* said: "Like meddlesome clerics the world over, Cardinal Ratzinger is inflaming an important political debate. He is elevating religious differences over political process and personal beliefs over values that are universal, not a Judeo-Christian monopoly."

Ratzinger was undaunted. He knew the editors of the *Times* wouldn't have a vote in the upcoming conclave; he continued to meddle in other people's political affairs. On September 19, 2004, Ratzinger gave a key interview to *La Repubblica* that outlined his objections to a pending law in Spain authorizing gay marriage. Cardinals from Spain thanked him for that.

Few noticed that the Ratzinger campaign train was gathering steam, though *Time* magazine did so in January 2005 when it quoted a well-placed Vatican insider: "The Ratzinger solution is definitely on. There was a stigma. He rises above that now." *Time* later called the Ratzinger effort, promoted as it was by "the conservative Italian intelligentsia," a stealth campaign.

The push for Ratzinger became clearer in February 2005, when the leaders of Communion and Liberation, who had ties to Italy's prime minister, Silvio Berlusconi, invited Ratzinger to Milan to deliver a eulogy at the funeral of their founder, Luigi Giussani. Normally, Cardinal Dionigi Tettamanzi, the archbishop of Milan, would give the homily at this event, and he did. But Ratzinger upstaged him with an eloquent tribute to Giusanni. Ratzinger had no script, but the members of Communion and Liberation did. They gave Ratzinger thundering applause and responded to Tettamanzi with silence. Politi said this was a blow to Tettamanzi's campaign, a boost for Ratzinger's.

On February 22, Ratzinger took center stage again, to present John Paul II's latest book, *Memory and Identity,* to a news conference in the Palazzo Colonna. It was the pope's fifth book, Ratzinger said, and it was going to press in eleven languages. The book talked a good deal about Mehmet Ali Agca, the pope's would-be assassin, who, Ratzinger said, had written to him frequently to ask if the mystery of Fatima contains an answer to what was apparently still a puzzle to him, why he shot the pope. (Ratzinger said it didn't.)

On March 25, Good Friday, Ratzinger stood in for the pope, too ill now to preside at a huge Way of the Cross ceremony at Rome's Colosseum. He delivered a little sermon at each of the fourteen stations of the cross. At the ninth station, the scourging at the pillar, a moment when preachers traditionally bid penitents to ponder their sins of the flesh, he delivered a bitter text about the need to cleanse the Church of "filth"—an apparent reference to the sex scandals now plaguing the priesthood across the globe.

Ratzinger was not only establishing himself as the man in charge, he was also nailing down a campaign theme, that it was time to get tough with God's enemies. He used the theme in an earlier interview in *La Repubblica:* "God has been put on the sidelines. In political life, it seems almost indecent to speak of God, as if it were an attack on the freedom of those who do not believe."

While cardinals from the party of change dithered, unable to come up with a credible candidate or a theme, Ratzinger proceeded to demonstrate his popability through the entire preconclave period, from April 2, the day the pope died, until April 18, the day of the first ballot. From his position as dean of the college, Ratzinger could seize every opportunity to take center stage. And he did—at the pope's funeral, as chairman of the cardinals' daily meetings, and finally at the mass on the first morning of the conclave. More important, he was in a position to turn down the volume on the only other campaign going on in Rome, the media's own campaign to find a proper pope.

For the first week, many American cardinals assisted in the alternate media campaign, by doing radio, television, and newspaper interviews implying they could pick anyone, their choice to be determined by the unseen power of the Holy Spirit, who, presumably, would tell them how to vote.

Michael Novak, who stayed in Rome after John Paul's funeral, didn't believe the bishops really meant that, and that, if they did, they were wrong. Novak wouldn't dare say this openly now (he has turned quite conservative), though he might have forty years ago when he was reporting on Vatican II for *Time* magazine and producing a brilliant book on the Council, *The Open Church*.

Novak's blog about the Holy Spirit, written during the interregnum, helped give a fine explanation of the widely misunderstood role of the Holy Spirit in the conclave:

> Don't try to imagine a puppeteer pulling strings. The better image is that of the novelist, creating free, living, breathing, conflicted characters who make choices, and in doing so tell with these choices a magnificent story of liberty. The novelist who plays puppeteer convinces few readers that his characters are real. Real artistry lies in creating characters who are free, and who act from within the depths of their own liberty. So it is with the Artistry of the Holy Spirit in the theater of the conclaves down the centuries—a free God, Who chooses to be honored by the flawed efforts of free humans to respond to Him in their own liberty. The God of liberty.

Reporters at the conclave should have been interviewing Novak. Instead, they flocked to the side of prelates like Ted McCarrick, the affable cardinal from Washington, D.C. "We couldn't pay for this kind of advertising," he said—in gratitude, perhaps, for all the priceless exposure. McCarrick and other American cardinals scheduled a spate of news conferences at the North American College for the print press, and they agreed to sit-down interviews with the television networks. They had nothing very enlightening to say, mainly banalities about the sense of high responsibility they felt going into the conclave, but like Hollywood starlets doing guest turns on late-night television, they enjoyed the attention. For more than two years, the sex-abuse scandal had won them a hugely negative press. Now they were heroes—for simply talking with the media.

They weren't heroes to Cardinal Ratzinger. Their coziness with the press made this conclave look like a political convention. Ratzinger wanted it to resemble a retreat. In 1996, he had helped John Paul II set rules to make this conclave a holy affair, where the cardinals would meet in prayerful solitude, far from the madding crowd, giving no heed to the media. To help lessen the media influence in the week before the conclave, Ratzinger seized leadership in the three-man troika supposed to be making key decisions during the interregnum. Seldom keen himself on giving interviews to the press, he used the rudeness of the press itself as an excuse to shut them off completely.

After someone complained to Ratzinger that broadcast reporters had begun setting upon stray cardinals while they were walking through Saint Peter's Square, waving microphones in their faces and demanding answers to questions that called for ten-minute-long replies or none at all, he made his move. On April 6, he suggested the cardinals lighten their burden by voting not to talk to the press. One cardinal objected: "How can we cut off our own reporters? We've already given them interviews. We intend giving them more." Another said, "The world's media is here. That means the whole world is here. You're suggesting we turn our backs on them?" A third cardinal said, "We can't disappoint the extraordinary interest the world has taken—in the papacy, and in the future of the Church."

Ratzinger pulled back, said he would take the matter under advisement, then returned the next day with a more palatable plan. "We can give interviews," he said, "that discuss the figure of John Paul II and his legacy. We can talk about the problems the Church faces, but we shouldn't be talking about the discussions we are having in here, or speculating on the candidates." He did not call for a vote on that recommendation until he was sure he had a majority on his side.

But he was working on that. During the preconclave, he had displayed winning skills as leader of the troika. (The cardinals did not see much of the other two members.) After the Scots cardinal Keith Michael Patrick O'Brien told Ratzinger he couldn't understand Italian, Ratzinger brought in simultaneous translators. When he noted that the Africans and the Asians were holding back, Ratzinger called for everyone to prepare seven-minute "interventions." The ostensible purpose: so they could talk about the problems in their churches and tell the conclavists what the next pope might consider doing about them. Many did so. And when Ratzinger noticed those who didn't speak up, he made a special point of inviting them to speak, addressing each of them by name.

Cardinal Zubeir Wako of Khartoum gave one of the most rousing speeches, about the blatant persecutions suffered by the Christians of all stripes in the Sudan at the hands of some Muslim warlords. Though he did not say that a religious war was going on in the Sudan, he complained that the warlords were well funded by Islam, while the needs of Sudanese Catholics were being ignored by their own Church and by the leaders of Western nations who did not see Sudan as having strategic importance. But Zubeir Wako's intervention did not suggest any concrete actions that his fellow cardinals (or a new pope) might take to help the people of Sudan.

Other than Zubeir Wako and one other cardinal who said that, whoever the next pope was, he should consider taking no foreign trips at all, most of those who spoke were rather boring, according to Cardinal Achille Silvestrini, who recalled what had happened in the conclave of 1978. "In nineteen seventy-eight," he said, "a number of cardinals had critical things to say about [the just-deceased] Pope Paul VI." (One of them was Ratzinger.) In 2005, according to Cardinal Silvestrini, only one cardinal had anything negative to say about John Paul II's policies; the charge was that the pope had exercised almost dictatorial control over the world's bishops.

If Silvestrini was right, then this preconclave wasn't bringing to a focus some of the Church's most crying needs, needs that had only grown more acute in a papacy dedicated to maintaining the status quo. Other cardinals confirmed this: no one spoke about the worldwide priest shortage, or made any suggestions about alleviating it. No one spoke about the alienation of women in the Church, particularly younger women who were leaving the Church in disgust because it had no use for them outside catechetics and motherhood. One cardinal said it was almost as if John Paul II himself were present in this assembly, frowning as he had done so often in the synods at anyone who sounded even slightly critical of his agenda. But as a theologian in Rome suggested, maybe the ghost of John Paul II did have a virtual seat in the conclave. "John Paul II was here inside the psyches of most of the cardinals he had appointed. Those who didn't carry Papa Wojtyla inside them were rare birds."

On Saturday morning, April 9, the day after his performance at the funeral, Ratzinger made a move that effectively stopped the rare birds from singing in public. He asked the cardinals to put themselves in silence with the media, making the case as he called for a vote that "the press is too much with us." He was seconded by an American cardinal in the Roman Curia who told one reporter that the press had made Rome "into a zoo." Not one hand went up in opposition, not even the hand of Godfried Danneels, who had told a news conference a week before that the electors had a natural right to speak to the press.

In a communiqué later that morning, Navarro-Valls, the papal spokesman, gave the press the bad news. The College of Cardinals had decided unanimously to avoid interviews and meetings with the media, so they could "enter a period of more intense silence and prayer." Possibly embarrassed—because the media had given the Vatican's show such a magnificent international staging for many days running—Navarro-Valls added, "This should not be interpreted as a snub to the media but a gesture of great responsibility." Now the cardinals who had been so gabby during the previous week went suddenly silent.

"It's a ridiculous move," said Thomas J. Reese, the Jesuit editor of *America* magazine, who had come to Rome to comment on the papal funeral extravaganza for CNN and other broadcast outlets. "The only cardinals who will go along with that are the American cardinals. Other cardinals will continue to speak on background to their favorite reporters."

Indeed, as the American cardinals turned mum with the media, curial cardinals continued to chat with the Italian press. Rome's Sunday newspapers were filled with articles about the preconclave's progress, some of them informed by a good many leaks "from sources inside the college." That afternoon, Cardinal William Keeler of Baltimore stood before a group of American religion editors (scheduled long before), uttered little more than a word of welcome, and said he couldn't answer any questions.

Reese tried to explain why all this was happening. "The Vatican loves the media when they cover the show. But it doesn't love the media when they start coming backstage to find out how the next show is being put together. Are you surprised? Every corporation in the world does this all the time. The Vatican doesn't want people to know the cardinals are squabbling over who's going to be the next pope."

Inside the preconclave, the cardinals were not squabbling over the potential candidates. South Africa's Cardinal Fox Napier said later, "We hardly heard any names mentioned."

"But CNN said they were squabbling," said Giovanni Avena, the veteran journalist who had been covering the Vatican for decades. "And that was enough to convince Ratzinger he had to quiet the media." Nor could the Internet betting sites that were making odds on the *papabili* have made Ratzinger happy either. Five days before the conclave, one such site in England made Arinze the number one favorite, at odds of 7–2. Asked about this, Arinze said with a modest smile, "I have always said my shoulders were too small for such a heavy weight." He noted that others on the list—Tettamanzi, Ratzinger, and Martini—were far more qualified than he. This was a perspicacious call; as we shall see, these three (plus one other) received most of the votes on the first ballot.

And only one of them, Ratzinger, did any serious campaigning. By early April, according to Sandro Magister, a leading Vatican reporter, Ratzinger had honed his message, that the Church had to stand up in God's defense, to a kind of "diamond hardness." Magister's evidence: the talk Ratzinger gave on the evening of April 1 at the Benedictine monastery of Subiaco, in which he talked about the debate in the European Union, which left God out of the preliminary draft of its constitution.

> The refusal of a reference to God is not an expression of tolerance which wants to protect non-theistic religions and the dignity of atheists and agnostics, but rather is an expression of a conscience which would want to see God definitively cancelled out of the public life of man and chained in the subjective ambit of the residues of past cultures. The relativism, which constitutes this point of departure, has become such a dogmatism that it believes itself in possession of the definitive understanding of reason, and that it has the right to consider all other viewpoints as a stage in this history of man which has been superseded and which can be thus reinterpreted. In reality, we have a radical need to survive and not to lose the vision of God, if we want human dignity not to disappear.

During the ten days of preconclave, Ratzinger took every opportunity to drill the message home. He did so publicly, at John Paul's funeral, and at the first of the nine masses that preceded the conclave, and privately in a score of meetings with other cardinals. When Ratzinger stopped by his office so his staff could help celebrate his seventy-eighth birthday on April 16, he told them, "My voice is tired because I've been talking all week." One of the staff, Gerald Cadieres Araújo, a Venezuelan, said, "His voice was almost gone." Another who worked in Ratzinger's office said, "This wasn't politics in any worldly sense of the word. The cardinal was simply trying to change the mood of the conclave. Some inner fire was lit, like God had chosen him."

Everything came to focus on April 18, the first day of the conclave, at the mass *pro eligendo pontifice,* celebrated by Ratzinger before all the cardinal-electors and thousands of others inside Saint Peter's, including the entire diplomatic corps. (Later that day, the scene would move to the Sistine Chapel, where the electors would cast their first ballots.) Ratzinger could have delegated anyone to give the homily, but he delivered it himself. It was, in effect, his campaign speech.

Ratzinger prayed God would give the Church "a new pope, like John Paul II, who will guide us to the love of Christ." The new pope would do that by making sure the faithful would not be "tossed about and carried here and there by any doctrinal wind." He didn't explain what a "doctrinal wind" was, but quickly shifted his metaphor. The real danger was more like a series of waves that tossed people about "from one end to the other." Then he ticked off a litany of scary abstractions that had long marked Ratzinger's rhetoric: Marxism, liberalism, libertinism, collectivism, radical individualism, atheism, religious mysticism, agnosticism, syncretism—while anyone who opposed these popular modern isms were charged with another ism, fundamentalism, a word of contempt in most quarters, but one that Ratzinger used triumphantly and unequivocally. For him, fundamentalism was "a clear faith, according to the creed of the Church." By that definition, he was a fundamentalist, and proud of it.

He scored "the dictatorship of relativism, which does not recognize anything as absolute and leaves as the ultimate measure only the measure of each one and his own desires." (Cardinal Martini would point out a week later at a mass in Milan, "Only God is absolute. All human efforts are relative to the end of time. Then all human works will appear in their true value, and all things will be made clear, will be illuminated, and will be pacified.")

Ratzinger's speech wasn't aimed at any particular individuals. This was campaign oratory, an attack on a set of abstractions, good rhetoric but meaningless, except as an inducement to defend God by voting for a man of God.

Ratzinger gave God a great deal of attention in this conclave. Any number of times, he reminded his fellows in the college of God's presence and insisted they repeat their solemn oath in the presence of almighty God that they would "not fail to affirm and defend strenuously the spiritual and temporal rights and the liberty of the Holy See."

By now, much of the Italian support was shifting to Ratzinger. For months, three Italian cardinals, Sodano, Re, and Sepe, hardly sure they wanted the head of the Holy Office to be the next pope and hoping to put an Italian in office, thought Tettamanzi might counter the tide that was running in Ratzinger's favor, and they pushed his candidacy with some of the moderates. Reporters for the *New York Times* in Rome got wind of this support, and so, five days before the voting was to begin, the *Times* ranked Tettamanzi as first among the *papabili*. An article by Ian Fisher of the *Times* pointed out that Tettamanzi was the son of a manual laborer, that he spoke in favor of those demonstrating against the G8 summit in Genoa in 2001, and that he had helped write some of John Paul II's social encyclicals.

In fact, Tettamanzi's support was not deep. Four days before the election, he may have lost votes after a vicious assault on him was published on the Internet by *Inside the Vatican*, a slick right-wing monthly. The article, written by Vittorio Messori, one of the four members of the press with access to Ratzinger, attacked Tettamanzi for sympathizing with Milan's gay community.

This was hardball. The publisher of *Inside the Vatican*, a lean, nervous American named Robert Moynihan, had been pushing Ratzinger's candidacy for weeks. But he didn't have to put Tettamanzi down in order to raise up Ratzinger. Those doing postconclave analyses discovered that the electors had been inclined to write Tettamanzi off for one simple reason: he didn't speak English.

On April 14, Ratzinger decided to gauge his electoral strength, and

Ratzinger. The senior man among the electors, William Baum, a seventy-eight-year-old American in the Roman Curia, hobbled up on his walker and said, "And I, William Baum, do so promise, pledge, and swear." Then, placing his hand on the book of the gospels, he added: "So help me God and these holy gospels which I touch with my hand."

Only when each of the other 114 cardinals had gone through this same exercise did Archbishop Piero Marini cry, *Extra omnes!*—"Everyone out." All of the noncardinals who had been assisting up to this point, except Marini and Archbishop Francesco Monterisi, then left the chapel. Marini closed the doors, then he and Monterisi distributed paper ballots. Each cardinal got one rectangular paper ballot printed with the words *Eligo in summum pontificem* —"I elect as supreme pontiff." Then, according to the strict protocol, each cardinal wrote a name on the ballot, taking care to disguise his handwriting as best he could, then folded the ballot and waited for his turn (in the same order of seniority) to proceed to the front of the chapel and place his ballot in a golden urn, with yet another oath. Each of them said, in Latin, "I call as my witness Christ the Lord who will be my judge, that my vote is given to the one before God I think should be elected."

This part of the exercise took the better part of an hour, during which time, by rule, there was no politicking (but, by exception to the rule, a good deal of whispering to one's seat mates). Then three cardinals chosen by lot (called "scrutineers") counted the ballots to make sure the number of votes corresponded to the number of voters. One scrutineer read each ballot out loud, a second kept a written tally of the number of votes going to each cardinal, and the third scrutineer pierced the ballot with a needle and secured it onto a piece of thread. Then three more cardinals (also chosen by lot) double-checked the ballots and the tallies to see if any mistakes had been made. Finally, the tallies were announced by the papal chamberlain. Only then did the electors know the results of the first vote.

Excommunication is supposed to be the automatic penalty incurred by anyone who reveals the count. Somehow, the tally is known and is always reported in the Italian press. As far as anyone knows, no one has ever been excommunicated for breaking the secret of the conclave. On the first ballot, a group of cardinals (including, no doubt, some Americans and some of the cardinals from Germany) gave Martini only nine votes. Ratzinger received forty-seven and Bergoglio ten. Tettamanzi got two votes, Ruini six, Sodano four, and Rodriguez Maradiaga three.

Soon those standing in Saint Peter's Square and millions of television viewers around the world saw puffs of smoke that could have been black. Or white. A phone call from Monterisi to the Vatican Press Office cleared up the ambiguity: *Non habemus papam*—"We do not have a pope."

That night, during the cardinals' supper in the Casa Santa Marta, Martini let it be known (how he did so is still a mystery) that he was really not well, not well enough to become pope. If elected, he would have to say he couldn't accept the responsibility. (Less than three weeks after the conclave, Martini had a heart flutter, was hospitalized, and sent home with a pacemaker.) No one—including Martini—would say whether Martini had thrown his support to Ratzinger or whether, more probably, he refrained from endorsing anyone.

(A nonelector came up to Martini the morning after the election and said, *Mi dica, que cosa è successo?*—"Tell me, what happened?"

"Lead me not into temptation," said Martini.)

There were two more ballots the next morning. On the first ballot, perhaps all nine Martini supporters transferred their votes to Bergoglio, the Jesuit from Argentina, and so did a number of others, giving Bergoglio thirty-five votes. Politi noted that if Bergoglio were elected he would become the first Latin American pope in history, the first non-European in the last nineteen centuries, and the first Jesuit. "Too many firsts," he wrote. In this ballot, however, Ratzinger picked up eighteen more votes. Now he had sixty-five, more than the fifty-eight needed for a simple majority. That almost did it. If necessary, according to the new rules written by John Paul II in 1996, that majority could hold on through another twenty ballots and get their man with 51 percent. But that wasn't going to happen. In the second ballot of the morning, Ratzinger got seventy-two votes, just shy of seventy-seven. Bergoglio received forty. No one else was even close. More black smoke.

The cardinals went off to lunch, then late that afternoon, they trooped back to the Sistine Chapel and cast their fourth ballot in all. By then, the landslide—with eighty-four votes for Ratzinger—was almost complete. Tettamanzi ended up with two votes.

Politi wrote, "Ratzinger's position had become so strong that it was up to the other electors—if they did not want to give an impression of great disarray, disastrous for the Church's international image—to take a step to give their votes to the most prestigious, and finally most unifying, candidate." Lopez Trujillo made that case with vigor.

During the last count, when Ratzinger reached the magic number of seventy-seven, there was an audible gasp in the chapel and everyone clapped. According to Murphy-O'Connor, Ratzinger had his head down, as if in prayer. When, after the last votes were tallied, Cardinal Sodano, the subdean, asked him if he would accept, he said, *Domine, non sum dignus, sed accipiam*—"Lord, I am not worthy. But I will accept." As they were burning the ballots and creating what they hoped was white smoke, Ratzinger was telling Sodano he would take the name Benedict XVI, because, he explained, Benedict XV tried to stop World War I, and he, the next Benedict, wanted to be a pope of peace.

It only remained for the new pope to don a pure white silk cassock, one of three (in three sizes) hanging in an anteroom, tailored in advance by Rome's Gamarelli brothers at a cost of $10,000 apiece, including the white zucchetto. Then he was ushered to the central balustrade of Saint Peter's and introduced to an estimated crowd of more than a hundred thousand people. *Annuntio vobis gaudium magnum,* said Cardinal Medina. *Habemus papam: Eminentissium ac Reverendissimum Dominum, Dominum Josephum. . . .* He paused for effect while his amplified words resounded through the square and on countless broadcast stations around the world. "I announce to you a great joy. We have a pope: the Most Eminent and Most Reverend . . . Cardinal Joseph Ratzinger."

The mob applauded, but for less than a minute. Some news photos showed young seminarians shouting and raising their arms in triumph, as indeed the new Benedict was doing at that very moment, clasping two hands above his head, like a winning prizefighter. Others in the square were less than excited. They had hoped for someone as wide as all outdoors, someone like John XXIII. Instead, they got a man they only knew as narrow.

A CNN/*USA Today*/Gallup poll of American Catholics conducted within hours of this moment found that 31 percent of its sample had a favorable reaction to the new pope, 9 percent unfavorable, and almost 60 percent said they didn't have enough information to make a conclusion. George Weigel may have spoken for the 31 percent. To him, the cardinals' choice was "a resounding affirmation of the pontificate of John Paul the Great, an overwhelming vote of confidence in Joseph Ratzinger, one of the great Christian minds and spirits of our time, and dynamic continuity in the world's oldest office." Colman McCarthy, an editorial columnist for the *Washington Post,* was just as hyperbolic on the other side. He wrote that Benedict, like his predecessor, was now "the secretly elected leader of a male-run, land-rich, undemocratic, hierarchic, dogmatically unyielding organization headquartered in a second-rate European country." Benedict would have as few worries about accountability, said McCarthy, as Pope John Paul II had had. He would rule as an autocrat.

Afterward, the new Pope Benedict invited the cardinals to join him in an impromptu supper at the Casa Santa Marta, where they would dine on bean soup, veal cordon bleu, and spumoni ice cream. Cardinal Joachim Meisner of Cologne was weeping tears of joy. The cardinals offered their new maximum leader a champagne toast and, after a hurried consultation trying to find a song everyone knew, they sang an old number from Roman seminary days. It was in Latin, of course. *Ad multos annos*—"For many years." Since the man they had elected was seventy-eight, the song was more of a hope than a prediction.

By then, Cardinal Danneels and nine other cardinals had already departed, not wanting to stay for supper. Danneels was driven directly to the Belgian College, where he met with reporters from seven countries. He was obviously nettled. As diplomatically as he could, he made it clear that he would have preferred someone else. Without much enthusiasm, he told more than twenty reporters, "This is the man the cardinals have chosen. So we have to trust him," not even mentioning Ratzinger's name. "As pope, he will be a different man than he was as a cardinal. As a cardinal, he had a special job to do, as a theologian, and he did it. Now, as pope, he has a different job to do. Now he is a pope for the whole Church. We have to have faith in him, as the pope."

Danneels said in answer to a question, "No, we don't have to accept the pope's theology. It may change. I hope it does. I change my theology every day, according to the things I see happening around me. Otherwise I wouldn't be a very good theologian."

Another reporter asked him if he approved of the college's choice. "I have a right to disapprove," he said, "for myself. But not as a pastor."

Most of the electors, however, seemed overjoyed. Some of them suggested later that they had only been listening to the people, evidenced by that tidal wave of humanity that had poured into Rome for John Paul's funeral. That, at least, was Opus Dei's spin. Thomas Bohlin, the Opus Dei priest-coordinator for the United States, said on Tim Russert's *Meet the Press* on April 24 that the cardinals "were shocked and even staggered by three million, four million people there, gathering there. And I think in that moment they heard the Holy Spirit speaking that what they wanted was continuity with John Paul."

Ratzinger had made his case for continuity, and like the board members of any major international conglomerate, the cardinals voted for a CEO who would give them that continuity.

Cardinal Murphy-O'Connor called the last ballot for Ratzinger "a unity vote," failing to mention that thirty-one electors did not vote with the majority. Curiously, three cardinals who had received no previous votes, Schönborn of Vienna, Biffi of Bologna, and Law of Boston, each received one vote, this according to an anonymous cardinal who leaked his conclave diary to *Limes,* an Italian monthly. It seems preposterous, but it is possible that the three of them each voted for the other, as a last-minute joke at the conclave.

On a more serious note, Cardinal Darmaatmadja insisted that, since the conclave had chosen Ratzinger, "it was the will of the Holy Spirit." Cardinal Tucci, who at age eighty-four didn't qualify as an elector, hoped that Ratzinger, as pope, would not resemble Ratzinger the enforcer. But even Hans Küng, a dissident, said, "We have to give Benedict a chance."

CHAPTER THIRTEEN

Benedict XVI

Keeping the People in the Pews

SOME POPES HAVE HAD HUGE EMOTIONAL REACTIONS, even breakdowns, when it dawned on them that they were being asked to assume their exalted role. There sits a room off the Sistine Chapel where a newly elected pope changes into papal white immediately after the vote; it is called *la sala delle lacrime,* the room of tears. *O mama mia, mama mama mia!* cried Giuseppe Sarto, the patriarch of Venice, when he went in that room on August 4, 1903, and emerged, shortly thereafter, as Pope Pius X, dreading what lay ahead for him.

Joseph Ratzinger shed no tears, but after his election, he told a crowd of German pilgrims he had prayed to God when the tally began to mount in his favor: "Don't do this to me." He said he felt "like a guillotine would fall on me. I was quite dizzy."

Few believed he had gotten this far by accident. Joe Napolitan, a political consultant in Washington, D.C., said Ratzinger's actions—given the constraints of custom and canon law—"demonstrated he wanted the job."

When Cardinal Angelo Sodano, the subdean of the College of Cardinals, asked Ratzinger what name he would take, he replied without hesitation, *"Benedictus."* Other popes had had to ponder that question. At seventy-eight, and with a history of heart trouble, the new pope had no time to waste. After making his brief appearance on the balcony of Saint Peter's to introduce himself as "a simple, humble servant in the vineyard of the Lord," then give his first blessing to the faithful, he turned to put the finishing touches on the major address he was scheduled to deliver the next day. Reginald Foster, the pope's Latinist, received the assignment to draft the speech, in Latin, four days before the conclave began. At that point, no one knew who the next pope would be, but Foster had this curious note from Ratzinger's office outlining some ideas the new pope might want to touch upon. In effect, Benedict XVI had outlined his acceptance speech four days before he was elected.

The pope said in that speech that his major goal was to work for Christian unity. Six times he emphasized the strength of his intention. He said he "must take charge of this project," that he had "a primary commitment to work without sparing energies." Good sentiments were not enough, he said. "There must be concrete gestures that penetrate spirits and move consciences." He would "do all that is in his power to promote the fundamental cause of ecumenism" and "cultivate every initiative that might seem appropriate to promote understanding with representatives of the diverse churches and ecclesial communities." And he would "spare no efforts and devotion to continue the promising dialogue" undertaken by his predecessors.

As prefect of the Holy Office, Ratzinger had a mixed history on the ecumenical front. He criticized a number of interfaith initiatives, including two meetings in Assisi of all the world's religious leaders that had been called by the pope himself; he never approved the final reports of the Anglican–Roman Catholic International Commission, and he wrote the infamous *Dominus Iesus,* so startling in tone to Christians of every stripe. On the other hand, at the funeral mass of John Paul II, he gave Communion to Roger Schutz, the retired prior of the Protestant monastery of Taizé in France, making it clear that he considered Schutz a fellow member of the mystical body of Christ, which is the Church.

It is just possible that, in the short time he had to work in, he could bring the Christian churches together in ways that John Paul II was not able to do. His dealings with the Orthodox in Russia would not be complicated by John Paul II's sentimental feelings toward the so-called Uniate churches in Eastern Europe, which the Orthodox have long regarded as Trojan horses within their walls. Now Benedict suggested that Cardinal Kasper, president of the Vatican's Council for Promoting Christian Unity, invite representatives from the Orthodox Church to the inaugural ceremonies, as well as leaders of other Christian bodies, and Jewish leaders, too. He made the same request of Archbishop Michael Louis Fitzgerald, the president of the Vatican's Council for Interreligious Dialogue. He wanted delegations from three of the world's major religions, Buddhism, Hinduism, and Islam, to be a part of his inauguration. Furthermore, he wanted to see them all in a private audience the very next day, so he could tell them personally of his determination "to continue building bridges of friendship with the followers of all religions" and "become peacemakers together with them."

Benedict was all too aware of his public image as God's chosen disciplinarian and of the references to his Nazi past, and he must have skimmed the standard packet of press reports a pope receives every day. One headline in a Jerusalem newspaper summed up his election: "White Smoke, Black Past." And he couldn't have failed to note the disappointed reactions of many—more from priests, actually, who had resented many of the strictures that had come out of the Holy Office over the years, than from the ordinary faithful. The negative reaction of two priests in Arizona was typical. Vernon Meyer, a priest in Scottsdale, told the *Arizona Republic,* "I believe his selection was one made out of force and fear. The last twenty years show what kind of pope he will be. The Holy Spirit did not choose this pope." Hugo Gonzalez, the pastor of a parish in Peoria, Arizona, told the *Republic,* "This is a sad rather than a joyous day. For better or worse, the Church must now live with this choice."

And so, in the pope's next major speech, the homily at his inaugural mass on April 24, it seemed he was trying to allay fears that he would be more dictator than democrat. "My real program of governance," he said, "is not to do my own will, not to pursue my own ideas, but to listen, together with the whole Church, to the word and the will of the Lord." What that meant, he said, could best be understood by meditating on two symbols that were part of the day's liturgy, the pallium and the Fisherman's ring.

The Fisherman's ring symbolized the fact that Jesus had made his apostles fishers of men, a charge, he said, that all Christians should consider sharing. "As we follow Christ in this mission to be fishers of men, we must bring men and women out of the sea that is salted with so many forms of alienation and onto the land of life, into the light of

God." To him, these men and women were worth saving. "We are not some casual and meaningless product of evolution. Each of us is the result of a thought of God. Each of us is willed, each of us is loved, each of us is necessary."

The pallium—a broad band of pure white wool that would be placed on the pope's shoulders at a moment in the ancient rite when past popes were given the triple crown—had the same significance, for it represented "the sheep lost in the desert that no longer knows the way," which Jesus, the Good Shepherd, had to rescue. "What the pallium indicates first and foremost is that we are all carried by Christ. But at the same time, it invites us to carry one another. Let us pray for one another, that the Lord will carry us and that we will learn to carry one another." Benedict said the pallium was meant to suggest "an image of the yoke of Christ, which the bishop of this city, the servant of the servants of God, takes upon his shoulders."

The media took note of these simple words, simply expressed, and began to look for stories that highlighted Benedict's humanity. A man had become a demigod, and the press's first instinct was to humanize him. Martin Mosebach, a German novelist, wrote a piece in the *New York Times* describing the new pope's "strikingly peculiar face, his large, child's eyes lurking in their shadowy sockets, and the eager glow that seems to radiate from them even when he is absorbed in contemplation."

> It's rare to see a face like that in his Bavarian homeland. The great novelist Heimito von Doderer once said that all of Bavaria can be divided into a small group of butchers and a larger group of people who look like butchers. And unlike many of my compatriots, the pope is unflaggingly courteous and appears to grow even gentler in the midst of debate, though he'd never relinquish so much as an inch of ground. His enemies call him cold because he refuses to feign cordiality. And it's true: his manner shows nothing of the effusive Dale Carnegie mold so admired in Germany.
>
> But his German is beautiful, which is particularly noteworthy for a German in a high position, since the language is not often

> spoken correctly, not even by native speakers. Although he is a philosopher and a theologian, he has developed a style that is crystal clear in its simplicity, but that never simplifies the complicated topics he needs to address. Is this, too, not a virtue befitting a shepherd of souls?

Sylvia Poggioli of National Public Radio quoted Augustine DiNoia, a Dominican priest and one of Cardinal Ratzinger's collaborators at the Holy Office. "The image of him as 'Panzer-Cardinal,' you know, is just completely ludicrous. He's a kind of simple person. He chuckles, you know. I mean there's a certain childlike quality." Some who had been called to answer Ratzinger's inquiries at the Holy Office must have had a chuckle over that.

Ratzinger's American publisher, Joseph Fessio, told the U.S. Catholic News Service it was wrong to label Benedict XVI a theological hardliner. "He has a tremendous breadth of vision that is recognized by his critics. But he's a Catholic. He believes in Catholic truth. He wants to preserve the integrity of the deposit of faith."

A reporter for the *Catholic Spirit,* the official newspaper of the diocese of Minneapolis–Saint Paul, found two local priests who recalled Cardinal Ratzinger's visit to the upper Midwest in 1984. One of them, Lee Piche, remembered the new pope as "a very gentle, soft-spoken, self-effacing man." Another, Michael Skluzacek, now rector of the Cathedral of Saint Paul, said that he was most struck by Ratzinger's demeanor. "He was so humble and gracious and friendly, and he smiled. And that's why I was always a little confused when people spoke of him as such a tough man because my experience of him was that he's a very gracious and friendly man."

And then there was Agnes Heindl, the housekeeper of Benedict's brother, Georg, a priest in Regensburg, Germany, who regaled a reporter from the Knight Ridder news service with stories about the pope's love of *Weisswurst,* the traditional white Bavarian sausage, and his predilection for cats. "When he was relaxing," said Ms. Heindl, "there was never a mystery about what would make him laugh. Cats. He loves them." She pointed up a staircase to a wall full of painted plates, each depicting a different cat. The brothers collected the plates together, she said. "When we were on vacation, a cat, a little kitten, would come by, and he'd be giddy, almost giggling with joy. Cats love him. They always go to him straightaway. And he loves them back."

Cardinal Ratzinger's neighbors living next to the Vatican's Saint Anne's Gate recalled his cats, too. They told reporters stories about his regular strolls down the Borgo Pio, the main shopping street near his apartment. "Stray cats seem to like him," one woman told a reporter for *Il Messagero.* "They come right up to him and purr when he pets them."

Two days after the election, several hundred people gathered in the afternoon outside the Ratzinger apartment at 1 Piazza Leoniana like so many swarming bees. Benedict XVI was inside the apartment, according to his spokeswoman, writing his speech for the Sunday inaugural at Saint Peter's.

Reporters were surprised to find the pope had a spokeswoman—not his priest-secretary, George Gänswein, not the papal spokesman, Navarro-Valls, but rather his fifty-five-year-old German housekeeper, Ingrid Stampa, who not only told the reporters the pope was upstairs working, but also announced she had his permission to talk about herself. She was a lay member of the Schoenstatt Sisters of Mary, an order founded in Germany, and she was something more than a housekeeper. Ever since the death of the cardinal's sister, Maria, in 1991, Ms. Stampa had served Ratzinger as a live-in personal assistant, ghostwriter, translator, and confidante. She had an advanced degree in ancient music, and for a number of years taught the viola da gamba, an ancient musical instrument similar to the modern cello, at the conservatory of music in Hamburg. She spoke German, English, and Italian. She was asked if it was true that Benedict had a cat. "Oh, yes," she said with a smile. "Two of them. They are porcelain."

On the day of the election, Stampa was working on her computer when she heard the pealing bells of Saint Peter's. She rushed to Saint Peter's Square and broke down in tears when she heard Cardinal Ratzinger's name announced. Wondering if she could see him that night, she walked over to the Casa Santa Marta and found him on his way to dinner with the rest of the cardinals. She bent down to kiss his hand. He stopped her, saying: "God wanted it this way. Let us both follow the will of God." She had been preparing herself for a quieter future as Ratzinger headed into retirement. Now her life had taken a dramatic new turn. Some hoped she would be part of the pope's inner circle, perhaps someone like Pius XII's German nun, Mother Pasqualina Lehnert, whose rule over the papal household in the 1950s earned her the title *la papessa,* the popess. Some believed Stampa, a woman of ideas, a scholar, and a translator of some standing, would serve the pope in different ways.

Less than a week after the election, Cardinal Martini told *La Repubblica:*

> It is certain that Benedict XVI has some surprises in store for us, in light of the stereotypes by which he has been defined a bit too hastily. The new pope is a man of great humanity, courtesy, and gentleness, ready to listen, even to ideas different from his own. I am sure he will not be rigid, but will listen and reflect. The other reason why we should expect surprises is simply the fact that a pastor is always being educated and formed by his people.

Martini predicted Pope Benedict would adapt his own views and pastoral practices to the needs of the people, "once he becomes more familiar with the problems in the hearts of believers and nonbelievers."

Not everyone was so sure about that. Michael A. Fahey, a Jesuit who is now the editor of *Theological Studies,* a learned quarterly in the United States, studied under Ratzinger at Tübingen. He wrote on his Web site:

> Can a man who shifted horizons at the age of 41 do so again (in another direction) at the age of 78? Some commentators on the election are convinced that his change of ministry from prefect of the Congregation for the Doctrine of the Faith to Roman Pontiff may occasion a shift from a relentless style to a more compassionate and flexible attitude. In these early days of media coverage we are being deluged with "opinions" from everyone, from his Munich University classmate, Uta Ranke-Heinemann (*Eunuchs of the Kingdom of Heaven*), to his "old friend and student," Joseph Fessio, about how he will grow in the Petrine office. Change is possible. After all, the much revered archbishop of El

> Salvador, Oscar Romero, underwent a dramatic change of heart because of his episcopal responsibilities. Time will tell, and Benedict XVI's curial replacements, especially the prefect of the CDF, will be one of the early signals.

Benedict's early signals could hardly have been a comfort to Fahey. Within days of his election, Benedict reappointed John Paul II's cabinet members, including Cardinal Sodano as his secretary of state, or prime minister. In effect, he was only fulfilling a kind of campaign promise. A month before the pope died, Ratzinger had told the chief of RAI's Vatican coverage that if he should become pope, he wouldn't attempt to reform the Roman Curia. "I don't know how," he explained, "because it's very complicated machinery. It's very difficult to repair complicated machinery. It requires great confidence, which I do not have." In fact, Ratzinger demonstrated huge self-confidence before, during, and after the conclave, and quite a bit of political cunning, too. Telling RAI before the conclave that he would make no curial changes would give him a better-than-even chance of winning the votes of some curial cardinal-electors; they represented 25 percent of the conclave, and stood to lose their positions in any administrative shake-up.

Fahey got a second, disquieting signal on May 13, when the pope named Archbishop William J. Levada of San Franciso to succeed him as prefect of the Holy Office. Levada had been on the right career course from the beginning. He took most of his seminary formation at the North American College in Rome, where he was ordained a priest, then obtained a graduate degree in theology from the Gregorian University. A degree in sacramental theology or in scripture would have marked him for later assignments teaching theology in a seminary. But Levada did his doctoral dissertation on a subject that was calculated to put him on the bishop track, "The Infallible Church Magisterium and the Natural Law." In it, he gave reasons justifying the power of Church teaching to bind consciences.

After his doctoral study, Levada took various assignments in his native Southern California; then, in 1976, he returned to Rome for a six-year assignment in the Holy Office. (His last year there was Ratzinger's first.) In 1986, he was appointed archbishop of Portland, Oregon, where he got the nickname "Darth" (after the villain in the *Star Wars* saga), then named archbishop of San Francisco in 1995, where he tried without much success to deal with a fractious gay community and with the sex-abuse scandal, which hit San Francisco as hard as it hit anywhere. He served on a commission of American bishops and Vatican officials charged with translating the bishops' zero tolerance policy into Church law. Levada said that this may have been why the new pope chose him to run the Holy Office—"to make sure [the cases] are handled in a proper manner."

Terrie Light, a San Franciscan and a national board member of the Survivors Network of Those Abused by Priests (SNAP), had his own negative interpretation of that remark. He told Alan Cooperman of the *Washington Post* that Levada "very much falls in line with how the Catholic Church has handled the problem. They've denied it. When they say he's an expert, he's only an expert on their way of dealing with things. In that way, he'll fit right in."

Like many American bishops, Levada had used all the right rhetoric to decry what abusive priests had done, but in some instances, he had protected them. In 1992, in Portland, Levada sent Joseph Baccellieri to a treatment program for child molesters and then reinstated him to ministry in 1994. His successor as archbishop, John G. Vlazny, removed Baccellieri in 2002. When Jim Jenkins, an Oakland, California, psychologist who chaired Levada's lay review board in San Francisco, learned how Levada was handling the sex-abuse protocols, he resigned.

Hugh O'Regan, a Bay Area coordinator for Voice of the Faithful, reported how Levada dealt with a priest who told him he caught his pastor engaged in erotic wrestling with a thirteen-year-old altar boy in the rectory. Levada said he should say nothing about it. When the priest reported the incident to the police, Levada suspended him. "This intelligent move by our archbishop," said O'Regan, "resulted in a lawsuit by the suspended priest, and a hefty confidential pretrial money settlement to the priest who is now secure for life." The priest was reinstated, but he received no new assignment until Levada left San Francisco.

On May 6, Thomas J. Reese told some five hundred media people in an e-mail that he was resigning after seven years as editor of *America* magazine. Many believed this was a routine move; the normal term of office for a Jesuit superior is six years. Soon reporters learned this was anything but routine. Reese had been sacked by none other than Cardinal Ratzinger, just two weeks before he became Benedict XVI. For those who had been willing to give Benedict XVI a chance to show how he could be kinder as a pope than he was as an inquisitor general, this was terrible news. They wondered what Reese had done to deserve this.

It turned out that Ratzinger had been complaining about Reese for five years over a number of articles in *America,* always addressing his objections to the superior general of the Jesuits in Rome, Peter-Hans Kolvenbach. Many of the articles, Ratzinger said, dissented from Church teaching. In 2002, moreover, Reese wrote an editorial that called for an end to the Holy Office as presently run; in that piece, he wasn't attacking "Church teaching," but he was attacking Ratzinger himself. At that point, Ratzinger told Kolvenbach that Reese would have to resign or submit every issue of the magazine to a board of censors appointed by the American bishops.

The Jesuits at *America* could not do that. Since 1909, *America* had made its reputation as a forum for every kind of ongoing adult discussion among Catholics in the United States. Its circulation was not large—37,951 subscribers when Reese took over in 1998, and 49,324 when he left in 2005—but that didn't equal even a tenth of a percent of the American Catholic population. *America* appealed to intelligent, adult Catholics, including the twenty-three United States senators and 130 members of the House of Representatives who are Catholics, many of whom counted on *America* to analyze almost every public policy issue that confronted lawmakers at local, state, and national levels, not on the basis of faith but reason.

Tom Reese felt the magazine had a duty to express reasoned opinions on a whole range of ethical issues—and on a good many Church issues that were open questions. Cardinal Ratzinger didn't agree. For him, once the magisterium took a position on anything to do with faith, morals, or Church discipline, it was no longer an open question. And yet, Reese kept publishing articles in *America* like the essay by two Jesuit moral theologians approving the use of condoms in AIDS-torn Africa. He ran several critical analyses of Ratzinger's *Dominus Iesus.* He printed a troubling essay about homosexual priests. Reese had always been careful to present opposing points of view, including articles by American bishops and even by Ratzinger himself in a celebrated exchange with Cardinal Kasper about the authority of local churches. But that didn't mollify the prefect of the Holy Office.

The Reese affair came to a head shortly before the death of John Paul II. In mid-March, Ratzinger sent off a note to Father Kolvenbach. This time, after an article criticizing the American bishops' involvement in the presidential election campaign, it was not a question of either-or. Reese simply had to go. Kolvenbach said nothing to Reese, even though Reese was living under the same roof at the Jesuit headquarters in Rome, waiting to see what would happen in the conclave. When Ratzinger was elected, there was never any question about carrying the fight any further. The Jesuits do not argue with a pope. The general told Brad Schaeffer, the American superprovincial in Washington, D.C., that it was time for Reese to resign. "So, give it up," said Schaeffer. "You've had a great run, seven great years."

So Reese resigned. Benedict XVI had the kind of electoral mandate to do almost anything he wanted with the Jesuits. He could suppress them (as Clement XIV had done in 1773) or put them into receivership (as John Paul II had done in 1982). Far easier, he could take Vatican Radio out of their hands and give it to Opus Dei, which would be happy to take control of the world's single biggest radio operation. (It has four hundred employees, broadcasting in thirty-four languages.) Or he could give Opus Dei direction over the Jesuits' Gregorian University and the Biblical Institute, still the most prestigious training ground in Rome for future bishops.

The spectacle of the pope himself going after Reese created an uproar among other Catholic journalists. *Commonweal* and the *National Catholic Reporter* wrote fiery editorials protesting Reese's ouster. *Commonweal* said the whole affair proved that "the Catholic Church is a backward-looking, essentially authoritarian institution run by men who are afraid of open debate and intellectual inquiry."

> Those calling for the strict regulation of Catholic discourse argue that public dissent from Church doctrine creates scandal, confusing or misleading "the simple faithful." What really gives scandal to people in the pews, however, is the arbitrary and self-serving

> exercise of ecclesiastical authority. What the CDF has done to Thomas Reese and *America* is the scandal. Is it possible that not one bishop has the courage to say so? That too is a scandal.

NCR's editorial said, "The question is not about Rome's right to intervene, since someone in the end has to decide what Roman Catholicism stands for, but about the standards applied in deciding when, how and against whom action is taken. In this case, most American Catholics cannot help but feel it's the wrong target for the wrong reasons."

> In one bullying move, the congregation has compromised a journal that has been a centerpiece of Catholic intellectual life in the United States. A forum for rational discussion, debate and exchange of ideas now has to look over its shoulder to make sure that Rome will not be offended. Some applaud the decision, saying it brings clarity to how a Catholic publication should conduct itself. What the Vatican move against Reese conveys, however, is fear, not clarity or certainty.

NCR's editors seemed anxious not to pin responsibility for all this on the new pope (even though that is where it belongs) because *NCR* operates out of a Catholic context that still maintains respect not only for the office but for the person of the pope. They respect the pope, and they mute their criticism when they cannot accept everything he says. Many in the Catholic world would feel as they do.

Few criticized Benedict XVI on May 7, for example, when he took possession of his cathedral in Rome, the Basilica of Saint John Lateran, and delivered what had to be the most uncompromising statement of his first six weeks in office. During that period, he spoke or published roughly 43,500 words. Those words came in the form of one *urbi et orbi* blessing, sixteen addresses delivered to various groups visiting the Vatican, six homilies, six catechetical addresses from his Wednesday general audiences, five Sunday messages given at noon appearances at the window of his apartment in the Apostolic Palace, three addresses to groups of bishops on their *ad limina* visits, three written messages to different groups, one welcome to a new ambassador to the Holy See, two addresses to visiting dignitaries, and one document enacting a change in Church law.

Most of what Benedict said reflected his quiet, clear certainties about the condition of the Church, and the state of the world as well. This is probably why he was elected by the College of Cardinals—he was a theologian/administrator who had been "keeping the faith" for twenty-four years in the Holy Office, promising he would follow John Paul's right-thinking program. He had a superb understanding of the Church's tradition, or at least the strain of the Church's tradition currently in vogue with the kind of men John Paul II picked to serve in his college. It is a particularly unworldly strain of Catholicism that dates all the way back to Saint Augustine. Ratzinger wrote one of his two doctoral dissertations on Augustine, and he seemed entranced ever since his student days with Augustine's particular take on the world, divided between the forces of good and evil, symbolized as the City of God and the City of Man. Ratzinger has an either-or approach to the world, even to the members of his own Church.

At Saint John Lateran on May 7 he said:

> The bishop of Rome sits on his chair to give testimony of Christ. Thus the chair is the symbol of the *potestas docendi,* that teaching authority that is an essential part of the mandate to bind and to loose conferred by the Lord to Peter and, after him, to the twelve. In the church, sacred scripture, whose comprehension grows under the inspiration of the Holy Spirit, and the ministry of authentic interpretation, conferred to the apostles, belong mutually to one another in an indissoluble way.

Benedict maintained that this teaching power was "a mandate to serve" the people with the message of Christ. He said, "The pope must not proclaim his own ideas, but bind himself constantly and bind the Church to obedience to the Word of God, in face of attempts to adapt and water down, in face, as well, of all opportunism."

The trouble is that, in the contemporary world, teaching is one thing and a power that binds is another. If someone teaches us the Pythagorean theorem, why does he or she have to bind us to it? We've learned it, and we possess the truth of it, and it possesses us. If we haven't learned it, no one can bind us to it.

Furthermore, when Benedict XVI talked about "the binding power of the magisterium," he did not distinguish between faith and reason. On matters of faith, there is little dispute over his right (and duty) to say what a teaching means. Most Catholics do not have a very clear idea of the Church's doctrine on the Trinity, for example, but they accept the Church's teaching on it nevertheless. That is a faith issue. Or rather, for most Catholics, not an issue at all.

But Benedict seemed to insist that Catholics owed the same assent to every one of the Church's "binding teachings" on moral issues as well, and many Catholics couldn't be "bound" by something that they didn't understand, and that might well be wrong. Church teaching on moral matters does not have the same authority as its teachings on matters of faith. The Church (or to be more precise, the pope) currently says that artificial contraception is "intrinsically evil," and that anyone who uses it is guilty of a grave sin. Catholics who consider this a "binding teaching" should, logically, avoid the sacraments. They may even want to leave the Church on this account, and since 1968, when Pope Paul VI reaffirmed this binding teaching, many have done just that.

The vast majority of Catholic couples, however, do not consider the pope's position on birth control binding. It is a classic example of a teaching that has not been received. Therefore, argues James A. Coriden, a priest and a canon lawyer who once served as president of the Canon Law Society of America, in a white paper called "The Canonical Doctrine of Reception," it is not a teaching at all.

As the Catholic scholar and jurist John T. Noonan Jr. explains at length in his book *A Church That Can and Cannot Change,* Catholics have been through all this before. The Church once taught that usury, the lending of money at interest, was a sin, and it continued to do so for four hundred years, even as Catholics proceeded to lend (and borrow) money at interest without a qualm of conscience.

Most intelligent Catholics put this so-called teaching on birth control in the same context. They know the pope's position has been challenged and rejected by some of the Church's own best moral theologians, including a majority of the scholars, scientists, and loyal Catholic couples who were members of the papal birth-control commission in the 1960s. The fifty-six members of that commission voted down the classic teaching, fifty-two to four.

Today's Catholics are split over moral, social, and political issues that have little to do with their faith in Jesus, and much to do with their own personal histories and their own genetic codes. They disagree mostly on the issue of how they can live in the modern world as Christians—whether they should really be a part of that world, getting into all the messiness of politics, for example, which often demands they fudge Church teachings, or condemn politics as something evil and withdraw, leaving it more evil for their absence.

Benedict XVI has implied Christians would be better advised to go live on mountaintops (like the ancient Benedictines) and chant psalms rather than try to live a life of purity in an impure world. Those who agree with Benedict find his Church a comfortable place, and take some guilty joy (Michael Novak calls it *Ratzenfreude*) in the discomfort of those Catholics who expected the conclave of 2005 to choose a people's pope for a people's Church.

One can detect such *Ratzenfreude* in George Weigel's writings after the election of Pope Benedict XVI. He wrote in *Newsweek:*

> In the long view of history, April 19, 2005, may mark the moment at which the forty-year effort to force Catholicism to tailor its doctrine and its message to the tastes of secular modernity crashed and burned.
>
> Ever since the Second Vatican Council, some Catholics and most of the world media have expected—and in certain cases, demanded—that the Catholic Church follow the path taken by virtually every other non-fundamentalist western Christian community over the past century: the path of accommodation to secular modernity and its conviction that religious belief, if not mere childishness, is a lifestyle choice with no critical relationship to the truth of things.

Now Weigel has a pope who got elected after a campaign speech that declared his fundamentalism and attacked an abstraction, relativism.

Two weeks later, at an April 30 conference of Catholic philosophers in Chicago, Alasdair MacIntyre said, "In the entire universe, there are absolutely no relativists who are not American undergraduates."

Many Church liberals grumble when they hear the pope identify himself as a fundamentalist, but they will not leave the Church. They will pay as little attention to Benedict XVI as they did to John Paul II, whose cause for sainthood officially began on June 28 after Benedict waived a rule stipulating that no cause can begin until the man or woman in question has been dead five years. They will stay and battle for a people's Church, not because they enjoy fighting with Catholics who prefer a clerical Church, but because they think it is the only way they can live honorably in a reasonable world. Soon after Reese was sacked, Fay Vincent, the former baseball commissioner, resigned from the board of trustees at the Jesuits' Fairfield University in Connecticut, and refused to accept an honorary degree from Sacred Heart University in Hartford, to protest what happened to Reese. "I'm really worried that some Catholic organizations, especially universities, are at some risk," Vincent told a local newspaper. "How can you call yourself a university without free debate?"

There is, of course, another side. Richard John Neuhaus, once a liberal Lutheran pastor and now a conservative Catholic priest, makes a forceful case for clear boundaries. Writing in the *Boston Globe,* Neuhaus argued that because *America* is "a Catholic magazine in the service of the Church and its mission," it has a special obligation to uphold orthodoxy as defined by the pope. That's especially true, he said, on "publicly controversial questions such as the moral understanding of homosexuality, same-sex marriage and the exploitation of embryonic stem cells. On such questions, the Church has clearly defined positions." He asked *America,* "Whose side are you on?"

Some hope Catholics from both parties might learn to listen to one another. Timothy Radcliffe, recently retired after serving nine years as master general of the Dominicans, suggested at a talk to a Catholic group in New York in April 2005 that Catholics had little reason to fight one another and much to agree on. They needed something he called "conversion."

> The conversion required all around will be appropriately expressed in how we speak to one another and listen to one

> another. There can only be dialogue if we take time to listen to those with whom we tussle. Don't just hear the words, but inquire about the experiences from which the words come. It's not just a clash of ideas, but of different human experiences that give rise to the words we use.
>
> We need to stand in each other's shoes and avoid taking each other to court. We must dare to live not just on the side of black or white, but to step upon occasion into a demilitarized zone marked by some gray. We must find new words, and give our common search for the best way forward some time.

Pedro Casaldáliga is the bishop of São Félix in Brazil. He is a member of the Claretian Order who was once called to the Holy Office to answer for his continued support of liberation theology and a people's Church in his poor part of Brazil. After the election of Benedict XVI, he, too, had some wise words.

> We as Catholics have to learn how to define the figure of the pope. The pope has a ministry . . . but he is not the Church, he is not God. We have to relate to him and be adults in our faith and continue on the journey and insisting. The big institutions only change if there is strong pressure at the bases. The Church, divine and human, will only change if there is a coherent force, universal at the bases, and these are necessary for ecumenical and interreligious dialogue, coresponsibility, enculturation, keeping an open ear and mind to the world's needs.

Joe Hill, a legendary character in the history of the American labor movement, said the same thing more succinctly: "Don't mourn. Organize."

Epilogue
Modest Proposals

I HAD ONE LAST MEETING with Cardinal Murphy-O'Connor in the spacious office of the Archbishop's House on Ambrosden Avenue in London. We could talk little about the conclave because, as he reminded me, he had taken an oath of silence. "I wouldn't want to be excommunicated," he said with a twinkle in his eye.

I took the occasion to tell him I was disappointed with the conclave's choice of Benedict XVI. In my view, we now had a pope who was taking us back to the nineteenth century, when Gregory XVI was condemning something he called "liberalism" and Pius IX was condemning freedom of speech, freedom of the press, and freedom of religion. Trying to give me some perspective, he said, "Perhaps we put too much emphasis on the pope. Real reform in the Church doesn't come from the top. It comes from below, from the people. We need more saints. Yes, men like Saint Francis of Assisi and women like Saint Catherine of Siena. And the Jesuits."

Later, I pondered the cardinal's words, thinking of the saints I had met in my wanderings of the past five years, men and women who, with their minds and hearts firmly fixed on Jesus, went about their quiet witness in the world with hardly a thought about the pope. I thought of a Jesuit in the Syrian desert who had become a Muslim at heart, and a nun in Jakarta worshiping five times a day in the mosque across the street from her Sacred Heart convent, and the president of a Benedictine college in Manila gathering all of her community together to celebrate their own mass, and I thought again about Murphy-O'Connor's insight, that the real strength of the Church lay in its faith-filled people.

There are millions of Catholics all over the world who are making their own independent moves—feeling free in a new kind of people's Church, working out new ways of being and loving, and doing so without drawing upraised eyebrows or incurring excommunications from Rome. They're asserting their freedom, spurred on in many cases by their best priests, secure under the trusting, watchful eyes of their bishops, who want to mean it when they tell their people this is their Church.

I once asked Cardinal Jean-Baptiste Pham Minh Mân, archbishop of Ho Chi Minh City in Vietnam, what he thought of a people's Church. He said, "I would love to have one if someone can just tell me how to get it." I suggested he give his people some proof that they own it and make it ever more their own by adapting it to their own culture, making it more catholic, less Roman.

By now, most Catholics, even most of the officials of the Roman Curia, applaud the enculturation they see or read about in Africa—in the Congo, for instance, where the people's Church has created its own masses, with drums, dancing, and song. The Vatican didn't create those liturgies for the people of the Congo; they did it for themselves.

Up to now, however, America's Catholic pastors, buying too deeply, perhaps, into Rome's way as the only way to be Catholic, haven't done much hard thinking about enculturating their mission in the United States. Nor have they encouraged their people to think they have any special stake in the process. If they realized how important their share is, they would demand their Church be run better.

In November 2004, James Carroll, the novelist and historian, told a Catholic reform group meeting in Boston that they had to insist that the American Church be run by a consensus of the governed. "God may be love," he said, "but the polis isn't, and neither is the Church. Everyone must be protected from the unchecked, uncriticized, and unregulated power of every other, including the well-meaning leader. The Church's own experience—its grievous sin in relation to the Jews, for example, its long tradition of denigrating women, and, lately, the inability of clerical leaders to dismantle an autocratic structure that enabled priestly child abuse—proves how desperately the Catholic Church is in need of democratic reform."

Earlier, in July 2004, a group of Catholic business leaders and academics—all staunch Catholics meeting under the banner of something they called the Church in America Leadership Roundtable—met at the Wharton School in Philadelphia to confront a dozen American bishops with some hard facts. Taken collectively, they told the bishops, the 193 American dioceses have more than a million employees and a yearly operating budget of almost $1 billion, making the American Church as large as many of the nation's largest corporations.

As a corporation, however, they said the American Church was headed toward ruin. Fred Gluck, a former director of McKinsey and Company, one of the world's leading management consulting firms, told the bishops,

> On the personnel side, your workforce is rapidly aging. Your ability to recruit has declined dramatically over the last forty years. You are no longer first choice of the best and the brightest. Your people are demoralized by internal conflict and public scandal. On the financial side, your traditional sources of revenue are drying up. Your costs are escalating rapidly as you no longer are attracting high-quality cheap labor. Your plant is rapidly obsolescing. Your potential liabilities as a result of the recent scandals are large and growing. Your processes for financial management seem to be highly fragmented and uncoordinated and much too underdeveloped to deal with the problems enumerated above. On the marketing side, many of your faithful customers no longer feel committed to your product line and openly reject portions of it as irrelevant to their lives, though most of them remain highly committed to your basic message and thirst for sure-handed leadership and dramatic change in the delivery system.

It was not entirely fair for the Leadership Roundtable to look upon their Church as it might look at any business corporation. In fact, each American bishop (appointed by the pope in a secret process that remains a mystery even to most American priests) is on his own, an absolute ruler until retirement—unless, of course, he is caught in some crime. Since 2000, six American bishops have resigned, five of them for aberrations of a sexual nature that became public and one after he was charged (and later convicted) with leaving the scene of a fatal hit-and-run auto incident, a felony. In none of these cases did the pope intervene. He didn't have to. Local public opinion told the misbehaving bishops what to do.

A bishop who behaves himself, however, and remembers to pay a visit to Rome every five years with an envelope of cash for the pope can exercise a rule that is close to absolute, hardly diminished by his diocesan finance council, whose members he appoints and whose advice he need not follow, or by the United States Conference of Catholic Bishops, an organization he supports with annual contributions but whose resolutions he can, according to canon law, safely ignore.

If any wonder why the American Church is in such a parlous condition, they must, therefore, lay the blame on the bishops who have enjoyed such extraordinary control—and on the pastors who support them. Some bishops say canon law blocks various initiatives recommended by the forces of reform, which quiets some reformers but should not, since canon law itself says a bishop need not follow those rules that in his judgment are overridden by his people's needs. If he insists on following the letter of Church law, one can only conclude that he is using it as an excuse to stave off cries for reform out of a simple, perverse desire to maintain his absolute power.

Why a bishop would want to cling to this kind of absolutism is puzzling. He would live a far less anxious existence, and his people would be better served if he shared governance in an enculturated Church with, by, and for the people.

How would he do that? Leonard Swidler, a distinguished professor of theology at Temple University in Philadelphia, has long argued that the Catholic Church in the United States will enter a new, more vital existence when it can make a declaration of independence—not independence from the pope (for American Catholics tend to love their pope, no matter who he is) but independence from a system of governance that is entirely man-made, and made in another time and another place that bears no resemblance to twenty-first-century America.

Swidler is referring to the Church's canon law, written by a foreign monarch, the pope, so that he can exercise absolute power absolutely. Americans do not understand how and why a pope, with the assistance of his courtiers, can make the laws, enforce the laws, and be the judge of his own justice, all in secret. "If canon law isn't helping the Church achieve its mission, then," he says, "the American Church should write some new law."

The new law he has in mind would not deal with changes in doctrine but in discipline. Other theologians are beginning to see a way out for the American Church, which they suggest could become an autochthonous Church, modeled on the ancient Churches of the Middle East—the Chaldeans, the Maronites, the Melkites, the Armenians, and the Copts, for example, who are Catholics united with Rome, with their own patriarchs, their own liturgies, and their own mostly married clergy.

But could they create an autochthonous Church in modern times? It is not unthinkable. In 1925, the Belgian cardinal Désiré Joseph Mercier proposed that the Anglican Communion be brought back into union with Rome whole and entire, as an autochthonous Church—with its own patriarch, the archbishop of Canterbury, its own married clergy, and its own English liturgy. Mercier was ahead of his time: Pope Pius XI wouldn't hear of it. A little more than seventy years later, however, Indonesian bishops at the 1998 Asian synod in Rome called for an autochthonous Church in southern Asia on the stated grounds that Rome had "neither the knowledge nor the competence" to make their pastoral decisions for them. In 2001, at another synod in Rome, Indonesian bishops called for a new ecumenical council, one that would launch the radical decentralization implied in the concept of autochthony. "Only then," one of them said, "can we be free to proclaim the gospel." The Indonesian bishops justified their position by harking back to the new charter that was written for the Church at Vatican II. They cited the series of enactments that dealt with the Church's need to make the gospel come alive everywhere on the planet, and in every culture.

Francis Hadisumarta, the tall, patrician Carmelite who was bishop of Manokwari-Sorong, stood up in that Roman synod of 2001 and said, "In many crucial pastoral areas, we need the authority to interpret Church law according to our own cultural ethos, to change, and where necessary, to replace it." He mentioned the decades-long pleas from Indonesian bishops to ordain married men, always turned down by Rome. And he cited the issue of liturgical translations and adaptations. "Why," he said, "do we have to go to Rome for approval by people who do not understand our language?" This is a case, he said, where local Churches can become truly local—"when its laws are not only in line with the spirit of the gospel and ecclesial norms but also with the ethos and legal tradition of the local people." In general, he asserted, "Theology, spirituality, law and liturgy should be as diverse as our languages and cultures."

Surprisingly enough, even a leading curial cardinal in Rome has said as much. Cardinal Walter Kasper of the Vatican's Council for Promoting Christian Unity has suggested "giving relative autonomy to the local Churches." Kasper's willingness to apply the principle of autochthony to other local Churches around the world suggests to some theologians that other Churches may consider it, too. They say the bishop of Rome cannot hope to have the world's billion-plus Catholics marching in lockstep. If Tip O'Neill was right, that all politics is local, then that practical wisdom ought to also apply to Church politics, from Jakarta to Johannesburg.

As we have already seen, the Church in the early history of the United States, led by the bishops of Baltimore, Maryland, and Charleston, South Carolina, could have become a democratic Church. John Carroll was appointed by Rome only after he had been elected by a vote of the nation's priests. John England ran his sprawling diocese, covering what is now the states of North and South Carolina and Georgia, under a constitution that made him accountable to his priests and his people, not to the pope. The democratizing moment faded away when the American hierarchy rejected England's leadership, more comfortable with their status as something very close to feudal lords, an arrangement that worked well for them.

It worked, that is, until the sex-abuse crisis forced Catholics to take a closer look at the stewardship of their bishops. Now organizations are springing up all over the country that are taking that close look. On March 14, 2005, the Church in America Leadership Roundtable called a press conference to issue a set of recommendations for a more accountable Church, and to announce the formation of a new organization, the National Leadership Roundtable on Church Management. The *National Catholic Reporter* hailed their move:

> The clergy sex abuse crisis has ricocheted in unanticipated ways, giving a voice to those once content to "pray, pay, and obey." Among them are American Catholic business leaders—highly educated, hugely successful in the secular world, used to making decisions for large organizations after hearing diverse views on complex issues, possessing a call-'em-as-they-see-'em attitude. They don't claim their expertise is sufficient to cure what ails the Church, but they think it is necessary.

Other organizations are gathering momentum. In July 2005, the national organization Voice of the Faithful (VOTF), with 30,000 members in all fifty states and forty-six countries, held a national convention in Indianapolis to determine its next moves toward a more accountable Church. One item on its agenda: to discuss ways they might push for the election of American bishops, which they claimed had ample precedent in the very early Church. Joseph O'Callaghan, a delegate from Bridgeport, Connecticut, cited the words of Saint Cyprian, a bishop of Carthage who died in 258, writing in his Epistle 67 that a new bishop "should be chosen by the whole people," according to an ancient principle: "what concerns all must be decided by all."

Other VOTF delegates argued that any bishop elected by the people would conduct the Church's business like any city mayor or state governor, openly and accountably, subject to the normal checks and balances of his collaborators in the ministry. "If everyone is doing his job," said O'Callaghan, "we would have an accountable Church."

This is not pie-in-the-sky theology. It is not theology at all. It is politics, pure politics. When the people of God wake up to the fact that they can exercise the art of politics and remain good Catholics, changes will start to occur in a Church where they can claim ownership, and, just as important, citizenship. O'Callaghan said, "Before too many more dioceses go bankrupt, the American bishops could decide to give the Church back to the people. But the people have to ask for it."

When they do, their asking will mark a new kind of drama in the American Church. Rome may not be happy. Benedict XVI may write a new encyclical inveighing against an old ism, Americanism. But what, in the final analysis, can Rome do to stop the move toward a people's Church in America, especially if the American bishops see the Spirit working in these movements toward a democratic consensus on most of the questions that vex American Catholics? Who can say that the process itself—bishops, priests, sisters, laymen, and laywomen acting in concert—will not give the Church a new vitality and the Jesus message a new credibility?

This is arguably the time to make the Church less Roman, more catholic—and more American. First, however, the people of God in America have to wake up and stand up. About half of the people go to mass and Communion every week, but many of them continue to grumble quietly (not knowing what else to do) about prelates who do not listen to them. The other half stay away, still believers deep down, but lodging by their absence an unspoken indictment of those running an institution they cannot support. Both halves of the people's Church saw the top leadership—the American cardinals—on television during April 2005. The television viewers were looking, perhaps, for Jesus. But all they saw were mighty princes of the Church, quite satisfied with themselves and their symbols of power, apparently oblivious of the battle for the future.

Where, then, is the battle? We can see forces gathering now in a unique new freedom-space—online. There, young people (of all ages) are finding others who want to seize ownership and citizenship in a Church that is, after all, theirs. Their numbers are small at this point, but this is how all revolutions start, with a happy few. Readers of this work can visit some of them on a Web site—www.takebackourchurch.org—where they make no secret of their plans to build an accountable Church that gives everyone a voice and a vote.

What do they want? A Church they can be proud of, a simpler Church, the kind of Church Jesus the carpenter might like to drop in on.

Acknowledgments

THIS IS A BOOK about papal politics and Church politics as well. I distinguish between the two because, in writing about them both as I have, I have two sets of acknowledgments to make: to those who helped take me behind the scenes during the month of April 2005 to report on the election of a new pope, and to literally hundreds of people from five continents who helped me understand the Church beyond the Vatican, the people's Church.

I couldn't even think of reporting on a papal election unless many people were willing to take me behind the scenes. I must thank them here without naming them, because, in all probability, these insiders would quickly become outsiders for daring to reveal how power is parceled out inside a Church whose hierarchs maintain their power by creating an illusion about it, drumming in the message that their doctrinal and disciplinary decisions come directly "from God." Those who diminish that message by relating the human power plays that attend the election of a pope could well expect swift retribution for undermining the myth that the Church runs according to orders that come directly from on high.

Fortunately for my readers, I found sources inside the system who enjoyed taking me on little iconoclastic trips without crossing the border into heresy. The Church's authority, as one of them said, may indeed come from God. But he quickly added, "In a world where God sustains our every breath, what doesn't? It would be foolish for us to think God doesn't reveal himself in thousands of ways." He cited no less an authority than Pope John XXIII, who suggested that God speaks to us through contemporary history, or what he liked to call "the signs of the times."

As a reporter during the Second Vatican Ecumenical Council, which met for four years from 1962 to 1965, I saw how God may have been revealing things to the assembled bishops through the vocal bishops around them; many of them weren't afraid to speak out in the kind of back-and-forth discussions that prevail in any healthy family or corporate board meeting. I saw, then, the overturning of the papal pyramid myth, that God told the pope what to say and do, so the pope could tell the bishops, and the bishops the priests and nuns, and the priests and nuns could tell the people. In fact, the pope had called the bishops to Rome to advise *him* on the major work of this Council: updating the Church, which is what Pope John XXIII called his aggiornamento.

The Fathers of Vatican II wrote a new charter for a Church that didn't have all the answers. Those answers, they said, would have to come not only from the pope and the bishops but from the people of God as a whole, over time. As a result, Catholics began to grow up—reconciling themselves to the fact that they could not expect the pope or the bishops to provide them with magical solutions to the personal and societal problems facing them in a century of escalating change. They had to think their solutions through, just as the bishops did in writing their conciliar charter, hoping they were heading in the right direction, trying to find the words and the ways that make the old Jesus message come alive in new ways, and in places it hadn't previously penetrated.

This conclave to elect a new pope was something like a Council, in one respect, at least: for all of its otherworldly trappings, it was a human event that I could observe, and analyze, and write about as I have here, just as if I were reporting an election campaign anywhere in the world—except, of course, that a conclave is not much like other election campaigns anywhere. In order to maintain the illusion, that their choice of a new pope comes from on high, the College of Cardinals established an unprecedented secrecy that would have made the reporting impossible without the help of my sources inside who felt the people of a people's Church had a right to know what was going on in their own Church—even what was going on in the Church's corporate boardroom. Readers can judge how valuable they were to the unfolding of this story and, if thanks are in order, thank them.

With me, readers should also acknowledge the work of all the members of the Vatican press corps, whose dispatches before and during the conclave itself and on everything that surrounded it during the hectic spring of 2005 helped me produce the many-sided account you see here. Thanks, first, to that special group of Italian journalists who have been covering the Vatican full-time for decades with such high expertise, the men called *Vaticanisti:* Luigi Accattoli, Giovanni Avena, Sandro Magister, Orazio Petrosillo, Marco Politi, Luigi Sandri, and Giancarlo Zizola.

Special thanks should also go to the men and women reporters who filed their stories in English—John Allen, Robert Mickens, Gerry O'Connell, Peggy Polk, Phil Pullella, Victor Simpson, John Thavis and Cindy Wooden and their reportorial staff at the American Catholic News Service in Rome, and David Willey, who all reported on the Vatican full-time during the momentous last days of John Paul II's papacy and the first days of Benedict XVI's. Thanks also to my colleagues who covered the conclave with me: Chris Dickey and Edward Pentin at *Newsweek,* and Carol Eisenberg, Matt McAllester, Letta Tayler, and Paul Vitello at *Newsday.*

It is hard to know where to begin acknowledging all the help I received in writing what is almost a second book about the condition of the Church today. To begin my research on that book, in August 1999 I traveled for a month across the continental United States, from San Francisco to San Antonio to Minneapolis (with a side trip to Toronto), to Chicago, Notre Dame, Saint Louis, Boston, and New York, in an effort to meet articulate Catholics who cared enough about their Church to have opinions about it. In September 1999 I took up residence in Rome, which turned out to be a crossroads for people of every race and nation; many were eager to tell me about the Church they knew, and it wasn't long before I realized how appropriate was James Joyce's description of the Church: "Here comes everybody."

In Rome in 1999, away from friends back home and family, I took to writing a diary about my exploits and sharing parts of it with them on the Internet. My friends and family forwarded my candid e-mails to their friends, and they, in turn, forwarded them to their friends, and soon I was getting e-mails from hundreds of people asking me to put them on my Rome Diary list. I did so, and in giving of myself to them, I soon found them giving back to me, a large network of friends from Pittsburgh to Perth, mostly Catholics, who could and did tell me what was happening in their Church. I now have more than sixteen hundred people on my Rome Diary list. With many of them, communication goes both ways. I am now well wired to Catholics on every continent.

I also became a member of a number of Listservs, electronic bulletin boards for Catholics of all kinds (and former Catholics and would-be Catholics, too) who were daring to think new thoughts and try them out in cyberspace, where they found thousands of people (who knows, maybe millions) listening—and responding. I became part of a new kind of people's dialogue in a new kind of people's Church.

The people I met in cyberspace helped me write a different kind of book than I would have been able to write otherwise. I began to see the people's Church envisioned at Vatican II take on a new reality in the first decade of the twenty-first century. The catechisms before Vatican II told us about "a teaching Church" and "a learning Church." Now, on the Internet, I began to see that distinction disappear. We all became learners and teachers together.

I cannot (and maybe should not) name them all here, and therefore, I won't try to name any of them. But I would like to thank them. They know who they are: men, women, humble, proud, builders, bankers, saints, sinners, gays, straights, right, left, and center, laypeople, and members of countless religious orders. I even corresponded with one hermit.

I can and should thank one special man, my editor at Knopf, Jonathan Segal, who stuck with me on a project that took several years longer than we thought. If you put me in a box, I am the kind of man who has to jump out of it. Segal needed to keep putting me back in his Knopf box, so we, together, could produce a work that, pardon the expression, "made some sense" out of the worldwide institution that grew out of Jesus' simple pun, "On you, Peter-the-Rock, I will build my Church." I hope readers will e-mail me, to tell me how successfully we made sense.

rbkaiser@justgoodcompany.com

Rome, May 2005

Index